The Illustrated Encyclopedia of

ELEPHANTS

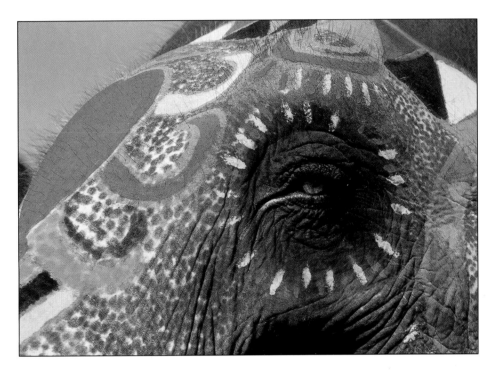

An Asian elephant waiting for the ceremony to begin.

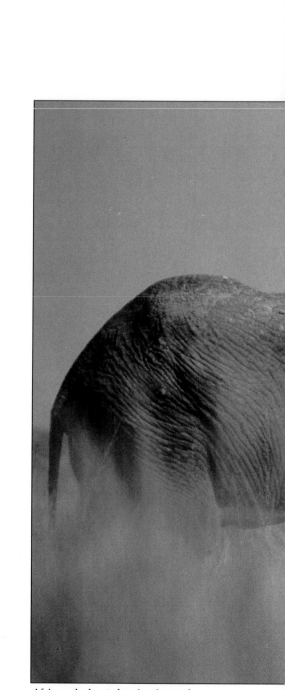

African elephants keeping in touch – an important part of their social life.

The Illustrated Encyclopedia of

ELEPHANTS

*From Their Origins and Evolution to Their Ceremonial
and Working Relationship with Man*

Consultant: Dr. S. K. Eltringham

CRESCENT BOOKS
New York

A SALAMANDER BOOK

© 1991 Salamander Books Ltd., 129-137 York Way,
London N7 9LG, United Kingdom.

This 1991 edition published by Crescent Books, distributed by Outlet
Book Company, Inc., a Random House Company, 225 Park Avenue
South, New York, New York 10003.

ISBN 0-517-06136-8

8 7 6 5 4 3 2 1

Credits
Edited and designed by Ideas into Print,
  Geoffrey Rogers and Stuart Watkinson
Copy-editing: Maureen Cartwright
Illustrators: Bob Bampton (Bernard Thornton Artists, London),
  Andrew Beckett (Garden Studio), Rod Ferring, Matthew Hillier,
  Maggie Raynor, John Sibbick, Glenn Smith, Todd G. Telander
Picture research: Diana Morris
Colour reproductions: P&W Graphics Pte. Ltd.
Filmset: SX Composing Ltd.
Printed and bound in Hong Kong

Endpapers: Bathing in the Uaso Nyiro River, Kenya.
This page: Dawn patrol on the Luangwa River, Zambia.
Opposite contents page: Asian elephants – tame but still proud.

THE AUTHORS

Jeheskel Shoshani B.Sc., Ph.D.
Jeheskel Shoshani's interest in the natural sciences began in Israel, where he became a Head Zookeeper at the Tel-Aviv Zoo in 1966. In 1969 he went to the USA, where he studied mammalian comparative anatomy, ecology and evolution, and developed an interest in the natural history of elephants. In 1977 he established the Elephant Interest Group – an international non-profit organization to promote interest in elephants for research and conservation. Dr. Shoshani has travelled widely, studying wild elephants as well as fossil remains of proboscideans. He has prepared many articles about elephants for both scientific and popular publications and continues to conduct research on a number of elephant-related topics. He shares his home in Michigan with his wife Sandra and their pet rock hyrax, one of the elephant's closest living relatives.

Phyllis C. Lee, Ph.D.
Phyllis Lee is a zoologist based in Biological Anthropology at the University of Cambridge. Her early work was on the behaviour of free-living primates, with Dr Jane Goodall at Gombe in Tanzania. After completing her Ph.D on vervet monkeys, she moved on to working with elephants in collaboration with Cynthia Moss and the Amboseli Elephant Research Project. Her research interests centre on early physical and social development, and life histories of mammals. She continues to work with the Amboseli elephants, as well as with primates.

R. Sukumar M.Sc., Ph.D.
R. Sukumar was born and raised in Madras, India. In 1979, after completing Bachelor's and Master's degrees in Botany from the University of Madras, he joined the doctoral programme in Ecology at the Indian Institute of Science, Bangalore. His doctoral thesis on Asian elephant ecology and interactions with people in southern India was accepted in 1985 and later published as a book. He is currently on the faculty of the Centre for Ecological Sciences, Indian Institute of Science. He is also Deputy Chairman of the Asian Elephant Specialist Group of the IUCN – the World Conservation Union – and heads the Asian Elephant Conservation Centre in Bangalore. As well as his work on Asian elephants, his academic interests extend to tropical forest dynamics, palaeontology and conservation biology.

James Barnett B.Sc., B.V.Sc.
James Barnett graduated in Environmental Biology from Aberystwyth University in 1983 and then studied Veterinary Science at Bristol University. While at Bristol, he spent a period of time in Africa, where he developed an affinity with African wildlife. In July 1989, he took up the post of veterinary House Surgeon for the Zoological Society of London based at Whipsnade Wild Animal Park. He is responsible for the veterinary care and management of the collection, which includes Asian elephants. He has lectured on elephant nutrition and the veterinary management of elephants in captivity.

Lyn de Alwis B.Sc. F.Z.S.
Lyn de Alwis, one of Sri Lanka's best-known conservationists, was Director of Wildlife Conservation for 12 years and concurrently Director of her National Zoo. Always developing innovative techniques in dealing with human-elephant conflicts, he has organized successful translocation operations of problem elephants into national parks, both by drug immobilization and, in 1980, by the then untried method of driving whole herds to safety, sometimes over distances of up to 50 miles. For his contribution to conservation he was made a Member-of-Honour of the World Wide Fund for Nature (WWF) in 1983. He has been Chairman of IUCN's Asian Elephant Specialist Group since 1985, spearheading the raising of funds for the conservation of this beleagured giant. He is also Consultant to the Singapore Zoological Gardens, which he designed in 1970-71, and which is today regarded as one of the most beautiful and successful zoos.

Dhriti K. Lahari-Choudhury, M.A., Ph.D.
Dhriti K. Lahari-Choudhury took his M.A. from Calcutta and Ph.D. from Leeds (1966), specializing in Medieval and Early Tudor English Literature. He is currently Professor and Head of the Department of English at Rabindra Bharati University in Calcutta. His lifelong interest has been the ecology and management of larger mammals, especially the Asian elephant, with which he has been familiar since childhood. He was the Principal Investigator of the IUCN/WWF Project on the Status and Distribution of Elephants in northeast India, and is on the Steering Committee of the Asian Elephant Specialist Group. He was appointed a member of the task force set up by the Government of India in 1990 to prepare proposals for Project Elephant in India, has served on various government wildlife advisory bodies and committees, and was a member of WWF (India) Eastern Region Committee from 1976 to 1990. He is also a keen wildlife photographer.

Richard A. Luxmoore M.A., Ph.D.
Having studied at Cambridge University, Richard Luxmoore obtained his Ph.D. in marine ecology while working for the British Antarctic Survey. After a brief period in commercial fish farming, he returned to Cambridge to join the Wildlife Trade Monitoring Unit of the World Conservation Monitoring Centre, which he now heads. This international organization, jointly managed by the WWF, the IUCN and the United Nations Environment Programme, collects and analyzes data on all aspects of trade in wildlife products. In 1991 he was appointed by CITES to the panel of experts to assess proposals to resume trading in ivory.

THE CONSULTANTS

S.K. Eltringham, M.A., Ph.D., F.I.Biol.
Keith Eltringham started his research career as a marine biologist, before moving to the Wildfowl Trust as pilot-biologist in order to evaluate the use of aerial survey in wildfowl ecology. After a spell as lecturer in zoology at King's College, London, he moved to Uganda as Director of the Nuffield Unit of Tropical Animal Ecology, where he began his involvement with elephants, as well as with other large mammals and birds. It was during his investigation of the need to cull elephants that the first indications of the widespread escalation of ivory poaching became apparent. Since returning to England he has been successively a lecturer in the Applied Biology and Zoology Departments of Cambridge University, from where he has made frequent visits to Africa to continue his study of elephants.

David Ward B.Vet .Med., M.R.C.V.S.
David Ward graduated from the Royal Veterinary College in 1974 and worked for 14 years as a small animal veterinary surgeon in southern England. He spent most of his spare time collecting fossil vertebrates worldwide and in 1987, he and his wife participated in a British Museum (Natural History) expedition, collecting dinosaur remains in sub-Saharan Africa. Since then they have themselves led expeditions to Niger and Mali, as well as to the USA. In 1988 he retired from veterinary medicine in order to devote his time more fully to palaeontology.

CONTENTS

ORIGINS & EVOLUTION

Although looking most unlike an elephant, the hyraxes, or conies, are considered to be one of the elephant's closest living relatives. The clues lie not in the enigmatic expression, but in the shape of their feet and other characters. Biochemical evidence confirms the connection.

The fossil history of the Proboscidea – the order of mammals that includes the modern elephants – is one of the most complex stories of mammalian evolution ever told. It contains examples of parallel and convergent evolution, giants, dwarfs, and bizarre forms. The vast array of species in the Proboscidea was 'moulded' through adaptive radiations during the geological times of the Cenozoic era, a spread of approximately 55 million years from the Eocene to the present day. Although elephants are the only proboscideans alive today, they are just one of many proboscid families. During the course of evolution, proboscideans spread to all parts of the world, except Australia, Antarctica and some islands, and occupied terrestrial environments that were just as varied as the species themselves. This section briefly explores the twists and turns of their development on earth – a chronicle that continues to fascinate and engage evolutionary scientists throughout the world.

The relationship between elephants, sea cows and hyraxes

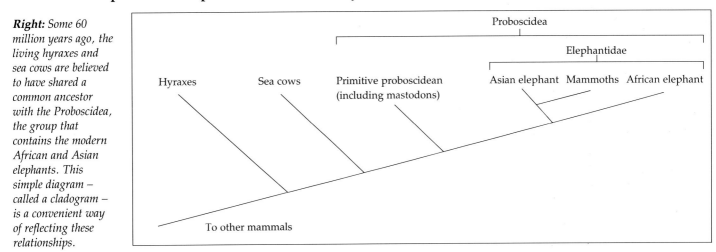

Right: Some 60 million years ago, the living hyraxes and sea cows are believed to have shared a common ancestor with the Proboscidea, the group that contains the modern African and Asian elephants. This simple diagram – called a cladogram – is a convenient way of reflecting these relationships.

This overview of the origins and evolution of elephants begins with a simple clarification of the term 'Proboscidea' and then considers the elephant's closest living relatives. The survey is then broadened to encompass the basic groups within the order Proboscidea and consider how they have radiated in time and space over the past 55 million years. Here, the narrative pauses occasionally to consider points and trends of particular interest. The chapter concludes with an animal-by-animal review of extinct and living species that represent 'milestones' along the evolutionary journey. Sometimes aspects referred to earlier in the text are re-examined and developed. To the non-scientist, this chapter may

Below: A family group of manatees. Together with the more marine dugongs, these herbivorous mammals are aptly known as sea cows. Now adapted to a fully aquatic lifestyle, sea cows may have evolved from the same ancestors as the elephants. Fossils of both can be found in the sediments of north Africa.

seem to be confusing territory. Every discipline has its own terminology, and 'leading edge' investigations into evolution carry a particularly heavy burden of jargon that is difficult to avoid completely. The scientific names of long-dead species of animals seem particularly difficult to understand at first, but there is a simple logic to their compilation which is explained where possible. Although complex, this section, and the chapter on *Anatomy and Physiology* that follows, provide a foundation for further reading and act as a fitting introduction to the fascinating world of elephants that this book is dedicated to explore.

Defining Proboscidea

The name 'Proboscidea' was coined by the naturalist Carl D. Illiger at the beginning of the nineteenth century from the Greek words *pro* for 'forward' or 'in front of', and *boskein* meaning 'to feed' or 'mouth'. Direct evidence for a trunklike organ has been known in the living elephants and woolly mammoths for many years. Indirect evidence for the presence of a trunk in extinct species comes from our knowledge of the skull. The upper part of the front of the skull contains an opening that is the beginning of the nostrils. In mammals, this single opening is normally situated at the front of the skull. In members of the elephant family – the Elephantidae – it is much further back. Thus, finding a similar arrangement in other mammals may be interpreted as the possible presence of a trunk. However, fossil evidence suggests that the earliest proboscideans did not have trunks, and so other characters are used to define members of this group. These include the pattern of cusps on the teeth, the loss of a tooth, enamel bands on the tusks and the architecture of the bones, especially in the skull.

The elephant's nearest relatives

The earliest known ancestors to the elephants were pig- to cow-sized herbivores. Little is known of the roots of the proboscidean family tree; new fossilized remains are still being found. One group, called the moeritheres, inhabited north Africa 40 million years ago and appear to be true proboscideans. Moeritheres and some other north African Eocene proboscideans are, however, too specialized to be the direct ancestors of later proboscideans. The search for the latter continues. Also about 55 million years ago in India and Pakistan lived an older and more primitive group, the anthracobunids. Some authors have considered anthracobunids to be true Proboscidea, but because there is some uncertainty they have been excluded here. Being unspecialized mammals, others have suggested that anthracobunids may include the ancestors of both moeritheres and the purely aquatic sirenians (see below).

These proboscideans lived close to the shores of an ancient seaway called the Tethys, of which the present-day Mediterranean Sea is a remnant. They were only one of many groups of animals that inhabited these shores; another was the Sirenia, the manatees and dugongs,

Above: *Fossil remains of early proboscideans are still being discovered and meticulously examined in the arid, windswept hills of north Africa. Fifty to forty million years ago this area would have been a lush subtropical coastline.*

commonly known as sea cows. In addition to sharing similar habitats, these earliest members of Proboscidea and Sirenia also shared some anatomical features that indicate that they are related. Sea cows have adapted well to a shallow water, herbivorous lifestyle and are now strictly aquatic.

A third order of mammals traditionally grouped with the Proboscidea and Sirenia is the Hyracoidea, containing the hyraxes, or conies. Living representatives of hyraxes resemble overgrown guinea pigs. Superficially, there would be no reason to suspect that an elephant, a manatee and a hyrax would have something in common, except of course that they all are mammals. Clearly, these groups of mammals look very different. Elephants are the largest living land mammals; manatees and dugongs are the size of dolphins and aquatic; whereas hyraxes are rabbit-sized creatures that live among rocks or in trees. In fact, so different are these mammals that 18th- and 19th-century investigators classified elephants with rhinoceroses and the hippopotamus, manatees with seals and sea lions, and hyraxes with rodents. Recent fossil, anatomical and molecular data, however, suggests otherwise.

BASIC GROUPS WITHIN THE PROBOSCIDEA

The moeritheres
These bizarre animals were widespread across north Africa in the late Eocene and early Oligocene (40 to 35 million years ago). They stood about 1m(39in) tall and were probably amphibious, living on a diet of aquatic plants, rather like the modern-day hippopotamus. There is no evidence to suggest that they possessed a trunk. Although classed within the Proboscidea, they were an evolutionary side branch and were not ancestors of the modern elephants

The barytheres
Barytheres are known only from the African late Eocene and Oligocene(40 to 35 million years ago). Whether or not they should be included in the Proboscidea has been debated over the past 90 years, a problem aggravated by the scarcity of fossil material. More recent fossil finds have settled their position as a side branch of the proboscidean tree. Barytheres had two pairs of short incisor tusks in both upper and lower jaw; the former protruded vertically, and the latter projected horizontally. They had diastemas (gaps) between their tusks and the cheek teeth, which were lophodont, i.e with occlusal (grinding) surfaces consisting of ridges formed by the elongation and fusion of cusps. The front cheek teeth were probably used for crushing vegetable matter and the back teeth may have been adapted for shearing. Cheek teeth were present all together at the same time in the mouth, unlike those of modern elephants, where one, two, or sometimes three teeth are present at any one time and are replaced from behind as though on a slowly moving 'conveyor belt'.

The deinotheres
The deinotheres were reported from the African Miocene (about 24 million years ago) and only became extinct in the Pleistocene (less than 2 million years ago). They spread out over Europe and Asia but not to the Americas. Their origins are uncertain, but there is no doubt that they are true proboscideans. Deinotheres had lophodont teeth and a large diastema. They lacked tusks in the upper jaw but had curious downwardly curved lower tusks. Like the barytheres, they were a side branch of the proboscidean tree, albeit a fairly successful one. From their African beginnings their only real change was to increase in size, some species reaching 4m(just over 13ft) in height.

Palaeomastodons and other ancient proboscideans
Palaeomastodons are currently known only from the late Eocene (40 million years ago) of north Africa. They had cheek teeth with cusps arranged transversely in pairs along the tooth, and upper and lower tusks that were oval in cross section. Between the tusks and the cheek teeth there was a diastema resulting from the absence of anterior premolars. At the same time in north Africa, another lineage of proboscideans had evolved in a different direction. This lineage, represented by the genus *Phiomia*, had cheek teeth with cusps arranged in staggered pairs. The lower tusks of *Phiomia* were flattened in cross section and there was a diastema similar to that of *Palaeomastodon*.

Long- and short-jawed 'gomphotheres'
'Gomphothere' is a rather imprecise term used for some of the more primitive members of the proboscidean family tree. The evolution of the gomphothere stocks proceeded in two different directions. The first evolved in such a way that the lower jaws became increasingly long, whereas the second had short lower jaws. Those that lived in marshy and swampy habitats usually included species with long jaws equipped with shovel-type tusks that may have been used for digging soft vegetation. In contrast, those that inhabited open or wooded savannas usually included species with short jaws, with or without tusks. The savanna dwellers are thought to have evolved trunks longer than those that lived in the marshy and swampy landscapes. Long trunks were an advantage and were probably used to reach high foliage. Examples of long-jawed gomphotheres include *Gomphotherium*, *Amebelodon* and *Platybelodon*. Examples of short-jawed gomphotheres include *Anancus* and *Cuvieronius*.

The teeth of long-jawed gomphotheres included accessory cusps that developed on the sides of the main molar cones. This increased the effectiveness of the teeth as grinding mills. The lower tusks changed from round through oval to flattened and chisel shaped, while the upper tusks became large and curved strongly upward.

Impressive examples of the long-jawed gomphotheres were *Amebelodon* of North America and *Platybelodon* of Asia, the so-called 'shovel tuskers'. In these Miocene-Pliocene proboscideans, the lower tusks were very broad, forming huge scoops on the front of the jaws, presumably used for digging up plants in shallow waters.

The short-jawed gomphotheres, with almost tuskless lower jaws included the mastodon, *Mammut americanum*, one of the best-known of fossil vertebrates in North America. Its premolars and molars had sharp ridges placed transversely. It had both upper and lower tusks, although the latter were very short and only present in presumed males. In contrast, the upper tusks were long and strongly curved upwards; some reached 3m(almost 10ft) in length and 25cm(10in) in diameter at the base. Many skeletons of American mastodons have been recovered from Pleistocene swamps, where the bones are often well preserved and articulated. Associated plant material reveals that they browsed upon twigs and leaves of trees. Radiocarbon dating indicates that they were contemporaneous with early man, some 10,000-12,000 years ago. Archaeologists have

The rise and fall of the Proboscidea

These maps plot the rise and fall of the Proboscidea, from their origin in north Africa about 50 million years ago, through their worldwide dispersal, to their reduced distribution about 10,000 years ago.

1. *Moeritherium*

2. *Palaeomastodon*

3. Gomphotheres

4. *Mammut*

5. *Mammuthus*

6. *Stegodon*

7. *Elephas*

The 'D' symbols on the middle map represent Deinotherium.

7. *Elephas*

8. *Loxodonta*

■ General distribution   ■ Dispersal of different types

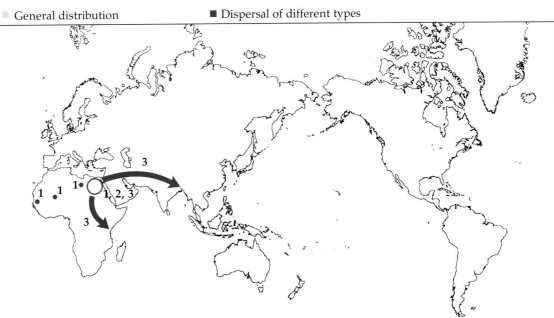

Eocene – Oligocene   55 to 25 million years ago

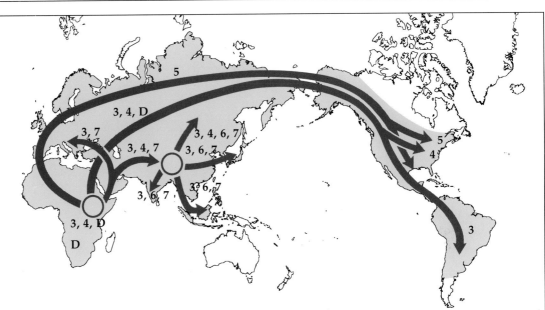

Miocene – Pliocene – Pleistocene   25 million to 10 thousand years ago

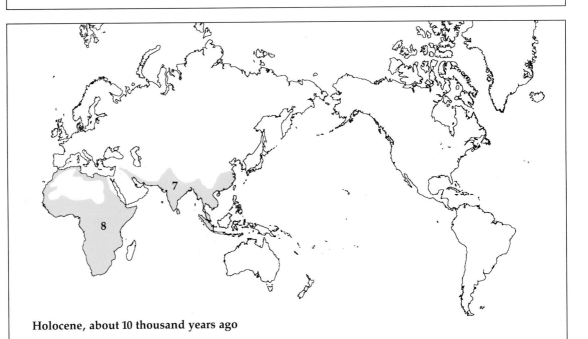

Holocene, about 10 thousand years ago

The proboscidean family tree

This family tree shows the relationship between modern-day elephants and their ancestors over the last 50 or so million years. Anyone encountering a Moeritherium would find it quite difficult to believe that this was one of the earliest relatives of the modern elephants. With a short trunk, the Oligocene proboscidean, Palaeomastodon, had acquired the more familiar elephant-like appearance. The exotic Deinotherium and the bizarre Platybelodon are examples of early specializations that were doomed to eventual extinction. The ice ages,

with rapid climatic and habitat changes, may have led to the extinction of the mammoth (Mammuthus) and the American mastodon (Mammut), leaving just the Asian and African elephants in the proboscidean line. The reconstructions used in this tree are reduced versions of those featured on the following pages, where details of the possible size and anatomy of the creatures are given, along with further clarification about how they fit into the evolutionary story of the elephants. It has not been possible to reconstruct Barytherium.

PLEISTOCENE

PLIOCENE

MIOCENE

OLIGOCENE

EOCENE

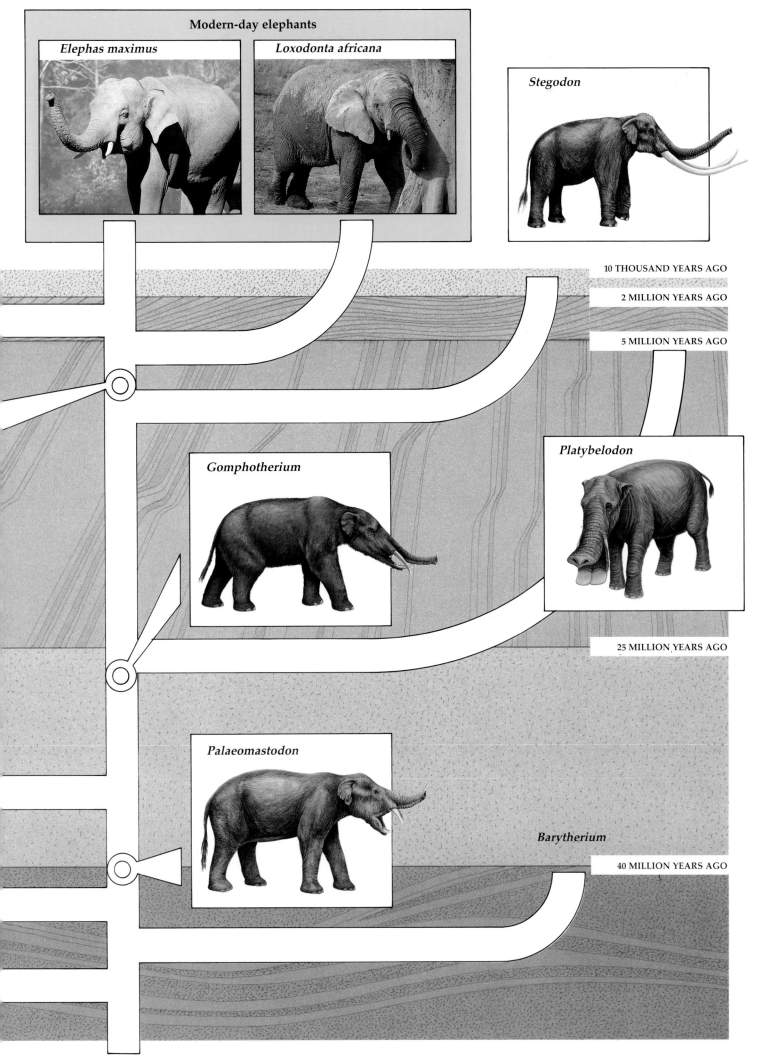

Modern-day elephants

Elephas maximus

Loxodonta africana

Stegodon

10 THOUSAND YEARS AGO

2 MILLION YEARS AGO

5 MILLION YEARS AGO

Gomphotherium

Platybelodon

25 MILLION YEARS AGO

Palaeomastodon

Barytherium

40 MILLION YEARS AGO

Evolutionary trends in the proboscideans

Perhaps the most significant trend in proboscidean species is a progressive increase in size. In association with this came the enlargement of the tusks and the elongation of the trunk. In conjunction with the variety of habitats occupied, natural selection through adaptive radiation produced extraordinarily varied groups of proboscideans. Despite these extreme variations, changes were marked by certain dominant trends.

1. Increase in size. Except for the earliest forms, most later proboscideans became giants.
2. Lengthening of limb bones and the development of short, broad feet. This is a common evolutionary trend among very large mammals.
3. Growth of the skull to an extraordinarily large size. This growth is particularly evident in the cranium, where air cells (diploe) developed.
4. Shortening of the neck. Since the skull and its associated structures (tusks and trunk) became large and heavy, the neck was reduced in length to shorten the lever between the body and the head.
5. Elongation of the lower jaw. In many of the later proboscideans, there was a secondary shortening of the lower jaw, but lengthening of the jaw was an early, primary trend.
6. Development of a proboscis. Elongation of the upper lip and the nostril appear to have evolved along with the elongation and then shortening of the lower jaw. Subsequently, the nostril was further elongated to form a very mobile trunk, or proboscis.
7. Secondary shortening of the jaws and the shift of the centre of gravity of the head posteriorly.
8. Forward/horizontal replacement of cheek teeth.

9. Reduction in number of teeth. This trend started with *Moeritherium*. Throughout the history of the Proboscidea, there is a decrease in tooth numbers.
10. Excess growth of the second incisors to form tusks. They have functioned in food gathering, defence, offence and display.
11. Enlargement and specialization of the cheek teeth by increasing the number of lamellae (loops) accompanied by a thinning of the enamel, thereby molarifying the deciduous (milk) premolars. This trend is an adaptation for chewing and grinding plants.

As the size of the animal increased from *Moeritherium* to *Phiomia*, and later to other members of the Proboscidea, the growth in size and height did not correspond proportionately with the lengthening of the neck. Without other adaptive changes in anatomy, it would have been difficult for such newly evolved species to eat and drink with the mouth placed so far above the ground. These adaptations began with the lengthening of the skull and then, when a lighter and more flexible structure like a trunk began to evolve, the process was reversed and the skull became progressively shorter. The elongation was most pronounced when the lower jaw housed the spoon-shaped tusks protruding forward (in *Platybelodon* and *Amebelodon*), a feature that probably led to the evolution of the extraordinary shovel-tuskers such as *Platybelodon grangeri*.

Later in evolution, when the shortening of the lower jaw had taken place, the upper tusks lost their enamel band and then turned upward, greatly increasing in length and diameter, and moving out of the way of the newly evolving proboscis.

and the mammoth. Currently, this family includes six genera and 26 elephant species. The African elephant (*Loxodonta africana*) and the Asian elephant (*Elephas maximus*) are the only living representatives; the other four genera are extinct. The mammoth (*Mammuthus*) is the next best-known genus. The other three genera, namely *Stegodibelodon*, *Stegotetrabelodon*, and *Primelephas* are more primitive forms from the latest Miocene-Pliocene (7 to 5 million years ago).

Most of the evidence supporting the relationships between the elephantids is based on cranial and dental characters. Examination of non-dental characters supports the classical dental-based hypothesis, i.e., *Mammuthus* and *Elephas* are closer to each other than either of them is to *Loxodonta*. The skulls, particularly the teeth, of earlier species of *Mammuthus* and *Elephas* closely resemble each other. This has resulted in differences in identification and nomenclature; many specimens now considered as *Mammuthus* were originally described as *Elephas*.

REPRESENTATIVES OF THE PROBOSCIDEA

Introduction

Much of our knowledge of the evolution of Proboscidea is based on the teeth, because they are more durable than bones and are the most common fossils. Adult *Moeritherium* is believed to have had a total of 36 teeth. The cheek teeth were separated from the canines by a gap (diastema), and the molars were broad and of a simple tetrabunodont type. Tetrabunodonty – literally 'four bumps' – was a common feature in moeritheres and other early proboscideans, in which the molars were doubly cross-crested, each crest being formed by two large cones, or cusps, placed side by side. These cheek teeth were composed of dentine (soft, dull and situated internally) and enamel (hard, shiny and situated externally); there was no cement present. These teeth had short crowns and relatively long roots, and grew to a certain height and stopped. Deciduous (milk) premolars and molars were replaced by permanent ones in vertical fashion, from below in the lower jaw or from above in the cranium, similar to tooth replacement in many mammals. In more advanced proboscideans, tooth replacement was in a horizontal fashion. Specialization was apparent in the second pair of incisors in the upper jaw, which were much enlarged, suggesting that the formation of tusks had already begun to evolve. Small tusks were likewise present in the lower jaw, a common condition in many of the later proboscideans. Upper and lower second incisors, or 'tusks', were of roughly equal size and in many types they rubbed against each other, as in the rodents.

provided firm evidence that man hunted and probably ate their flesh, supporting the hypothesis that Palaeoindians contributed to their extinction, although a much more important factor was their over-specialization in a changing environment.

Stegodontids and elephantids: how are they related?

Until relatively recently, *Stegodon* was thought to represent a more primitive stage than *Elephas* and *Mammuthus*, and was believed to have given rise to other elephantid lineages. As additional fossil material came to light, it was evident that *Stegodon* itself was also too specialized for this. During the 1960s, a wealth of elephantid (and other proboscid) fossil material was discovered in sub-Saharan Africa, much of it in Kenya. This material shed new light on the diversity and evolution of the Elephantidae; many of the species proving to be intermediate forms between known advanced elephantids and earlier gomphothere species. These transitional species, *Stegotetrabelodon syrticus* and *Primelephas gomphotheroides*, provided the evidence that the roots of Elephantidae should be sought within the Gomphotheriidae and not within the Stegodontidae.

The Elephantidae

The family Elephantidae was established by J.E.Gray in 1821. At that time, only three elephant species were known: the African elephant, the Asian elephant,

Dental features of the 'mega' proboscideans

As we have seen, an important evolutionary trend among the Proboscidea has been their increase in size. Compare, for example, the 125kg(275lb) *Moeritherium* to the 5,000+kg (11,000+lb) *Mammuthus*. With the increase in body size came an increase in tooth size and complexity of the chewing surfaces. A natural development resulting from the elongation of the cheek teeth was the evolution of the horizontal tooth replacement system. This process is believed to have begun at about the Eocene-Oligocene boundary (40 million years ago).

The ground plan of gomphotheres' cheek teeth was relatively simple, consisting of ridges with two cusps each. In contrast, the cheek teeth of the Elephantidae were and still are composed of plates. Each of these plates is composed of a complete loop, or lamella, made from enamel on the outside and a dentine filling inside the loop. With a little imagination and correlated scientific evidence, one can build up a scenario whereby two cusps on a transverse ridge as seen in the gomphotherids may have evolved into four to six conelets on a transverse ridge typical of the stegodontids, or into the complete flattened loop seen in elephantids. The latter stage, from conelets to a loop, required the 'dissolving of the borders' between adjacent conelets. Correlated with these changes came the lengthening of the cheek teeth and the increase in number of ridges or plates per tooth. The third molar of *Gomphotherium* had up to 5-7 ridges, that of *Stegodon* had 12-13, and *Mammuthus* may have had over 30 plates.

The more specialized Pleistocene stegodons had deep skulls and extremely long and curved upper tusks. The lower jaws were short and bore no tusks. The cheek teeth grew so large that the simultaneous arrangement of all the teeth in longitudinal rows within the cranium and lower jaw was no longer possible (as in *Moeritherium*). Once the teeth of pro-

Skull of *Palaeomastodon* to show teeth

Skull and lower molar (inset) of the primitive proboscidean, Palaeomastodon. *Compare the tooth structure with those shown below.*

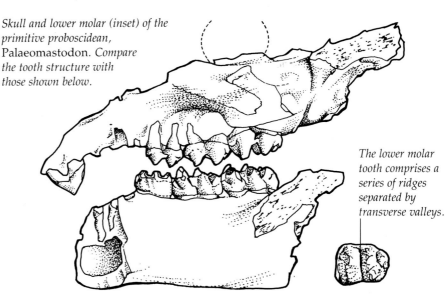

The lower molar tooth comprises a series of ridges separated by transverse valleys.

Evolutionary trends in proboscidean molar teeth

In Gomphotherium *normal wear has removed the tops of the two rows of enamel 'bumps', exposing the dentine and giving a file-like surface. (Black indicates enamel in these top views.)*

Gomphotherium

Primelephas

In Primelephas, *the two rows of cusps have fused into enamel-bounded plates. In the Elephantidae the number of plates has increased, with a thinning of the enamel and cement.*

Loxodonta africana

Elephas maximus

Mammuthus primigenius

Below: *A top view of the molar tooth of the extinct mammoth,* Mammuthus columbi. *Like those of the modern elephants, it was made up of a stack of enamel plates that formed at the back of the jaw and moved forward as the leading plates wore away. The jaw could only accommodate one to two teeth at once.*

boscideans became longer and taller, there was a need for an alternative mechanism to replace the old ones. There were two possibilities: either the skull could become long to accommodate all of the teeth at one time, or the tooth succession could be conducted in a 'conveyor belt' system, with the one from behind replacing the one in front. This mechanism is termed horizontal, as opposed to vertical, tooth replacement. Mammutids, gomphotherids, stegodontids and elephantids evolved the horizontal replacement approach. In these advanced proboscideans, the skulls were greatly deepened and the teeth were formed in the alveoli (small sockets in the jaw) and came into the occlusal, or chewing, position one at a time. It is possible that there was more than one tooth at a time in the jaws, especially when these were the smaller premolars rather than the molars. Those teeth at the front of the mouth eventually reached the edge, fragmented and broke away. Pieces of teeth either fell away or were swallowed, as occurs in the living elephants (see page 41).

A cast of characters

Rather than describe proboscidean evolution in great detail, it may be helpful to illustrate the general trends by looking at species that show the representative stages of evolution. For our purposes, the following species have been selected:

Moeritherium lyonsi
Barytherium grave
Deinotherium giganteum
Palaeomastodon beadnelli
Phiomia serridens
Mammut americanum
Anancus arvernensis
Cuvieronius humboldtii
Gomphotherium angustidens
Platybelodon grangeri
Primelephas gomphotheroides
Loxodonta africana
Elephas maximus
Mammuthus primigenius

These are not listed in evolutionary order but they are intended to show gradual trends in evolutionary processes within some of the well-known groups. Where the family is known, this is included in brackets after the specific name.

Moeritherium lyonsi (Family Moeritheriidae)

Moeritherium, named after the ancient Lake Moeris in the Fayum Basin, Egypt, was a primitive proboscidean that lived in the Eocene, about 50-55 million years ago. Subsequently, it has also been found at localities on the fringes of the Sahara from Libya to Mali and Senegal. Moeritheres are believed to have inhabited environments intermediate between those of the semi-aquatic hippopotamus and the purely aquatic sirenians (manatees and dugongs). They were comparatively small, pig-sized animals, heavily built, with long bodies, moderately short tails and stout legs. They did not possess trunks, although *Moeritherium* may have had a thick upper lip. The structure of the skull, particularly the teeth, reveals proboscidean affinities.

The skull as a whole was specialized; it was long, with the eye set far forward. The back of the skull was broad and forwardly sloped, giving a large area of attachment for strong neck muscles. The lower jaw was deep, and its articulation with the cranium placed high above the level of the teeth, a feature common to many herbivorous mammals. There were also some signs of air cells in the skull, a feature typical of the modern elephants. Although *Moeritherium* was about the size of a pig, its limbs already showed indications of increased size, and some of the bones, such as the femur, were distinctly elephantine.

Barytherium grave and other barytheres (Family Barytheriidae)

Much of our understanding of the Barytheriidae is based on the material collected in the Fayum Basin, Egypt, during the early 1900s, and in Dor el-Talha,

Below: Moeritherium *stood less than 1m(39in) at the shoulder and is thought to have spent most of its life in and around water, browsing on aquatic vegetation. The symbol at right compares* Moeritherium *to a female African elephant 3.2m(10.5ft) at the shoulder.*

Deinotherium

Libya, during the 1960s. The two localities are about 1,500km (just over 900 miles) apart and are interpreted as being part of a semi-aquatic environment. The Egyptian specimens were described soon after their discovery but the Libyan specimens, initially unstudied, eventually yielded additional information.

Both localities contained skeletal remains of mammals of proboscidean proportions, of approximately the same geological age (middle to late Eocene – 45 to 40 million years ago) and of similar environment, i.e. near shorelines and marshes. The Libyan material proved to be extremely valuable for comparison, because it included partial skeletons of animals of different ages and possibly of different sexes. More significantly, it is likely that there are two barythere species from Libya. One is *Barytherium grave*, the same species that was found in Egypt, and the other is a smaller, undescribed species. The larger one was about the size of the modern Asian elephant, and the smaller one was about the size of a cow.

It is possible that both also lived in Egypt, especially since the distance between the two localities (for a proboscidean) is relatively small. A scapula (shoulder blade) collected in the Fayum does not match any of the remains of the large species, *Barytherium grave*; rather, it matches the size of the smaller species from Dor el-Talha.

Deinotherium giganteum (Family Deinotheriidae)

The first deinotheres that were discovered, from the Miocene of East Africa, exhibited both primitive and highly

Above: Standing as much as 4m(13.1ft) at the shoulder, the largest of the deinotheres, Deinotherium giganteum, would have dwarfed a modern elephant, as is clear from the symbols shown at right. The downwardly curving lower tusks were possibly used for digging roots, or even as 'anchors' during overnight rest periods at the river's edge.

specialized characters. Other discoveries were made in Asia and Europe; none in the New World. These fossils were of the middle-late Miocene, Pliocene and Pleistocene epochs (between 15 and 2 million years ago). Based on the elevated position of the external nostrils, they probably had a developed trunk, perhaps shorter than that of living elephants. If they had survived to the present time, it would probably be very difficult for a layman to understand why the African and the Asian elephants would not have been classified in the same family with them. The differences lie in the skeletal anatomy, particularly the teeth, which are quite different in *Prodeinotherium* and *Deinotherium* compared to those of *Loxodonta* and *Elephas*. The former had only two or three ridges, with very simple cusps, whereas the latter have up to 29 ridges, with complex patterns. The enamel on deinothere teeth was thicker than on those of elephantids (about 5-8mm/0.2-0.3in compared to 1-5mm/0.04-0.2in).

Naturalists of the early 19th century believed that this 'terrible beast' (as the name 'deinothere' implies, from the Greek *deinos*, 'terrible' and *therion*, 'beast') was a herbivorous sea monster or, with its pair of formidable down-curved 'canines', a carnivorous beast.

Other characters of Deinotheriidae, some of which render it more primitive than Elephantidae, include:

(a) A dorsally flattened skull with an upper jaw with no tusks (most advanced proboscideans have had a high, domed cranium).
(b) Long, down-recurved lower jaw and tusks. No other proboscidean has this unique character.
(c) The dentition was replaced in a vertical, rather than the horizontal fashion found in elephants.
(d) A number of primitive skeletal features that deinotheres shared with moeritheres but which do not occur in members of the Elephantidae.

The function of the unusual tusks protruding from the lower jaw is unknown. It has been suggested that they were employed for digging and extracting roots or more fancifully that deinotheres, living in rivers, used the tusks to anchor themselves to the bank where they rested during the night.

Because of their mixture of extremely primitive and specialized characters, it is believed that deinotheres evolved very rapidly, and their successive changes were principally manifested in their size.

Palaeomastodon

Above: Palaeomastodon, *one of the earliest proboscideans, stood at least 2m(6.6ft) tall and is believed to have been a forest and savanna dweller. The size symbol shown above is based on a height of 2.5m(8.2ft) at the shoulder.*

Deinotheres may have had rapid initial evolutionary development, followed by a long period of evolutionary stability at a high level of specialization. Fossil evidence suggests that their stature was comparable to those of present-day elephants. One species, *Deinotherium giganteum*, was a giant, towering over even the modern African elephant, being 4m(just over 13ft) or more at the shoulder.

The bizarre appearance of deinotheres and some of their primitive characters caused some researchers to remove them from the Proboscidea but, based on osteological characters, they are now accepted as members of the order. They were well adapted; the persistence of the single genus *Deinotherium* through about 20 million years is the best testimony for its ability to adapt to changing environments. The disappearance of deinotheres during the Pleistocene epoch is believed to be a part of a pattern of extinction; other proboscideans became extinct at the end of the Cenozoic era.

Palaeomastodon beadnelli (Family unnamed or Palaeomastodontidae)

This was one of the first proboscideans to be described from the Oligocene (35 million years ago) of the Fayum Basin and was appropriately given the name *Palaeomastodon*, namely the 'ancient mastodon'. Measuring about 2m(6.6ft) at the shoulder, it was an Oligocene contemporary of *Phiomia* (see below). It is believed that *Palaeomastodon* was a forest and savanna dweller, whereas *Phiomia* lived in the lowlands. The low preservation potential of the bones of forest-dwelling animals may explain its comparative rarity in the fossil record.

Palaeomastodon is believed to have been

of the same general body structure and size as *Phiomia* (it reached about the size of a cow), and it may have had a less developed trunklike structure. In evolutionary terms, *Palaeomastodon* had less specialized dentition than *Phiomia*. The differences in the teeth between the two species are subtle, with *Phiomia* possibly one or more stages higher in the evolutionary tree.

Phiomia serridens (Family unnamed)

Phiomia was an Oligocene proboscidean (about 35 million years ago), a contemporary of *Palaeomastodon* and *Moeritherium*-type mammals. *Phiomia* had two pairs of tusks, two above and two below, that projected only a short distance beyond the jaws. The lower tusks were probably used to assist in feeding, whereas the upper ones showed the first stage in the development of offensive and/or defensive weapons. This was a relatively common evolutionary trend that reached its peak in the Pliocene and Pleistocene, and can still be seen in today's magnificently tusked African elephants.

Although smaller than the living elephant species, *Phiomia* was considerably larger than any of the moeritheres, standing perhaps as much as 2.4m(8ft) tall at the shoulder. The skeleton of *Phiomia* exhibits elephantine features, including an enlarged cranium. This increase in cranial size was accompanied by very little increase in weight, a condition possible because of air-filled compartments (diploe). The functions of these diploe and associated bony structures were multiple: to provide expanded surface area for muscle attachment; to better protect the braincase; and to equip the skull with the strength needed to support the

weight manifested by the developing proboscis and tusks. The presence of the short trunk is surmised from the retracted position of the nasal bones. The incisor teeth in the upper jaw developed into sharp and recurved tusks with an enamel band on their outer sides; these were possibly used for offence and defence and not for feeding. In the elongated lower jaw, there were two tusks projecting horizontally. Molars and premolars were low crowned, with central conules between the transverse ridges. The molars were trilophodont, i.e. equipped with three transverse pairs of bluntly conical cusps.

Mammut americanum (Family Mammutidae)

Mastodons were prehistoric elephant-like mammals that were separate from the family Elephantidae, including the two living elephants and the extinct mammoth. Neither the American mastodon nor the mammoth was a direct ancestor of the living elephants; they are placed at different branches of the 'elephant family tree' (see pages 16-17).

The vernacular name 'mastodon' is derived from the Greek meaning 'breast-shaped tooth', an appropriate description of the cheek teeth. This was intended to be its scientific (generic) name but a prior name, *Mammut*, had been coined. This was unfortunate, as *Mammut* is very similar to *Mammuthus*, the name used for mammoths, and invites confusion. Apparently, *Mammuthus* and *Mammut* originated from a Tartar word 'mamut' – a legendary giant rat whose bones could be found under the ice. Here the term 'mastodon' is used only for the American mastodon. Those mammutids and gomphotherids that were often called 'mastodonts' are referred to by their specific names or simply as 'mammutids' or 'gomphotheres'.

Dental morphology and the fossil record suggest that *Mammut* is more primitive than *Gomphotherium*, which is closer to Elephantidae. Fossil specimens of *Mammut* were found in the early Miocene (some 25-20 million years ago) of East Africa. Their ancestors therefore lived earlier, probably during the Oligocene (some 35-30 million years ago). *Gomphotherium* is early Miocene in age (about 25 million years ago), although its ancestors could have appeared in late Oligocene (some 30-25 million years ago).

Distribution of *Mammut americanum* in the New World

The miminum estimate of the number of specimens of *M. americanum* discovered in the New World up to 1990 is 1,473 individuals. The vast majority (just over 80 percent) were found in the formerly forested eastern half of North America. Radiocarbon dates indicate that it became extinct close to the Pleistocene-Holocene boundary, about 10,000 years ago. Some of the specimens of mastodons and mammoths were trawled up by fishing boats

Below: Mammut americanum, *the American mastodon, was about the same size as an Asian elephant. Possibly a forest dweller, fossil evidence suggests that the mastodon may have had an underfur and a covering of long blackish to auburn hair.*

Comparing mastodons and mammoths

MASTODON	MAMMOTH
SKELETON	
Generally stockier, with a heavier frame	More delicately built
Head and shoulders slightly above hindquarters	Head and shoulders considerably above hindquarters
More thoracic vertebrae (20-21 pairs)	Fewer thoracic vertebrae (18-20 pairs)
SKULL	
Flattened on top and bottom (low-domed)	Flattened on front and back (high-domed)
Eye borders rounder	Eye borders squarer
Tusks project slightly below horizontal, curve outward and then inward	Tusks project much below horizontal, curve outward then much more inward
LOWER JAW	
Elongated	Shortened (brevirostry)
Sometimes possess a pair of incisors (tusks) at front	No incisors (see under dentition)
DENTITION	
Nipple-like chewing surface (bunodont)	Flat chewing surface with ridges (lophodont)
Low-crowned (brachyodont)	High-crowned (hypsodont)
Crown without or with very little bonding material (cement)	Crown with cement
Thicker enamel	Thinner enamel
Fewer ridges per given length (low laminary index)	More ridges per given length (high laminary index)
Dental formula:	Dental formula:
$\dfrac{1033}{0033}$ or $\dfrac{1033}{1033}$ A total of 26-28 teeth	$\dfrac{1033}{0033}$ A total of 26 teeth
FEEDING HABITS	
Fed on a variety of plant material, mainly twigs and leaves (mostly a browser)	Fed on a variety of plant material, mainly grasses (mostly a grazer)
Feeding mainly involved a crushing action in an up-and-down motion	Feeding mainly involved a grinding action in a forward-backward motion

Mammut americanum

off the eastern seaboard of the United States. These records provide us with valuable information on the habitat, topography and overall concentration of these proboscideans in North America.

It is evident that mammoths (*Mammuthus*) were more prevalent in the western than in the eastern portion of North America. When we superimpose the distribution map of *Mammut americanum* onto that of *Mammuthus*, they overlap in the areas along the Mississippi River Basin, and that overlap appears to be less dense as we move away from the river to the east or the west. For example, it was reported that for the state of Michigan as of 1989, 219 remains of *Mammut* were found, compared to 47 of *Mammuthus*. The corresponding numbers for Nebraska and Florida are 49 and 408, and 249 and 290, respectively. It is possible that this 'lopsidedness' is more prominent north east of the Mississippi River than in the southeastern USA.

EXAMPLES AMONG THE 'GOMPHOTHERES'

This group of proboscideans contains a variety of genera and species, making it the most heterogeneous assemblage of gomphotherid species. There is perhaps more disagreement among proboscidea-nologists about the taxa that should be included among the gomphotheres than about other groupings within the Proboscidea. Some authors divide this assemblage into two major groups: the trilophodont and the tetralophodont gomphotheres. As the names imply, the first had three lophs, or crests, on their cheek teeth, whereas the second had four. Others argue that this division is artificial, and that environmental factors may influence similarities (such as parallelism) in dental characters. The following brief summary features some of the better known gomphothere taxa arranged alphabetically. They are *Anancus*, *Cuvieronius*, *Gomphotherium* and *Platybelodon*.

Anancus arvernensis
(Family unnamed)

Anancine proboscideans are one of the experimental side branches of the main evolutionary trunk. There may be between four and thirteen species, the synonymy has not yet been worked out. One of these, *Anancus osiris*, was unearthed in Egypt and was named after the Egyptian god Osiris. In these Miocene, Pliocene and Pleistocene taxa, the lower jaws became shorter than in basal gomphotheres, and they lacked lower tusks. The upper tusks became longer than in their Miocene ancestors. One well-known species, *Anancus arvernensis*, from the Pliocene of Europe had extremely long (3m/10ft) straight tusks.

Cuvieronius humboldtii
(Family unnamed)

Cuvieronius humboldtii (named after the celebrated anatomist and palaeontologist Cuvier and explorer Humboldt, respectively) was one of the few proboscidean genera to reach South America. It was an advanced gomphothere in the sense that it was of elephantine proportions, and its cranium contained air-cells, found also in *Mammut*, *Elephas* and *Mammuthus*. As in other advanced gomphotheres, the cheek teeth may have been replaced in a horizontal fashion. The premolars and molars of *Cuvieronius* had four to five ridges, and these included complex trefoil patterns. The lower jaw was short, devoid of tusks, yet in the upper jaw, the tusks were long (over 1m/39in), rounded, straight or upturned, with a reduced or no enamel band. Closely related genera include *Stegomastodon*, *Haplomastodon* and *Rhynchotherium*.

Based on the rocks in which *Cuvieronius* was found, it is believed to have inhabited plains, and was probably a grazer as well as a browser. It apparently lived until the end of the Pleistocene, and there is at least one report of a cranium of *Cuvieronius* with supposed flint spear holes, presumably inflicted by South American natives.

Gomphotherium angustidens
(Family unnamed)

Gomphotherium is the type genus of gomphotheres. It is a well-known and widespread member of this group, whose remains were discovered in Miocene deposits in Africa, Asia, Europe and North America. It is estimated that *Gomphotherium* was nearly as large as an Asian elephant, with two pairs of tusks; one in the upper jaw and the other in the lower jaw. Based on the position of the external nasal opening, the short neck and long limbs it is also believed that *Gomphotherium* had a short well-developed trunk. Dental characters of gomphotheres, and particularly those of *Gomphotherium*, were of the generalized elephantid type; the teeth of subsequent elephant genera and species included features already found in gomphotherids. On the chewing surfaces, the cheek teeth were multicusped, each of which was composed of dentine and covered with thick enamel; many teeth have three transverse ridges, or lophs. In side view the teeth have low

Below: Gomphotherium *was about 2.5-3m (8.2-9.8ft) tall at the shoulder, about the size of a small modern elephant. It is unknown whether it had a shaggy coat, but its form of teeth make an important link between those of* Palaeomastodon *and the modern elephants.*

Gomphotherium

(brachyodont) crowns. The length of the combined tooth sockets in the lower jaw indicates that three teeth may have functioned simultaneously. Each successive tooth is larger than previous ones, so that tooth replacement is believed to have involved horizontal as well as vertical components.

The first two molars had three pairs of transverse, conical cusps. When worn, these display clearly defined, narrow closed loops of enamel, and within them the typical dentine found in all proboscideans. Enamel and dentine are distinctly contrasted by their colour and durability; the former is shiny and dark, whereas the latter is dull brown. Enamel is more durable than dentine. The third molar of many gomphotheres was elongated by the development of a 'heel' (cingulum) behind the last two of the paired cusps.

Platybelodon grangeri (Family unnamed)

Perhaps one of the best-known gomphotheres was the shovel-tusked *Platybelodon*. Soon after it was discovered in the 1920s, it was a celebrity in the scientific and popular literature because of the clear similarity between its lower tusks and a shovel. Uncovered in the Miocene of Asia (about 20 million years ago), *Platybelodon* had small upper tusks but lower tusks completely flattened and growing in juxtaposition to form a shovel, presumably to uproot marshy vegetation. A contemporaneous gomphothere that filled a similar niche in North America was *Amebelodon*. Although superficially similar, the tusk cross section of *Amebelodon* reveals dentine lamellae, whereas in *Platybelodon*, the cross section consists of minute dentinal rods, believed to be a derived or specialized feature that functioned as reinforcement.

THE STEGODONS (Family Stegodontidae)

The Stegodontidae appears to have originated in Asia during the late Miocene and early Pliocene epochs (between 8 and 4 million years ago) from a gomphothere-like ancestor. Some lineages spread into Europe, others migrated to Africa. Certain members of this family were so extremely derived, or specialized, in the morphology and architecture of their skull and teeth that they truly represent a successful lineage. Their molars, however, were low-crowned.

The unspecialized stegodons could easily be placed as intermediate forms between certain gomphotheres and the least advanced elephantids. For example, *Stegolophodon* had a short lower jaw and large upper tusks. The cheek teeth were composed of transverse ridges, or lamellae, and each of these was made up of tiny cusps, or small cones, known as conelets. Each conelet was placed in direct contact with an adjacent conelet and all

Platybelodon

were arranged in rows across the ridges, similar to the four fingers on our hands. Like their ancestors and descendants, stegodons replaced their cheek teeth horizontally. This trend began to manifest itself in members of the family Mammutidae at least 30-25 million years ago.

Stegodon ganesa

Perhaps the best-known of all the stegodons is *Stegodon ganesa*. The generic name

Above: *The upper tusks of* Platybelodon *were relatively small, but the lower tusks were vertically flattened and juxtaposed, hence the popular name 'shovel tusker'. Platybelodon was a small proboscidean, standing about 2m(6.6ft) high at the shoulder.*

Below: *The skull of* Platybelodon *from the Miocene of Asia, exhibited in the Beijing National History Museum in China. The lower tusks are thought to have been used to uproot water plants. A similar-looking gomphothere that flourished on the other side of the globe was the* Amebelodon *of North America. The 'shovel-type' lower tusks developed through parallel or convergent evolution in response to its similar habitat, not because of any genetic lineage between the creatures.*

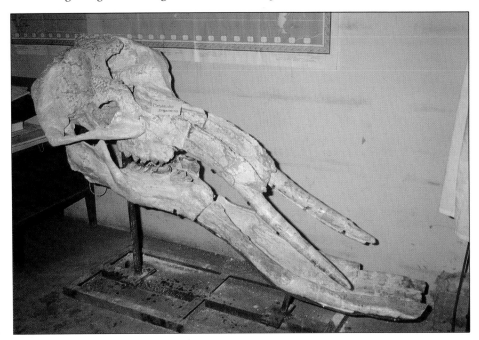

Stegodon

Above: Stegodon *is recognizable by its stature (3.5m/11.5ft) and formidable tusks. The stegodontids are believed to have arisen in Asia and spread to Africa and Europe, but not to the Americas. They may have lived in forests.*

is derived from the Greek *steg* for 'roof' and *odon* for 'tooth', probably referring to the arched occlusal surface of the teeth. The species name refers to Ganesa – the elephant-headed Hindu god of success.

This species grew to a height of over 3.5m(11.5ft). Its height, however, was not its most attractive feature but rather its upper tusks, which were formidable in size and architecture. They almost reached the ground and were curved sideways and upwards. They were placed inside the premaxillary bones in such a way that they appear to have been too close to each other at their base to permit the trunk to be held between the tusks. If this is true, then an adult would have had to have held its trunk on the outside of either the left or the right tusk – an uncomfortable position to hold for a long time and an awkward direction to feed. It is likely that they rested the trunk on the tusks, as has been observed in the living elephants. Young stegodons may not have had to behave in this manner because the tusks would have been small and would not have obstructed their trunks.

Fossil evidence suggests that stegodons evolved in Asia parallel to the true elephants in Africa. Stegodons are believed to have inhabited forested areas, close to water sources, and their diet may have consisted of bamboo shoots and leaves, among other foliage.

THE ELEPHANTS (Family Elephantidae)

The family Elephantidae may be divided into two subfamilies (Stegotetrabelodontinae and Elephantinae), with a total of six genera (the four discussed below plus *Stegotetrabelodon* and *Stegodibelodon*) and 26 species. Most proboscidean characters are found in the skull. All extinct members of the family Elephantidae are pre-

sumed to have possessed a well-developed trunk. This assumption is based on the elevated position of the external nostrils. The presence of the trunk is particularly important in those species whose lower jaws were extremely shortened. With the trunk, elephantids could reach foliage high above bushes and short trees, as well as grasses low to the ground. Similarly, one may hypothesize that the trunk was also important in the evolution of social behaviour, particularly in those species that inhabited open savannas.

Fossil elephantids have been collected from sites in Africa, Europe, Asia, North America and Central America, but no authentic indigenous material has been reported from South America, although other proboscidean taxa – 'gomphotheres', for example – are known to have lived there. All four genera discussed below, although not necessarily the same species, were found in Africa, which is believed to be the cradle of elephantid evolution.

Primelephas gomphotheroides

This species is based on a specimen discovered in Chad, originally named *Stegodon korotorensis*, later reclassified as a true elephantid and named *Primelephas gomphotheroides*. The differences between stegodons and true elephants include the architecture of the crown of the molars (taking into account the spacing between the ridges – in stegodons the ridges are narrowly spaced), the V-shaped valleys between the ridges (stegodons have Y-shaped ones), and the presence of incisors in the lower jaws of *Primelephas*. Remains of *P. gomphotheroides* date from the latest Miocene of East Africa. Its environment was open wooded savanna. *Primelephas* is presumed to have given rise to later Elephantidae taxa, including *Loxodonta*, *Elephas* and *Mammuthus*.

Loxodonta africana and Elephas maximus

The two living species of elephants, the African elephant (*Loxodonta africana*) and the Asian elephant (*Elephas maximus*), are the end results of over 50 million years of evolution. The African elephant is the largest land mammal living today. Up to a certain point, being large is a definite advantage against predators, but more importantly, larger animals lose less heat per unit of their surface area than smaller animals. Loss of heat implies increased search for food and subsequently being exposed to the hazards of nature.

The African elephant is believed to have migrated in prehistoric times throughout the African continent but did not venture out of its boundaries, whereas the Asian elephant evolved in Africa and later migrated to Eurasia. One of the most fascinating questions in the evolution of the Proboscidea is how these two living species of elephants managed to survive to the present day while all others became extinct. One reason is that both possessed a mixture of specialized and generalized characters. These are the key to survival because they enabled the lineages of *Loxodonta* and *Elephas* to adapt to an ever-changing environment. Although it shared more characters with the Asian elephant than with the African, the mammoth was apparently too specialized and doomed to extinction.

Mammuthus primigenius

Perhaps the most familiar of all mammoths is the extinct woolly mammoth, *Mammuthus primigenius*, which lived until

Above: The fossilized skeleton of an extinct elephant, Elephas recki, lying as it was found and excavated in Kenya in 1974. Similar to but larger than a modern Asian elephant, this particular elephant appears to have lived and died about two million years ago.

Below: Primelephas lived in the African savanna about 5 million years ago and is the presumed ancestor of both the mammoth and the modern elephants. It was slightly smaller than modern elephants, measuring about 2.8m(9.2ft) at the shoulder.

Primelephas

Mammuthus primigenius

the very end of the Ice Age, about 10,000 years ago. Pictographs of mammoths are found on walls and ceilings of caves in Europe. Drawings were only one form of evidence that man and mammoths were contemporaneous; bones and, more significantly, frozen well-preserved carcasses of the woolly mammoth found in Siberia and Alaska are other reminders. The latter provide us with direct evidence of the external and internal anatomy of these proboscideans. The dense coat of hair may explain how they survived in the arctic climate.

Discovered in 1900, the Berezovka mammoth (named after the river in Siberia where it was found) became a famous frozen carcass at the time. It took a year to reach the desolate area and bring it to Petrograd (now Leningrad), where it is now exhibited in the Zoological Museum. Another almost complete mammoth carcass was that of 'Dima', whose frozen body was discovered in the Soviet Union, in 1977. It was found in one piece in permafrost in the basin of the Kolyma River. Radiocarbon dating has provided conflicting ages, one of which was 40,000 years old. Its tissues were so well preserved that it provided a unique opportunity for scientists, who were able to demonstrate intact red blood cells and ancient proteins.

The extinction of mammoths and mastodons

Sheer numbers are no guarantee of the survival of a species. It has been reported that since the year 1600 AD, more than 50 mammals and 100 bird species have dis-

appeared or become extinct from our planet as a result of human activities. In these cases, it was possible to document these events, although it is unknown how many more species disappeared before the 1600s.

Exactly what the factors were that contributed to the extinction of mammoths, mastodons and other megafauna at intervals during the Cenozoic era and at the end of the Ice Age, no one will ever know. Climatic changes have been cited as a principal cause for Pleistocene extinction. Other factors may include competition with species that have similar ecological requirements, and hunting by man. Palaeoindians of North America and indigenous inhabitants of other continents, including Stone Age man, left their marks on bones and implements they made. Because of the longer generation times and smaller population sizes in larger species compared to smaller ones, the effect of any of these possible factors would be greater on the megafauna than on the microfauna. The demise of mammoths and mastodons seems to have been caused by many events. They have been trapped in tar pits, killed with heavy deadfalls, and exploited as a source of food, clothing and dwelling material – archaeologists have found their bones with butcher marks, charring and embedded projectile points, as well as finding remains of shelters built with their bones and tusks.

Although the evidence for man's contribution to the extinction of mammoths and mastodons is unequivocal, his impact was probably small. The causes of

Above: *At 3m(9.8ft) high at the shoulder and armed with long, curved tusks, the woolly mammoth,* Mammuthus primigenius, *must have been a daunting prey for early man. Nevertheless, it seems to have been an unequal match, for hunting by man seems to have been at least partly responsible for the demise of these magnificent creatures.*

the extinction were probably complex, yet they may be summarized in one word; overspecialization. Regardless of what the body size of a particular species was, mammals that were adapted to a particular habitat and diet were likely to be affected more than those that were generalists.

The message we must convey as a result of these observations is that the fate of the remaining two species that survived through the Holocene must not be the same as that of their cousins, the mammoths and other giants. Our love for elephants extends beyond regarding them as collector's items; it is our conscientious obligation to do our utmost to ensure that these noble mammals do not disappear from the planet Earth.

Above: *Preserved for thousands of years in the permafrost of Siberia, this almost complete body of a mammoth was discovered in the basin of the Kolyma River in 1977. Later given the name 'Dima', this carcass provided a wealth of material for scientific analysis.*

Right: *Scientists at Leningrad's Zoology Institute of the USSR Academy of Sciences study the body of a baby mammoth found in the soil of the Yamal Peninsula, well within the Arctic Circle. The frozen carcass had retained the proboscis, head, legs and some of the fur.*

Left: *An electron micrograph of a blood cell recovered from the soft tissues of 'Dima', the frozen mammoth discovered in Siberia. Other investigations and detailed biochemical tests revealed telltale evidence of ancient proteins – or at least fragments of them.*

ANATOMY & PHYSIOLOGY

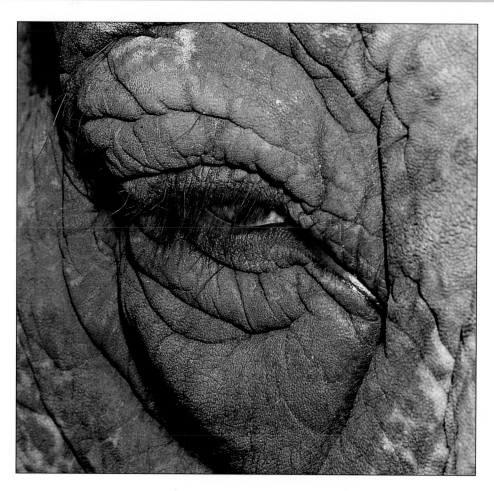

*For the size of its head, an elephant has small
eyes, with long lashes. There is only a vestigial
tear gland but another gland has taken over its
function. There is no tear duct and the 'tears'
simply evaporate, although they sometimes
overflow and run down the cheek.*

The most obvious difference between the African and the Asian elephant is the size of their ears – those of the African are larger. There are, however, many other anatomical differences, and these are considered in more detail on pages 32-33. To help us understand the similarities and differences between the two living African and the Asian species, however, let us first go back in time and briefly examine the entire 'elephant family tree', not just two of its twigs. This 'holistic' approach is crucial because it not only provides us with practical comparisons between them, but also yields a wealth of information for determining which of the two living species is more primitive (generalist) or derived (specialist) than the other, a decision that cannot be made simply by comparing the two species alone. This determination of generalist versus specialist between the African and the Asian elephants can form a useful foundation for our understanding of the differences in their anatomy, behaviour and ecology.

As we have seen on pages 12-29, at the base of the elephant family tree, some 50-60 million years ago, scientists believe that pig-sized mammals made up the basic stock from which other elephant-like creatures, collectively known as proboscideans, evolved. The roots of this tree go further back in time to the closest relatives of elephants and their ancestors. Based on morphological and biochemical evidence, it appears that manatees and dugongs (dolphin-sized, strictly aquatic mammals) and hyraxes, or conies, (rabbit-sized, terrestrial mammals) are the closest living relatives of elephants, even though all three groups have sharply contrasting external appearances and occupy extremely different habitats.

If we look at an evolutionary tree of the Proboscidea (on pages 16-17), we note that the branch of the American mastodon (*Mammut americanum*) reaches a 'dead end'. Mastodons, therefore, were not the predecessors of mammoths or other members of the family Elephantidae. It is also evident from the evolutionary tree that mammoths (genus *Mammuthus*) were more closely related to the living Asian elephants (genus *Elephas*) than the living African elephants (genus *Loxodonta*). The two proboscidean species found in the Rancho La Brea tar pits in California are *Mammuthus imperator* and *Mammut americanum*. They are believed to have arrived here in two separate lines of descent via the Bering Land Bridge.

The mosaic advantage
It is generally accepted that among the four proboscidean taxa mentioned above, *Mammut* is the most primitive, followed successively by *Loxodonta*, *Elephas* and *Mammuthus*; the last being the most specialized. How then, can one explain why *Loxodonta africana*, and *Elephas maximus* are the only two to survive out of the 352 proboscideans identified? A review of the literature and personal observations indicate that elephants exhibit a mosaic, or mixture, of characters that enable them to adapt to mild and extreme environmental conditions. Among these mosaic characters are the primitive (generalized) low metabolic rate and features found in the heart and vessels, such as the presence of paired anterior venae cavae (large veins returning blood to the heart), and in the feet, such as the pentadactyl arrangement – the presence of five digits. (The visible 'toe nails' are not attached to the digits and vary in number – see the tables on pages 32-33). The specialized proboscidean characters are found mainly in the head and include the teeth, trunk and musth (temporal) glands. In terms of evolutionary advantage of a species, the generalized features are probably more significant for survival than the specialized ones. Once a species specializes, its chances for success in the long-term are reduced.

The skeleton
As in all mammalian species, the skeleton of an elephant is divided into four major parts: the skull, vertebral column, appendages, and the ribs and sternum. The skull includes the cranium with the upper jaw and teeth, and the mandible, or lower jaw, and teeth. Five sections make up the vertebral column. Beginning

Above: Heads of Asian (upper) and African (lower) bull elephants. Note the prominent dome on the head of the Asian species and the different sizes and shapes of the ears. Patches of skin lacking pigmentation are typical of the Asian species and are variable in extent. The trunk of the African elephant has more 'rings' (annulations) and is generally more 'floppy' than that of the Asian elephant.

COMPARING ASIAN AND AFRICAN ELEPHANTS

The subspecies of the living elephants described here are based mostly on external characters and are a synthesis of the many more subspecies assigned in the past. The forest African elephant (*Loxodonta africana cyclotis*) occupies a habitat with generally more canopy forest than that of the savanna, or bush, African elephant (*Loxodonta africana africana*). The so-called 'pygmy' elephants attracted much attention for centuries, but recent work has shown that all the 'pygmy' and/or 'water' elephants were varieties of the forest and/or savanna African elephant subspecies.

Characteristics of the Asian elephant
(*Elephas maximus*)

Weight: 3-5 tonnes (6,615-11,025lb)
Height at shoulder: 2-3.5m(6.6-11.5ft)
Highest point: At top of head
Shape: Back – Convex or level
       Belly – Almost horizontal or 'sagging' in the middle
       Head – Compressed antero-posteriorly; has dorsal
          bulges, dished forehead
Ears (pinnae): Smaller, do not exceed height of neck.
In mature individuals dorsal edges of pinnae fold laterally
Skin: Smoother
Number of ribs: Up to 20 pairs
Teeth: Narrow compressed loops on chewing surface
Tusks: Males have tusks; absent or reduced in females
Trunk: Less rings, more rigid. Tip of trunk has one 'finger'
Number of nail-like structures: Forefeet 5
                         Hind feet 4 or 5

Subspecies within the Asian elephant

Sri Lankan subspecies	Mainland subspecies	Sumatran subspecies
(*E. m. maximus*)	(*E. m. indicus*)	(*E. m. sumatranus*)
Weight: 3-5 tonnes (6,615-11,025lb)	**Weight:** 2.5-4.5 tonnes (5,512-9,922lb)	**Weight:** 2-4 tonnes (4,410lb-8,820lb)
Height at shoulder: 2-3.5m (6.6-11.5ft)	**Height at shoulder:** 2-3m (6.6-9.8ft)	**Height at shoulder:** 2-2.5m (6.6-8.2ft)
Skin colour: Darkest, with large and distinct patches of depigmentation on ears, face, trunk and belly	**Skin colour:** Colour and depigmentation inbetween the other two subspecies	**Skin colour:** Lightest, with the least depigmentation
Size of ears: Largest	**Size of ears:** Inbetween	**Size of ears:** Smallest
Number of ribs: 19 pairs	**Number of ribs:** 19 pairs	**Number of ribs:** 20 pairs

A female Asian (left) and a male African elephant. Some obvious differences are the leaner look of the African species and the squarer, more chunky appearance of the Asian elephant. Tusks are vestigial in the female Asian elephant and hardly protrude beyond the lip line. The ears are clearly smaller in the Asian elephant compared to the African species. The two-fingered tip of the trunk is obvious in the African species; the Asian elephant has only one 'finger'.

Characteristics of the African elephant
(Loxodonta africana)

Weight: 4-7 tonnes (8,820-15,435lb)
Height at shoulder: 3-4m(9.8-13.1ft)
Highest point: At top of shoulder
Shape: Back – Concave
        Belly – Slopes diagonally downwards from
                front to back
        Head – No compression; no bulges, no dish
Ears (pinnae): Larger, do exceed height of neck
In mature individuals dorsal edges of pinnae fold medially
Skin: More wrinkled
Number of ribs: Up to 21 pairs
Teeth: Lozenge-shaped loops on chewing surface
Tusks: Both sexes have tusks; larger in males
Trunk: Has more rings, less rigid. Tip of trunk has
two 'fingers'
Number of nail-like structures: Forefeet 4 or 5
                                   Hind feet 3, 4 or 5

Subspecies within the African elephant

Savanna subspecies *L. a. africana*	Forest subspecies *L. a. cyclotis*
Weight: 4-7 tonnes (8,820-15,435lb)	**Weight:** 2-4 tonnes (4,410lb-8,820lb)
Height at shoulder: 3-4m(9.8-13.1ft)	**Height at shoulder:** 2-3m(6.6-9.8ft)
Skin: Darker, has more hair, especially on the trunk and around the mouth	**Skin:** Lighter, not so much hair, except in the young elephant
Shape of ears: Triangular or trapezoidal	**Shape of ears:** Rounder
Tusks: Curved, thicker	**Tusks:** Straighter, slender
Number of nail-like structures: Forefeet 4 or 5 Hind feet 3, 4, or 5	**Number of nail-like structures:** Forefeet 5 Hind feet 4

from the front, they are cervical (neck), thoracic, lumbar, sacral, and caudal (tail). The number of vertebrae in each section may vary according to the species. For *Loxodonta africana*, the vertebral formula is cervical = 7, thoracic = 20-21, lumbar = 3-4, sacral = 4-6, caudal = 18-33. For *Elephas maximus* the vertebral formula is cervical = 7, thoracic = 19-20, lumbar = 3-5, sacral = 3-5, caudal = 24-34.

In a side view of a skeleton, it is clear that the legs are in almost a vertical position under the body – similar to the legs of a table. This arrangement, described as graviportal, provides a strong support for the vertebral column, the thoracic and abdominal contents, and of course for the great weight of the animal. In other mammals, such as a dog or a cat, for example, the legs are in an angular position. Some of the major apparent differences between the African and Asian species can be observed on the skeleton. These include the shape of the skull and the differences in the profile of their backs; that of the African is concave, while that of the Asian is convex. It is important to realize that the vertebral column between the fore and hind limbs is convex in both species, and only the outline of the tips of the spinous processes is different and this affects the external shape of the back.

Internal organs

The brain of an adult elephant weighs 4.5-5.5kg(10-12.1lb), and has a highly convoluted cerebrum and cerebellum. (In mammals, these areas control motor and muscle coordination, respectively). The temporal lobes, known to function as memory centres in humans, are relatively large in elephants. Most newly-born mammals have brains that weigh about 90 percent of the adult brain weight, but in elephants the figure is 35 percent (compared with 26 percent for the human brain). Hence, there is considerable growth of the brain after birth, which is probably responsible for the remarkable

learning ability of young elephants.

In absolute terms, the heart of an elephant is huge, weighing 12-21kg(26.5-46.3lb). In relative terms, however, it weighs only about 0.5 percent of the total body weight, a proportion normal for large mammals. (A human heart weighs about 300gm/10oz, thus for a person of about 80kg/160lb the heart weighs about 0.4 percent of the total body weight.) Unlike most other mammals, the heart of an elephant has a bifid (double-pointed) apex instead of the typical single-pointed heart shape. The double veins (anterior venae cavae) leading to the heart are unusual compared to those of most mammals. The bifid apex feature of the elephant heart is also common to sea cows, the elephant's closest relatives. The arteries are huge and, at junctions with other arteries, are strengthened with fibrous ridges that may become calcified with age and may even block the artery, giving rise to strokes or heart attacks. The walls of the veins are much thicker, proportionately, than those of smaller mammals and it is thought that this is due to the unacceptably high blood pressure that would otherwise be necessary to prevent these large vessels from collapsing.

The digestive system is of the simple type among mammals. The salivary glands produce a copious flow to soften the coarse food and ease its passage to the stomach, which is of an unusual cylindrical shape. It is essentially a storage organ, as most of the digestion takes place in the huge caecum, which acts as a fermentation vat where the cellulose in the food is broken down by bacteria. The combined length of the small and large intestines may reach 35m(about 100ft). On average, it takes about 24 hours to digest a meal. Elephants digest only about 44 percent of their food intake; the rest is voided in an undigested state. (For more on feeding and related aspects, see the chapter on *Ecology* starting on page 78.)

The lungs of an elephant are peculiar.

Above: *A bull African elephant with its penis extruded. During copulation, the penis is curved forwards into an S-shape in order to reach the downward- and forward-facing vaginal opening. Elephants frequently rest their trunks on their tusks, as shown here.*

There is no pleural cavity, as the lungs are partially attached to the wall of the chest and to the diaphragm. The elephant , therefore, breathes by direct muscular action and not by creating negative pressure within the chest cavity, as humans and most other mammals do. Its muscular power enables it to breathe easily under water and hence use its trunk as a schnorkel. Although the elephant draws water into its trunk to drink, it does not have to hold its breath while doing so, because it can also breathe through its mouth.

The kidneys of an elephant lie in the top of the body cavity on either side of the backbone at the level of the 'hips'. They are not kidney-shaped, but consist of a number of lobes bound together by a sheet of thick connective tissue. The region around the kidneys is an important site for storing fat. The rest of the urinary system, including the bladder, follows the typical mammalian pattern but is, of course, on a larger scale. The amount of urine produced by a captive Asian elephant averaged 5 litres (1.3 US gallons) per micturition, with a maximum of 11 litres (2.9 US gallons). The total production per day was about 50 litres (13 US gallons).

The reproductive organs

The male reproductive system consists of the typical parts found in other mammals. Unlike many mammals, however, the testes in elephants are permanently located inside the body, near the kidneys. In a fully grown male, the penis is long, muscular and controlled by voluntary muscles. It can reach a length of 1m(39in) and has a diameter of 16cm(6.3in) at the base. When fully erected, the penis has an S-shape with the top pointing upwards; the orifice is Y-shaped.

The female reproductive system is also typical of most mammals; the cervix in a non-pregnant elephant, however, is not

Left: *The mammary gland of an African elephant. In proportion to the elephant's body size, the breasts are about the same as those of a woman. They become swollen only when the elephant is lactating. Otherwise, they are shrunk and the nipples shrivelled. The calf sucks with its mouth, not its trunk. The forward position of the nipples is also found in primates, bats, some hyraxes, and in sea cows.*

Internal organs of a female African elephant

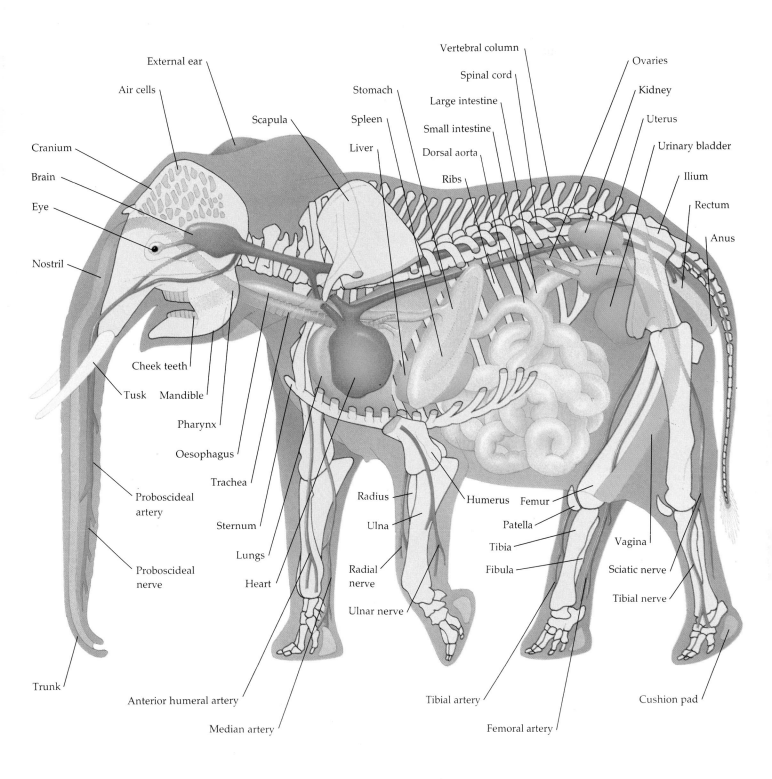

External ear
Air cells
Scapula
Cranium
Brain
Eye
Nostril
Cheek teeth
Tusk
Mandible
Pharynx
Oesophagus
Trachea
Proboscideal artery
Sternum
Proboscideal nerve
Lungs
Heart
Trunk
Anterior humeral artery
Median artery

Stomach
Spleen
Liver
Radius
Ulna
Radial nerve
Ulnar nerve

Vertebral column
Spinal cord
Large intestine
Small intestine
Dorsal aorta
Ribs
Humerus
Femur
Patella
Tibia
Fibula
Tibial artery
Femoral artery

Ovaries
Kidney
Uterus
Urinary bladder
Ilium
Rectum
Anus
Vagina
Sciatic nerve
Tibial nerve
Cushion pad

Above: *In this 'see-through' female African elephant, the respiratory system is shown in blue, the blood system in bright red, the nervous system in purple, the digestive organs in pale pink, the urinogenital system in green, and the main elements of the skeleton in beige.*

Looking at the skeleton, it is clear that there is a bridgelike backbone supported by stout limbs, one of the features of the so-called 'graviportal' arrangement. The leg bones are placed vertically above each other, forming a rigid column when at rest. This helps the elephant to sleep standing up without the risk of its legs buckling. As we have noted on pages

32-33, the Asian elephant has up to 20 pairs of ribs, whereas the African elephant has up to 21 pairs. It is clear from the illustration that the external shape of the back is influenced by the bony processes extending from the vertebrae. In the African elephant, the result is a concave shape; in the Asian elephant, the spinous processes give rise to a level or convex shape to the back. Note that the brain occupies only a small part of the skull. The development of air cells (diploe) in the cranium has enabled the skull to grow to a large size – an evolutionary trend in the Proboscidea – without enormous weight. Other features of interest include the

downward opening of the vagina, which led early observers to speculate that elephants copulated belly to belly. Note that the genital organs are located high up in pelvic region, as are the testes and related organs in the male elephant. The tubular stomach is mainly a storage organ and most digestion takes place in the caecum, which branches off from the large intestine. An interesting feature of the elephant's anatomy is the absence of a pleural cavity to contain the lungs. Because the lungs are attached directly to the chest wall and diaphragm, this means that elephants inflate and deflate the lungs by muscular action.

a distinct structure. The clitoris is a well developed organ; it can reach 40cm(16in) long and is manipulated by a dedicated muscle. The genital canal is very long, about 70-90cm(27.5-35.4in), and the vulval opening is located between the female's hind legs, not under the tail as, for example, in cows and horses. This unusual position of the female genitalia, which is similar to the male's position, has confused many elephant workers. In fact, there is a well-known case of a female that was considered to be a male throughout her 25 years of life and her true identity became clear only after she died. One way to distinguish between the sexes of the African elephant is to look at their heads in side view; that of a female has an angular profile, while that of the male is round. The mammary glands are located between the forelegs, a condition that enables the mother to be in touch with her calf while it takes milk. When not pregnant or lactating, the mammary glands are shrunk and the nipples are shrivelled and pointing downwards. During the later stages of pregnancy, the glands swell and the nipples distend diagonally downwards and sideways, enabling the newborn calf to reach them easily. Each nipple may have 10-12 lactiferous ducts. (The reproductive cycle in elephants is described in the chapter on *Reproduction*, starting on page 64.)

Can the two elephant species interbreed?

Theoretically speaking, since the African and the Asian elephants are classified in two distinct genera, they would not be able to interbreed because that would violate the biological concepts of species and genus. The geographical separation of these two genera is such that inbreeding in the wild is practically impossible. In captivity, however, conditions are artificial and inbreeding among species and genera may take place. An unusual crossbreeding occurred in Chester Zoo, England, in 1979, when a female Asian elephant ('Sheba') and a male African elephant ('Jumbolino') bred. The resultant hybrid – 'Motty' – died 10 days after birth. This is the only case on record of interbreeding between *Loxodonta africana* and *Elephas maximus*.

The musth or temporal gland

The word musth is almost a household word among elephant people in the Far East; in Hindi, it means 'intoxicated'. The musth gland has been known for hundreds of years. 'The Mad Elephant' in the medallion Jataka – a story carved on a stone railing in Amaravati, India – dates to about AD150-300 (late Andra Period); it is one of the most fascinating stories carved in stone. The carving depicts an elephant, apparently in musth, bowing in submission before Buddha. Musth is a phenomenon known to occur in both

Asian and African elephants. It is associated with a secretion from the musth, or temporal, gland. The exact function of this gland is not known but it might be associated with sexual activity and/or communication. Male elephants in musth are known to be uncontrollable, and they may attack and kill their keepers.

The musth gland is also known as the temporal gland because of its location – just below the skin midway between the eye and the ear on each side of the elephant's head. There is a web of intricate blood vessels between the gland and the deep muscles of the head. These vessels were more evident in the musth gland of a male Asian elephant ('Ziggy') examined after death at Brookfield Zoo in Illinois, USA, than in a female Asian elephant ('Iki') examined at a later date. The skin in the temporal region is about 2cm(0.8in) thick, and the orifice of the gland varies from 1.5 to 2.5cm(0.6-1in) long. The left gland proper of Iki measured 14cm(5.5in) long, 13cm(5.1in) wide and 2.5cm(1in) deep, and its central chamber was 5.0 x 3.2 x 1.1cm(2 x 1.25 x 0.43in) long, wide and high respectively.

A correction must be made here – the so-called 'musth secretion' of mammoths in cave drawings is a modified version of what was depicted in the original drawing. In the original, drawn with black paint on the light coloured wall of Rouffignac Cave at Les Eyzies in southern France, about 13,000 years ago, the artist(s) depicted two mammoths facing each other; both seem to have tusks, and both are drawn as though the outline of the lower jaws are in continuation with the tusks. As is usually the case with

Detail of the elephant foot

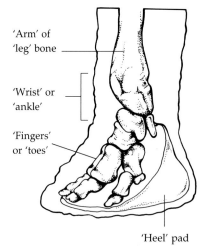

'Arm' of 'leg' bone

'Wrist' or 'ankle'

'Fingers' or 'toes'

'Heel' pad

Above: *Although the elephant appears to be flat-footed, it actually walks on its toes, as do ungulates. The 'heel' is really a pad of fatty and elastic connective tissues.*

Right: *The massive 'treelike' foot of the elephant. The toe nails are attached to the skin and not directly to the toe bones. The number varies among the subspecies of elephants.*

second and third generation information, a drawing of these two mammoths, with the one on the left having a dark line running down the side of its face as though it was 'musth secretion', appears in a book by D. Mazonowicz (*A Search for Cave and Canyon Art – Voices from Stone Age*, 1974). The illustration by D. Freeman (the author of *Elephants: the Vanishing Giants*, 1980) further accentuates this feature and, if the reader is not familiar with the original, it can be misleading. From discoveries of frozen mammoths in Siberia we know that they had long hair; if indeed the so-called mammoth 'musth secretion' was observed by Upper Paleolithic *Homo sapiens*, then this temporal secretion must have been so heavy that it poured over the long hair, a condition which may not be possible, or very rare, based on observations of temporal gland secretions in living elephants.

The skin

The old name of the order Proboscidea, 'Pachydermata', refers to their thick skin (*Pachys*: thick; *derma*: skin.). Thicknesses vary from paper thin on the inside of the ears, around the mouth and the anus, to about 2.5cm(1in) around the back and in some places on the head. Despite its thickness, the skin is a sensitive organ system, with sparse hair and bristles distributed unevenly on the body. Most noticeable hair concentrations are around the eyes, ear openings, chin, and the end of the tail. Young elephants are covered with brownish/reddish hair throughout, especially evident on the back and head profile. The amount of hair reduces with age and it darkens in colour.

The overall skin colour is usually grey,

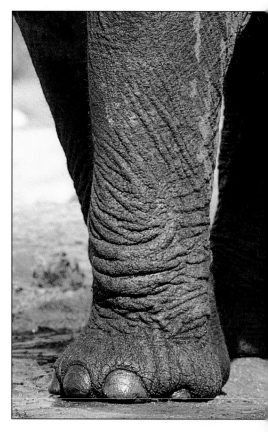

Above: A young Asian elephant. The Asian calf is much more hairy than the African and retains more hair in adult life. In this it is reminiscent of the woolly mammoth, although its hair does not help to keep it warm. Calves of this age are still dependent on the adults.

Right: The hide of an African elephant, showing the characteristic wrinkles, which, as here, tend to get filled with bits of grass. Despite its gnarled appearance, the skin is delicate and soft to the touch. No sweat glands have been found in the skin. The elephant cools itself by bathing and flapping its ears.

Below: A close view of the skin on the upper part of the trunk of a female Asian elephant. Lack of pigment, as seen on the lefthand side of the photograph, is typical of Asian elephants but is rarely seen in the African species.

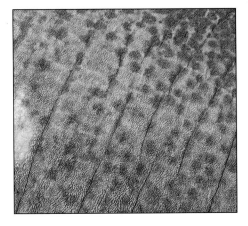

ears, whereas the woolly mammoth, having lived closest to the North Pole, had the smallest. That the ears of living elephants function as cooling devices can be demonstrated by the large number of blood vessels visible at the outer margins of the ear flaps, where the skin is about 1-2mm(0.04-0.08in) thick, and by the high frequency of ear flapping during warm days with little or no wind. Large ears also trap more sound waves than smaller

Left: An African elephant enjoying a good scratch on a termite mound in Kenya. The elephant's skin is sensitive and plagued by ticks and other parasites. Areas out of reach of the trunk are relieved in this way. Scratching also has a useful function of abrading the mound and returning nutrients to the soil.

although elephants in Africa often seem brown or even reddish from wallowing in mudholes of coloured soil that gets plastered on their skins. In Asia, wallowing usually results in darker or lighter tones of the original grey body colour. Wallowing appears to be an important behaviour in elephant societies; the mud seemingly protects against ultraviolet radiation, insect bites and moisture loss. Scratching against trees and bathing seem to be equally important behaviours related to skin care. It seems ironic that soon after bathing, elephants cover themselves with dust and the cycle repeats itself.

The ears

Generally speaking, the size of ears and other extremities is directly related to the amount of heat dissipated through them. On a global scale, those species that live close to the equator have, on average, bigger extremities than those species of about the same body size that live closer to the poles. The differences in the sizes of ears among the African elephant, the Asian elephant and the woolly mammoth (*Mammuthus primigenius*) can be explained based on their geographical distribution; the African elephant being closest to the equator, has the largest

Right: Bath time for a tame Asian elephant. Working elephants do not have the same opportunities as wild animals to splash water over themselves, and it is essential that their keepers should give them a daily bath to keep the skin in good condition. This activity also strengthens the bond between man and beast.

Below: A family unit of African elephants anointing themselves with mud. Why they do this is not altogether clear, but it serves to cool them and may help to control skin parasites and to keep the skin in good condition. Elephants certainly give the impression of thoroughly enjoying bathing in this way.

Subspecies of the Asian elephant

Right: Many subspecies of the Asian elephant have been described in the past but few have been accepted as valid by elephant biologists. The differences are not as distinct as those between the two African subspecies and the various types are best considered as belonging to a cline, i.e. a continuum, with no sharp divisions. The characters among these three forms of the Asian elephant change gradually from one extreme to another – beginning at Sri Lanka in the western part of their distribution and ending with Sumatra at the eastern limit. These illustrations reflect the main differences in body size and colour.

Elephas maximus maximus

Elephas maximus indicus

Elephas maximus sumatranus

The largest and the darkest of the three elephant forms, with largest ears. Patches of depigmentation on ears, face, trunk and belly – most evident among the three. Found in Sri Lanka and southern India.

Size, colour, and depigmentation inbetween. Found in Burma, Thailand, Laos, Vietnam, Cambodia and China.

Size smallest, colour lightest, with least depigmentation. Found in Malaysia and Sumatra.

Skull of young Asian elephant

Right: The skull of an elephant with bones cut away to expose the teeth. The only front teeth are the tusks, which are actually the incisors.

Below: The mouth of an African elephant showing what is probably the fourth molar in front and the fifth behind it. No more than two teeth in each half-jaw are in wear at the same time. Note the fleshy tongue and relatively small mouth.

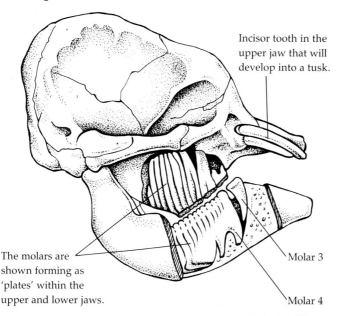

Incisor tooth in the upper jaw that will develop into a tusk.

The molars are shown forming as 'plates' within the upper and lower jaws.

Molar 3

Molar 4

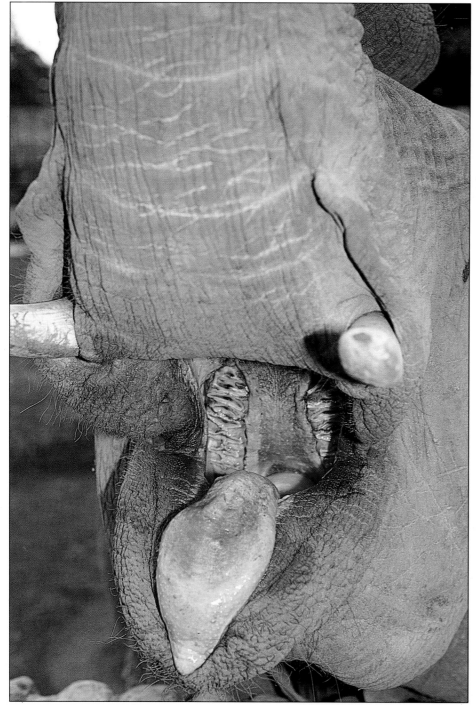

ones. It has been suggested that bull elephants in the wild use their ears to spread the odour released from their temporal glands, a smell to inform other males and possibly females of their presence.

The teeth in general

The number of teeth is identical for the two living elephant species in the lifetime of an individual; the total includes two upper incisors (tusks), no canines, twelve deciduous (milk) premolars, and twelve molars. These numbers are expressed in a simple dental formula to show one half of the jaws (in each pair, the numbers on the left represent the upper jaw and the number on the right the lower), and these numbers are then multiplied by two to give the total number of teeth. The dental formula is: incisors 1/0, canines 0/0, premolars 3/3, molars 3/3; a total of 26 teeth.

Unlike most other mammals, elephants do not replace their cheek teeth – the molars and premolars – in a vertical manner, i.e. by a new tooth developing and replacing the old one from above or below, but rather in a horizontal progression. A newborn elephant has two or three cheek teeth in one jaw quadrant and as it becomes older, new teeth develop from behind and slowly move forward. At the same time, the previous teeth are worn away, move forward and fragment. Pieces of teeth can be found in the field or enclosure, or in their faeces, if the animal swallows them. And so, as a conveyor-belt system, new and bigger teeth replace the old ones, six times in the life of an elephant.

Tusks, tushes and ivory

In living elephants, the deciduous incisors, or tusks, are replaced by permanent second incisors within 6 to 13 months after birth. Permanent tusks grow con-

Molar teeth compared

The African elephant has lozenge-shaped ridges on the surface (hence its generic name Loxodonta), whereas the ridges are parallel in the Asian species. During chewing movements the ridges act like the blades of scissors as the upper and lower teeth pass over each other.

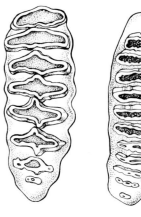

African   Asian

Progressive replacement of the molar teeth

Right: *The teeth erupt at the back of the mouth and move forward to fall out in pieces at the front. The blue arc shows the approximate ages at which the teeth are exchanged. The first three teeth are small because the jaw itself is small and they have to be replaced frequently to keep pace with the elephant's growth. Once the last tooth is lost, the elephant cannot feed properly and soon dies from malnutrition. By that time, the animal may be 60 years old.*

Below: *An African elephant in Samburu National Reserve, Kenya, feeding on a branch of an Acacia tree. The diet of an elephant is a mixture of grass and browse, which, as can be seen here, includes thorny vegetation. Elephants chew by moving the jaws fore and aft and not from side to side, as most mammals do. The elephant is adept at manipulating its food so as not to injure the soft parts of its delicate mouth. This type of feeding by elephants can severely damage trees and bushes, leading to habitat destruction.*

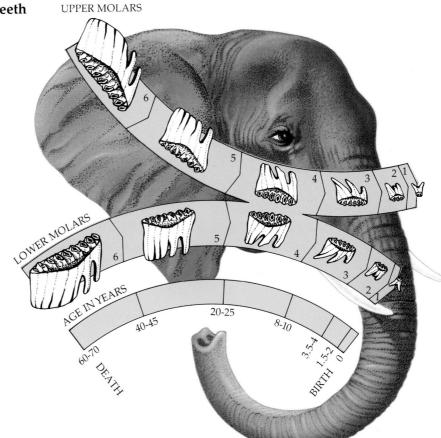

Above: This cross section of an elephant tusk shows the diamond-shaped striations, called 'engine turning'. These identify the material as genuine elephant ivory and distinguish it from the teeth of hippos, pigs, walruses and other animals with tusks – also called 'ivory'.

Below: Tusks of a large African bull elephant. About a third of the tusk is hidden within the upper jaw. The enamel cap is soon worn away to expose the dentine and is not replaced. Elephants tend to be right- or left- 'handed' so that one tusk is more worn than the other.

tinuously at the rate of 17cm(6.7in) per year, and are composed mostly of dentine. In cross section, a tusk shows a pattern of lines that criss-cross each other to form small diamond-shaped areas visible with the naked eye. This pattern has been called 'engine turning', and is unique to the Proboscidea. The tusks of pigs, hippopotami and walruses are canine teeth; those of narwhals are incisors. Since none of these mammals exhibit 'engine turning' in their tusks, the term ivory should be applied to proboscideans' tusks only.

Ivory carvers are familiar with this unique elephantine 'engine turning' and other properties. Even an uninformed layman who has examined a tusk a few times in different sections would be able to distinguish between real and fake ivory. Unfortunately, ivory substitutes, such as alabrite, celluloid, bone, ivoryite, ivorine, micarta and Galolith, are intended to be just that – substitutes; they will never replace the real thing. It has been noted that the hardness and, therefore, the carvability of ivory differs according to its geographical origin, and the habitat and sex of the elephant. For example, the ivory of elephants from West Africa (mostly forest African elephant, *Loxodonta a. cyclotis*, has been preferred by ivory carvers who noted that this ivory is harder than all other ivories, yet elastic and therefore more suitable for carving than those of the savanna, or bush, African elephant (*Loxodonta a. africana*) or the Asian elephant (*Elephas maximus*). Some also claim that female's ivory is superior to that of a male, as it has a closer grain. Data on volumes of carved ivory indicate that the vast majority comes from the savanna African elephant. These statements, although they come from reliable sources, should be viewed in context, because, on the whole, the Asian species has shorter and lighter tusks than those of the African species. It is possible that because the tusks that come from the savanna elephant are larger and available in greater quantities than those from the forest elephant (there are more of the former, and also the herds contain more females than males), ivory carvers developed a 'feel' for the ivory of female *L.a. africana* and therefore prefer it over that of *L.a. cyclotis* and *Elephas maximus*.

What exactly is ivory made of? Anatomically, ivory is a non-cellular matrix secreted by cells at the outer surface of the pulp cavity, called odontoblasts, that reach into the body of the tooth via microscopic tubes called dentinal tubules, or canaliculi. The secretion builds up a substance called dentine, a bonelike tissue found in the teeth of many animals that consists of up to 80 percent inorganic materials and 20 percent water and organic matter. The inorganic matter consists of deposits similar to the mineral hydroxiapatite (calcium, phosphate, oxygen and hydrogen), and the organic components are mostly collagen (a fibrous protein). The dentinal tubules are present along the radial section of a tusk, and their openings are visible in microscopic preparations. A cross section of a tusk that passes along the tubules shows the 'engine turning' pattern mentioned earlier. Theoretically, the greater the density of these dentinal tubules, the more flexible, and subsequently the softer, the tusk is. Electron microscope examinations of pulpal cavities seem to support this hypothesis, but only just. However, the earlier we go in the geological record, the harder the ivory becomes.

Early on in their development, the tusks bear a conical cap of smooth enamel that wears off at a later stage. Like all mammalian teeth, the pulp cavity of elephant incisors is well supplied with blood vessels and fine nerve branches; the tusks are thus sensitive to external pressure. On average, only about two-thirds of a tusk is visible externally, the rest is embedded in the socket, or alveolus, within the cranium. (This is shown in the diagram on page 107, in the chapter on *Disease & Mortality*.) Although elephants usually have one pair of tusks, three, four, five and even seven tusks have been observed. These supernumerary tusks may result from abnormal bifurcation of the permanent tusks, perhaps due to the effects of a bullet, a spear, or a splinter during calfhood.

Annual growth rings on tusks resemble those seen on the external surfaces of horns of sheep, for example, but differ from annual growth rings of trees, which can be seen only internally in a cross section. When viewed in cross section, a tusk shows concentric lines in addition to the criss-cross 'engine turning' pattern. The concentric lines are the edges of multiple cone-shaped structures whose annual growth layers were at one time visible at the external surface of the tusk during its development. Microscopic examinations of tusk show not only annual but also regular seasonal growth patterns. Once it is removed from an elephant body, ivory soon dries and begins to split along the concentric lines, unless it is kept cool and moist. Conversely, if it is kept in too hot and moist conditions, it will deteriorate. These water-absorbing properties of ivory are well known among certain African tribes, whose weathermen use the ivory as a rain predictor by planting it in the ground in selected locations.

To the living elephant, tusks are multipurpose instruments. Elephants may use their tusks to dig for water, salt and roots; to mark or debark trees; as levers for manoeuvring felled trees and branches; for work (in domestic animals); for display; as weapons of defence and offence; as trunk-rests; as protection for the trunk

(comparable to a bumper on a car); and may be akin to 'status symbols'.

Just as humans are left- or right-handed, so too are elephants left- or right-tusked; the tusk that is used more than the other is called the 'master tusk'. Master tusks can easily be distinguished since they are shorter and more rounded at the tip because of wear. In addition, master tusks are used, in combination with the trunk, to pluck grass blades. These tusks, therefore, usually have grooves near their tips, where the constant action of the grass wears a transverse furrow in the ivory.

For the record, bull elephants usually have longer and heavier tusks than cows; in African elephants, both sexes may have tusks of equal length. In Asian elephants, a tuskless bull is called a 'mukna' (sometimes spelled 'muckna') and small tusks that just protrude beyond the lips are called 'tushes'. The mere fact that the

Below: A bull elephant from Sri Lanka with exceptionally long and symmetrical tusks. This is a domesticated animal whose tusks would make it particularly valuable in ceremonial processions. The reduced pigmentation on the head is very typical in this subspecies.

words 'mukna' and 'tush' have been coined implies that there have been enough elephants exhibiting these characteristics. Contrary to common belief, some Asian bull elephants have huge tusks, bigger than the average size of the African species. One such male Asian elephant – the 'giant tusker of Udiapur' – was described by the celebrated zoologist Henry Fairfield Osborn as having tusks that ' . . . grew to such a length that he was unable to lie down and they were shortened at the extremities and encased in metal.' Another Asian bull elephant with huge tusks is Tommy (currently with the Ringling Brothers and Barnum & Bailey Circus, and called 'King Tusk'); although his tusks are trimmed at their tips, in 1985 his left tusk measured 145cm(57in), and his right one measured 157cm(62in) along the outside curvatures. For comparative purposes, the tusks of the legendary 'Ahmed' (an African elephant) measured 285cm(112in) and 297cm(117in). The longest recorded tusks of an African elephant measured 326.4cm(128.5in), and the heaviest weighed 102.7kg(226.5lb). Comparable figures for the Asian elephants are 302cm(119in) and 39kg(86lb). Data

collected during the last few decades indicates that African elephant average tusk weight has decreased at an alarming rate – about 0.4kg(0.9lb)/year, with an average of 12kg(26.5lb)/year in 1970 and 5kg(11lb)/year in 1989.

The trunk and how it works

The trunk, or proboscis (from the Greek and literally meaning 'before the mouth'), is the single most important feature of an elephant, and it is the character after which the mammalian order of elephants – the Proboscidea – was named. Anatomically, the trunk is a union of the nose and the upper lip. Its dexterity and its ability to perform various functions probably contributed to mankind's fascination with elephants.

A special flavour has been conveyed by artists and writers from the sixteenth through to the nineteenth century when they illustrated and described the trunk of an elephant. In 1715, the naturalist Hartenfels depicted it as a series of spiral rings similar to the 'horn of plenty'. The famous French anatomist Georges Cuvier and his colleagues examined the

trunk of an elephant and estimated the number of muscles at about 40,000. (Cuvier and Laurillard's exquisite volume was published in 1849.) On the other hand, in 1847, the Irish anatomist Harrison, when commenting on the number of muscles in the trunk, said that some people "... have attempted to count these muscles, but such an attempt is totally useless." One interesting description of an elephant trunk is that of a British writer, Nott, who wrote in 1886: "This trunk is composed of a mass of interlacing muscles, marvellously arranged, numbering, Cuvier estimates,

Right: The trunk of an elephant from the Aberdare National Park, Kenya. This shows that the African elephant is not as hairless as it might first appear. The wrinkles on the skin are more numerous than in the Asian elephant.

Below: An African elephant sniffing the air to gather information on its surroundings. Note how the skin on the upper surface wrinkles as the trunk is flexed. Also notice the two (very sensitive) fingerlike extensions at the tip of the trunk and the twin nostrils inside.

Cross section through an elephant's trunk.

Right: *The two large holes are the nostrils through which the elephant breathes and draws in water to squirt into its mouth. The great dexterity of the trunk, which can perform movements of delicate precision, is due to thousands of often tiny muscle units. These tend to be arranged either radially or longitudinally and by acting against one another, allow the trunk to be moved in any direction. Although so delicate in its movements, the trunk is also a very powerful organ that can lift heavy objects with ease.*

Proboscideal artery

Probiscideal artery

Skin

Nasal membrane

Nostrils

Proboscideal nerve

Proboscideal vein

Proboscideal vein

Radiating muscles

Longitudinal muscles

Septum between nostrils

Proboscideal vein

Proboscideal nerve

---

nearly forty thousand. Some running longitudinally and others radiating from the centre to the circumference, all so beautifully combined and adjusted to give it flexibility and strength, enabling it to be expanded or contracted, or wielded with that diversity of motion, and used in these manifold ways that must excite amazement when first seen, and from time immemorial have made the elephant's trunk an object of wonder and admiration. Some have described it as 'the elephant's hand', others as 'the snake hand', and the poor Kaffirs [members of a powerful group of South African Bantu tribes] regard it with such superstitious awe, that when they kill an elephant they solemnly inter [bury] the trunk.''

Recent research work suggests that there are over 100,000 muscle units in the trunk, which make it so extremely dexterous. It is said that an elephant can pick up a needle from the ground and bring it to its trainer. Although elephants are capable of picking up objects as small as a coin, however, the observations of mahouts and trainers suggest that elephants will pick up a small straw about the size of a needle, but not the needle itself. The degree of flexibility and manoeuvrability of the trunk as seen in the wild and in captivity is extraordinary and corroborates the underlying complex anatomical and physiological basis that enables elephants to conduct such a variety of functions and antics.

Photographs of elephant foetuses show how the upper lip and elongated embryonic nose combine to form the adult proboscis. The trunk has no bones or cartilage; it is composed of muscles,

blood and lymph vessels, nerves, little fat, connective tissues, skin, hair and bristles. There is a cartilage at the base of the trunk, which helps to divide the nostrils close to the single external bone opening on the cranium. The nostrils continue as separate openings from the base of the trunk to its tip, each lined with a membrane. The septum dividing the nostrils is composed of tiny muscle units

Below: *An African elephant picking up the fruit of a doum palm with its trunk. The two 'fingers' at the tip of the trunk can be clearly seen. In view of the time it takes to handle such small objects, wild elephants will feed on them only if they are numerous and highly tasty.*

horizontally stretched between the nasal tubes, as shown in the drawing above.

Like most of the body muscles, those in the trunk are also paired. They may be divided into two major groups: superficial and internal. The superficials are further subdivided into dorsals, ventrals and laterals. The deeper internal muscles have been described as 'radiating and transverse'. Detailed examination of the

Below: *The tip of the trunk of an Asian elephant, which has only one 'finger' at the end, but this does not seem to inconvenience the animal. It uses its trunk mostly by curling the end around objects and picking them up with the same dexterity as the African species.*

trunk layout confirms these overall divisions and also provides evidence for a more complex system, especially among the internal structures. The radiating muscles, for example, are organized from a hypothetical centre (the nostril) as spokes on a bicycle wheel. These interlock with the longitudinal muscles on the dorsal and lateral sides. On the ventral and lateral sides, the muscle fibres dovetail and interdigitate in many directions and can be viewed best when the trunk is sectioned.

The trunk of the African elephant has two fingerlike processes at the tip, on the dorsal and ventral sides, while that of the Asian elephant has only one, on the dorsal side. These processes are fleshy, mobile and extremely sensitive. The dorsal process of both species is a continuation of the *Maxillo-labialis* (*Lavator proboscidis*) muscle, which arises from the frontal bone and stretches through the entire length of the dorsal side of the trunk to its tip. The ventral process is a continuation of the *Pars rimana* of Bucci-nator (*Depressor proboscidis*) muscle, which arises from the premaxilla bone and the posterior surface of the proboscis. *Pars rimana* also stretches through the entire trunk, on the ventral side, to its tip.

Measurements show that the trunk of an Asian elephant can hold 8.5 litres(2.2 US gallons) of water, and a thirsty adult bull elephant can drink 212 litres(55 US gallons) of water in 4.6 minutes. Functions attributed to the trunk include: feeding, watering, dusting, smelling, touching, sound production/communication, lifting, and a weapon of defence and offence. It is, indeed, an indispensable tool – undoubtedly, the elephant's most important in everyday living.

Longevity

Sagacity is usually associated with long living, and because it was thought that elephants could live hundreds of years, it was also believed that they were extremely wise and experienced. The oldest recorded age in captivity is that of 'Jessie', an Asian elephant in Taronga Zoological Park, Sydney, Australia; her estimated age was 69 or 77 years. 'Raja', the male Asian elephant that performed for many years in the annual Peraherra Ceremony in Sri Lanka, was said to be '90 years old' when he died. Determining longevity in the wild is more difficult than in captivity because there is not enough accurate information available. Methods of age estimation include: condition and number of cross-loops (lamellae) on the cheek teeth, posthumous dry weights of the eye lenses and condition of the ears.

Right: The famous bull Ahmed, which lived in Marsabit National Reserve, Kenya. He was given presidential protection and on his death in 1974, his skeleton was mounted in the National Museum, Nairobi. Each magnificent tusk weighed 67kg(148lb).

Below: An elderly female elephant in Amboseli National Park, Kenya. At some time in her life she has broken her right tusk but it has continued to grow. These elephants are usually matriarchs, which lead family groups.

SOCIAL LIFE

A herd of African elephants moves in a coordinated body, with calves close to mothers and other family cows. A typical family is made up of animals of all sizes, from the largest, oldest cows to newborn calves. As they travel, they maintain this close-knit structure.

The social life of elephants, studied for the past 30 years, is influenced by individuals, by ecology and by population dynamics. Elephants are highly social animals, with a surprisingly complex repertoire of behavioural exchanges. For such a large, ponderous mammal, the delicacy and intricacy of their interactions are unexpected. Many different modes of interaction make up their social behaviour: elephants communicate through smell, sound and contact; they recognize each other as individuals and respond to others according to their relationship with that specific elephant. Their social life is thus complex and varied, revolving around some familiar and friendly individuals, and widening to include other less familiar or even disliked animals. Males and females live separately, with a different structure to the society of each sex. Bulls tend to lead solitary lives while most female elephants live in some form of small, stable social group incorporated within a larger network of groups.

In common with many grazing species of mammals, the social groups of females consist of a stable core of other related adult cows. These have been described as 'family units' and range in size from three to about 25 elephants. Among African and Asian elephants, most family units are made up of an old cow called the matriarch, her adult daughters, their suckling calves, and a number of juvenile and adolescent male and female offspring. The family units of African elephants average 8-10 animals, but Asian elephants tend to be found in smaller units of 4-8 animals, although there are consistent associations between some 10-20 individuals.

Adult bulls of both the African and the Asian species tend to be solitary, or associate with other bulls in small and relatively unstable groups. Bulls are frequently found with cow-calf groups, especially when females are reproductively active, but there are no long-term

Above: Asian elephants live in forests; their family units tend to be smaller but similar in structure to that of African elephants. Again, calves cluster around the adult females, with older juveniles and adolescents slightly further away. Cows, calves and older offspring make up the stable units, although cows with calves of similar ages will sometimes spend time together away from their families.

associations between bulls and family units. Young bulls leave the family unit of their birth (their natal unit) between the ages of 12 and 15. They then associate with bulls or other family units on a temporary basis. The patterns of basic social organization, kin groups of females and separate adult bulls, are similar between the two species.

The structure of family units

Most elephants thus spend a large part of their lives in a strongly female-centred world. Within their society, different in-

dividuals have specific social roles. The older cows head the family unit, and influence the movements and stability of their unit. They are active in defending the other members of the unit, and are alert to dangers as well. They also monitor the presence and identity of other elephants. The role of the matriarch is probably of major importance in the success of a family unit. Families composed only of younger, less experienced cows often fragment; they may have difficulty finding food and water during times of stress, and can be less successful at rearing their calves than older cows.

All the members of a family unit may be together for between 70 and 90 percent of time, and there are several reasons why families are not always together. Family units may split apart and rejoin over the course of several hours or several days, depending on the terrain, food supply and the activities of family members. During times of stress, such as a drought or even during the dry seasons of the year, mothers and offspring will feed independently, and the family temporarily fragments. Younger cows also tend to break away from the family to forage separately, possibly to feed with less competition from members of their unit. Cows sometimes leave their unit when about to give birth. It may be that they have lagged behind, moving more slowly than the rest, or they may choose to leave to find a sheltered spot to give birth.

Each female is highly individual; some will give birth in a large herd, others choose denser cover. The newborn elephant is highly vulnerable during the time immediately after birth, and needs the close protection and guidance of its mother and other family members. Calves do occasionally become separated from mothers shortly after birth if the mother is disturbed or alarmed, and the calf will invariably die of starvation or from predation if not reunited with its mother. A tiny calf is highly vulnerable to

Family unit size among African elephants

Right: The average size of an African elephant family unit is about 8-9, but some families can be very small (with 2-3), others very large (at 18-21). The largest groups tend to be less common than smaller ones. The figures shown here represent the means of observed unit sizes for three populations of East African elephants: Manyara(Tanzania), Amboseli(Kenya) and Luangwa(Zambia).

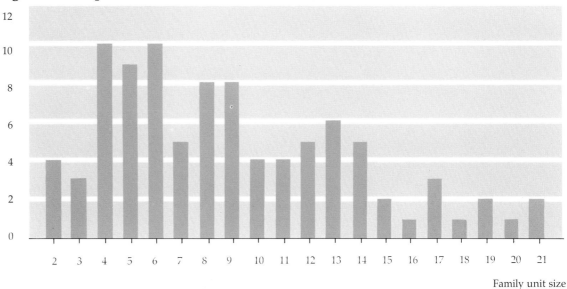

Family unit size

predators because it has no means of self-defence. Tigers are known to take the calves of Asian elephants, and lions may eat the occasional African elephant calf.

It appears that one of the essential functions of elephant families is to act as a defensive unit for the rearing of calves. All the cows cooperate to assist calves in movement and foraging and to protect them from threats, and they provide the important context for the social experience of the young. Younger cows before they have their own calves, and especially the juveniles and adolescents, are the main caretakers of calves. These females, called 'allomothers', will rush to protect or assist any calf in trouble. Young females stay near calves when mothers move away to forage, reducing the vulnerability of the calf when it is separated from its mother. They comfort distressed calves and will even allow a calf to comfort-suckle. However, such young cows are not producing milk, so it is unlikely that the calves obtain additional nourishment from this suckling. In captivity and in the wild, grandmothers also tolerate this suckling, and occasionally these older females may indeed be producing some milk. The number of young female allomothers in a family has been shown to affect calf survival. The more allomothers there are the higher the survival of calves, irrespective of the overall size of the family. Allomothers will adopt an older calf that has lost its own mother, becoming the primary caretaker of that calf. But if the calf is still highly dependent on its mother's milk (as are African elephants for the first two years, and Asian calves for at least the first year), it is unlikely to survive even with the help of an allomother.

Elephant calves remain dependent on their mothers and other family members for many years. Calves suckle for about three to five years, and their mother's milk forms the bulk of their nutrition for the first two years. They begin tasting solid foods at three or four months old, but they lack the coordination and trunk strength to eat tough fibrous foods in the quantities required for their growth until they are over two years old. Calves tend to forage on grasses, but they will take twigs and stems from their mother's or other animals' mouths. Young calves in

Effect of allomothers on calf survival

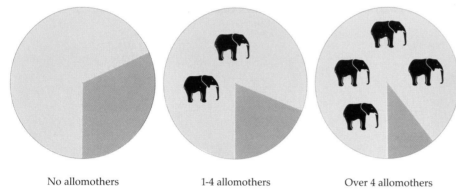

No allomothers   1-4 allomothers   Over 4 allomothers

■ Percentage of calves dying in the first two years of life

Left: As the number of young females available within a family to help rear calves increases, the survival of the calves goes up. With no such allomothers, calves are twice as likely to die as when there are many helpers. Even a few extra allomothers reduces calf mortality.

Below: Adolescent and juvenile females guard and assist young calves, and are frequently in contact with them. Greetings and body contacts are important ways of establishing the helper's relationship with both calf and mother.

their first year spend most of their time relatively close to their mother (within a couple of elephant lengths), becoming more independent during the next year.

While maturing physically and socially, calves engage in many social interactions. They greet other animals, touching their trunks to different parts of another elephant's body, and testing foods by placing their trunks into another's mouth. They will rub against others and rest in a heap. By far the most common interaction among calves is that of play. Calves play with objects, tossing and retrieving them, or rolling them over the ground. They will make mock charges at birds, buffaloes or twigs, and they frequently play together. Two or more calves will chase each other, push at each other, mount one another, and wrestle with their trunks. Elephant play is frequent and complex, and appears to serve functions as varied as gaining experience with objects, developing locomotor skills and assessing the abilities of other calves. During the early period of immaturity from birth to about five years of age, young elephants are acquiring a variety of social skills. They are learning about food plants, the locations of food and water, and, most importantly, they are learning about the other members of their family. As young females mature, they gain experience with calves that may be important when they come to reproduce, and their interactions with calves also enhances their relationship with the calf's mother. All these interactions maintain the integrity of the family as a reproductive unit.

What becomes of young elephant males? Although born into a female world, they will ultimately strike out on their own. From an early age, male calves are more independent of their mothers, often moving away from them to feed and play. They seek out 'novel' or unfamiliar young males from outside their own family as play partners, often having mock fights or sparring with other males. As young as six years, they will wander from their mother's family unit and associate for short periods with strange families. This trend accelerates with age; at 14 or 15 years old, most young bulls are spending over 80 percent of their time away from their own family. At this point they may become solitary, or form small temporary groups with other young bulls. Occasionally they will join another family unit for as long as a year before becoming fully independent.

Cows can be intolerant of young bulls, threatening, chasing them or poking them. Aggressive behaviour from cows can push the bull into being peripheral to the family, and initiate his decision to leave. While such aggression may be relatively rare, even isolated events can affect the young male's decisions. Aggression by cows towards young bulls is most

Above: *A young African elephant female stands guard over a sleeping calf, while the mother feeds close by. If the group moves off while the calf is still asleep, the female will gently wake it by pushing with her foot and raising the calf with her trunk.*

Below: *Elephant calves often spend over five percent of their time in play. Contact play such as mounting or play fights are common, as is chasing. Play is not only enjoyable, but it is also important for developing skill, strength and knowledge of other individuals.*

common towards those males that have formed temporary associations with a family other than their own. Alternatively, a young bull that has lost its mother may also be the target of female harassment, and again he is likely to become independent. Some bulls are tolerated within their families for up to 18 years. They maintain close and friendly links with their mothers and other female kin, even after short periods away from the unit. The mechanisms creating inde-pendence among bulls, and their decisions on when to leave and where to go are complex and deserve further study.

Each family unit thus goes through changes of membership as younger elephants mature and take up their new roles within that unit. While the cows remain within the unit of their birth to rear their own calves, bulls depart and establish new social relationships, primarily with other bulls. Elephants' social behaviour reflects aspects of these long-term changes. Individuals communicate with each other through very low-frequency vocalizations (called infrasound), by contact such as rubbing or entwining trunks, and by scent. Recent experimental work on wild African elephants has demonstrated that individuals recognize each other's vocalizations: their rumbles, bellows, trumpets and growls. Infrasonic calls can travel over considerable distances – 1-5km(0.6-3 miles) or even more – and thus animals that are out of sight or smell can be aware of the location, the identity and possibly the activity of others. It would appear that even when the members of family units are widely separated they can maintain some form of contact through their vocalizations.

An elaborate greeting 'ceremony' has also been described. When members of a family unit are reunited after a period of separation (as short as 20 minutes or as long as several days), they will all approach running, spinning, defecating and urinating, as well as rumbling and trumpeting. They will often touch each other's mouths, faces or genitals, clicking tusks and rub each others' heads or bodies. In this way they reaffirm their contact and friendly relationships, of

Sound perception among different mammals

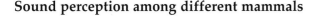

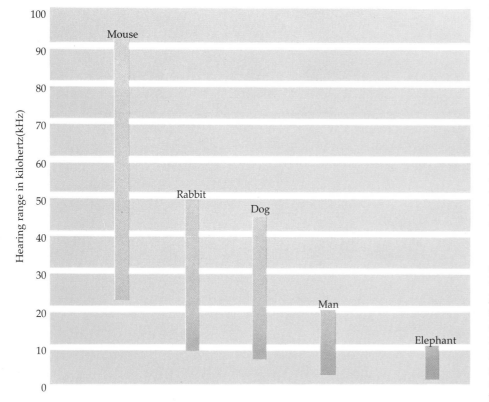

Left: Because of the long distance between their ears and large body size, elephants can both hear and produce sounds of very low frequency – known as infrasound. The power of sounds produced by elephants is strongest at 18 hertz (cycles per second), compared to 2,500Hz(2.5kHz) in mice and 100Hz in humans. Infrasounds have a long wavelength and thus travel long distances. Humans feel rather than hear deep sounds, although many elephant vocalizations also extend into the range of human hearing.

Detail of lower end of hearing range in Hz

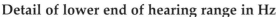

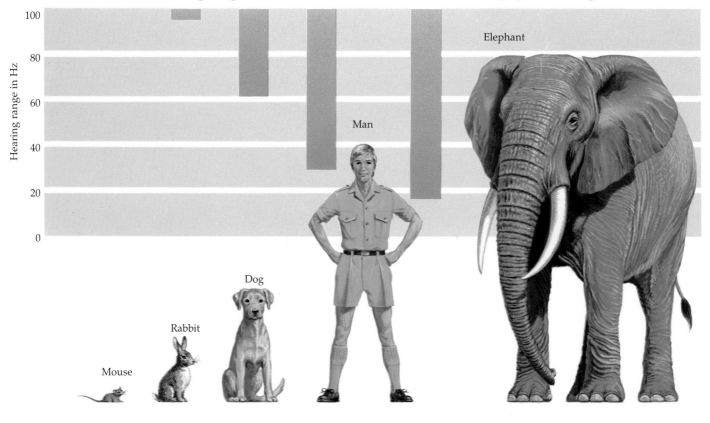

vital importance in a fluid society such as that of elephants. The greetings can be intense, with many loud vocalizations and contact lasting for several minutes.

Within each family, the cows typically interact in a friendly way, and competitive events are relatively rare. When family members do compete with each other, younger cows tend to defer to older cows. Such interactions may occur over access to a restricted waterhole, or over some choice feeding site. The approach of an older, dominant cow may be enough to cause the younger cow to move away, giving up her place at the food or water. Occasionally, the older cow will poke or shove the younger. Younger cows may find that life in a large family becomes stressful, especially when food or water are limited. Under such conditions, the younger, subordinate cows may temporarily leave their families. Competitive interactions, which define the dominance or subordinance of cows within a family, can be very subtle and infrequent, and thus the maintenance of a dominance hierarchy among elephants is difficult for the human observer to determine.

Elephant herds

The family unit, or indeed even the mother-calf unit, is not the only size of group that elephants experience. At times in some populations they will

Above: In open areas with ideal habitats, African elephant family units often congregate in groups ranging from a single unit to about six families, together with associated bulls. Families remain close and coordinated in activity, even in large herds. Along such a swamp, the location of each herd can reflect differences in core feeding areas between the family units. The flexibility of elephant society can be readily observed in these groups.

Below: Reunions between separated family unit members in African elephants are times of great excitement, as is clearly apparent in the elephants shown here. The individuals rush together, trumpeting and bellowing. Their open mouths indicate vocalizations, and the level of arousal is often evident from temporal gland secretion. Reunions are most intense and frequent within families and less marked but still friendly between bond groups.

gather into large herds or aggregations of as many as 500-1,000 individuals. A herd is defined as a concentrated body of animals, with coordinated activities and where no lone elephant is further away from others than the general diameter of the herd. In practice, a herd is easy to distinguish; several hundred elephants will be moving and foraging together, or resting near one another. Within a large herd, several levels of organization can

Right: *An Asian elephant family forages and interacts as a tight-knit unit. The close proximity of calves and adults within a family and friendly contacts are common to both species. Here they are eating salt from an artificial salt lick; many elephants dig for mineral-rich soils and will even enter caves to excavate important minerals such as calcium or potassium salts. Notice the baby elephant at the right of the photograph, clearly investigating something tasty in its mother's mouth.*

The social circles of elephants

In Cynthia Moss's definition of elephant society, a cow and her youngest calf form the central structure. The oldest cow, or matriarch, is the focal female around which the rest of the family revolves. She determines stability and ranging patterns.

The social circles widen to include the other cows related to the matriarch, which can be either daughters or sisters. These other adults spend the majority of their time in association with the matriarch, although they can spend time away as well.

The dependent offspring of the other family females and their older juveniles are tightly integrated into the family unit; they stay with the family and are usually very close to other family members, interacting primarily with them.

be determined. Initially, calves will be relatively close to mothers or other family calves; members of a family unit are also near each other.

Some family units have consistent associations with each other in herds. Individuals from these units will mingle, greet each other, and generally interact in a friendly fashion. These associated families have been described as 'kin groups' or 'bond groups'. Often such groups will be families that have grown over time as daughters mature and reproduce, and which then split into distinct and cohesive smaller family units. Thus, within a bond group will be cousins, aunts and nieces, while the family unit consists of mothers and daughters or sisters. The separate families that make up a bond group may spend between 35 and 70 percent of their time in association. Long-term studies have shown that close, stable and friendly relationships between

families are not invariably the result of kinship. Some bond groups are formed between unrelated females, that nevertheless maintain the high levels of friendly association and interaction. These may be the exception, while the rule is an extended family, or lineage descending from a long-dead matriarch. The bond groups formed between unrelated individuals may result from an attraction to young calves, or from a desire to form a potential feeding alliance against other family units foraging in the same area. Larger families could be at an advantage if they can feed undisturbed while smaller groups are excluded from choice foraging areas. A small family without any extended kin would be at an advantage, during feeding competition or in the cooperative rearing of calves, if they formed a stable friendly alliance with another such family. In Rwanda, African elephant juveniles left without any older

members of their real families after a cull formed themselves into new and stable 'families' made up of unrelated youngsters. The key to the organization of elephants is their complex social behaviour, which promotes flexibility in response to environmental or population changes over long periods.

Within a large herd, there may be a third level of organization. Among African elephants, family units are known to have specific small areas where they regularly feed and forage. No family has exclusive use of an area, and in that sense elephants do not have territories, but they do have core areas where they concentrate certain activities. A number of family units, bond groups and other unrelated families may share a similar core area of good feeding habitat. Obviously such individuals will be familiar with each other, and these animals are often found in aggregations together.

Adolescent bulls are at the social and spatial periphery of the main family unit circles. As bulls approach 15 years old, they wander from the family and their social ties weaken. They move outside the female social structure and associate with other young bulls. Some bulls are forced out, most leave of their own accord.

Large bull elephants live relatively solitary lives, often feeding and foraging separately from the cow-calf groups. They return to female groups when they are reproductively active. Large cow-calf herds tend to attract more males, and smaller families infrequently have males associated with them.

This is a second family circle, again with cows and dependent calves. This family is included within the larger circle of both families. Such groups are called bond groups, showing persistent associations and friendly greetings. Bond groups are thought to be made up of relatives that have formed separate units.

The family units that share areas have been called 'clans'. Within clans, individuals tend to be less friendly and lack the complex greetings of bond groups. Occasionally there will be aggressive interactions between the families.

At another remove, herds can consist of sub-populations, i.e. a number of family units all living within a larger shared geographical region. In some African elephants, sub-populations aggregate into large herds and forage away from specific family unit core areas during times of the year when young, growing grass is widely available. Such herds tend to be dynamic and flexible in their composition, with family units joining and leaving throughout the day. Relationships between the families within the herd can be friendly or competitive, or consist of mutual tolerance.

Herds can also consist of family units from any part of the overall area's population. Again, these types of herds are common during the wet or growing seasons. Often these herds will contain several reproductively active (oestrous) cows, which attract large numbers of bulls. Large herds may serve as a focal point for mating activities and concentrate the sexually active bulls together with the oestrous females. This can be essential when bulls are having to search over large areas to find females. With a large number of sexually active bulls together, cows can, potentially at least, in-

crease their ability to choose between those males that they might prefer to mate with. Large herds allow individuals to re-establish relationships and familiarity with animals that they rarely contact. They also provide opportunities for young bulls from different families to meet, and to test and assess each other's strength and size. Such contacts can be important in establishing the relative dominance of younger bulls. One conspicuous element of these larger herds is

Herd sizes in African elephants

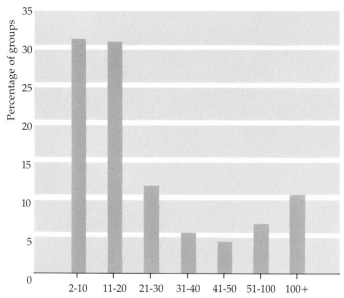

Right: In savanna populations such as those in Amboseli in southern Kenya, where herds can be counted over a long period, the average herd consists of up to 20 elephants. Large herds are much less common than small groups, which are usually made up of one or two families in association. Over 10 percent of groups are very large (over 100 elephants), and as many as 500 animals have been counted in a single herd.

Right: Elephant families often congregate at waterholes. A large herd can be made up of distinct families that show different behaviour. Some feed and await access to the water, while others rest, drink or mudsplash.

Below: A large herd of African elephants moves in a coordinated fashion through the bushland. In such a herd, elephants will be feeding, interacting, mating and playing, and individual family units are difficult to distinguish. Both sexes are present.

the frequency of vocalizations. Calves trumpet and bellow, adults give many different types of rumbles, and general communication is intense.

Large herds may also form when elephants have been subjected to intense poaching pressure. In open savanna ecosystems, there is safety in numbers. Potential predators (or poachers) can be spotted with many eyes, ears and noses, and avoided en masse. Larger groups may be able to defend themselves against human predators, at least until the advent of semi-automatic weapons. Unfortunately, an adaptive response to poorly armed predators proves to be a disastrous answer when entire herds can be mown down in a hail of bullets.

Forest elephants are less likely to be found in such large groups. In the rain forests of Africa, as in the forests of Asia, the most frequent group is the small family unit. Although genealogies are less well known for the more cryptic forest-dwelling animals, we can presume that the medium-sized groups occasionally seen are bond groups. Only infrequently, and often in patches of grassland or swamp within forests, will larger herds form from aggregations of family units. This does not imply a less complex form of sociality among the forest elephants; rather, the opportunities for expressing social behaviour are limited by infrequent contact. It may prove that forest elephants depend on infrasound vocalizations to a greater extent to maintain social bonds. Desert elephants, which also disperse over large areas of habitat in relatively small groups, are thought to use infrasound to monitor the movement and dynamics of other units.

The size of the 'average' herd of elephants thus differs between populations, between wet and dry seasons, and even between different habitats in the same general area. In regions with less food or very dispersed foods, elephants are more frequently found in their family units, or even in fragments of families. When food is more abundant, either overall or seasonally, family units group with others into

Average herd size in different populations

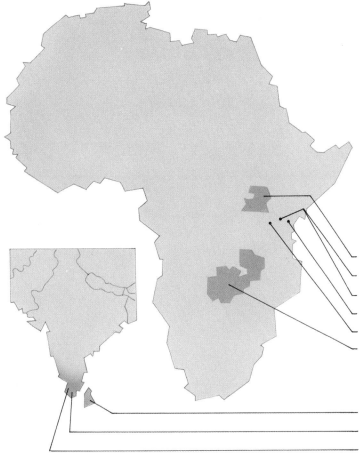

Below: Herd size depends on habitat, with small herds in the forests of Africa and Asia and large herds in open savanna. Food supply also affects herd size; when food is abundant in wet seasons, elephants congregate in larger groups, whereas smaller groups occur in dry times.

LOCATION						Group size	
AFRICA	0	10	20	30	40	50	60
Uganda							
Amboseli (Wet)							
Amboseli (Dry)							
Tsavo							
Serengeti							
Zambia							

ASIA	0	10	20	30	40	50	60
Sri Lanka							
Southern India (Wet)							
Southern India (Dry)							

Changes in group size over 24 hours

Group size (y-axis: 0, 20, 40, 60, 80, 100, 120, 140, 160, 180, 200, 220, 240, 260)

NIGHT

DAY

Time of day (x-axis: 18, 19, 20, 21, 22, 23, 24, 1, 2, 3, 4, 5, 6, 7, 8, 9, 10, 11, 12, 13, 14, 15, 16, 17, 18)

Above: *Monitoring a family unit over 24 hours shows the variability in group sizes experienced by elephants. Night groups are small, with families often splitting apart to forage or sleep. Day groups reflect the comings and goings of different families combining into a very large group for a short period.*

Right: *Young bulls face many stresses when they leave their families at about 15 years old. They range in less familiar areas, often alone, and some die during this time. Lone bulls are vulnerable to human hunters, and possibly to food stress during their adolescent growth period.*

larger herds. And in some types of habitat, such as those with more food or higher danger from predation, herds larger than the average family unit size also tend to occur more frequently.

During the course of a single day, an elephant may find itself in herds of many different sizes and compositions. Early in the morning, the members of a family that have spread out to feed or sleep during the night will regroup and begin to move to another feeding area. During their travels they may form temporary herds with other family units moving through the area. Upon reaching another feeding site, they can either disperse to feed in their separate units, or join with other elephants already in the area, forming an even larger herd. Throughout the rest of the day, there will be comings and goings by both family units and a variety of males. These continual contacts with new groups or individual elephants may be marked by interactions, either friendly or hostile. It is hardly surprising that elephants have a reputation for excellent memories when they use such skills in their daily contacts with many different individuals in many different places.

The social system of bulls

Although solitary females are sometimes observed among both African and Asian elephants, if an elephant is on its own it is highly likely to be a bull. Despite their apparent solitary nature, bulls also have a complex form of social organization. It used to be thought that there was a 'herd bull' with each cow-calf group. Most cow-calf groups do indeed contain at least one bull. On average, when an elephant group consists of 10 or more animals, about 10-15 percent of the group will be bulls. Small cow-calf groups are more likely to have no associated bulls, whereas a large herd of 50 elephants will have an average of six or seven bulls, and can have as many as 20. What has become clear through observations of known individuals is that bulls do not have preferences for specific, individual family units. Bulls associate with cow-calf groups at random; they will move between these groups searching for oestrous females. So, although most groups of cows will indeed have an associated 'herd bull', this bull will be different from day to day, or even from hour to hour.

Social relations between independent bulls and cows revolve around mating rather than any long-term affiliation. Cows may prefer certain bulls as mates (specifically, the older larger musth bulls – see page 77), but they do not appear to have any association preferences outside mating. From the bull's perspective, he increases his number of potential mates by moving around to find oestrous females. If he remains with a single family unit, his cows will be available as mates only once every three to five years (the interval between births). A herd bull would father a maximum of four calves in three years, whereas a successfully roving bull can find as many as 30 mates in a single year in a population of some 400 females. Again, the roving bull must find oestrous females and the long-distance infrasound probably plays a vital role in locating dispersed females. If females can monitor each other's location with infrasound, then the bulls can obviously use the same vocal cues.

Finding females is thus a major component of relations between the sexes. Bulls monitor females by listening for them, by smell, and by watching their behaviour. When bulls are with cow-calf groups, they assess the reproductive status of individual cows. If there are no oestrous cows, the bulls are likely to move on, changing group membership over short periods. However, most large bulls are not reproductively active throughout the year, but have specific active, or musth, periods. A bull's attitude to females and to other males depends on his reproductive state; it also changes according to the bull's age.

The younger bull elephants tend to be those that have recently left their own family units. These bulls are often found with cow-calf groups, although infrequently with their own family. Newly independent bulls tend to associate most frequently with females or with small groups of other young bulls. As bulls age, they spend less time with females and more time as solitary animals, returning to cow-calf groups to mate. There are

Below: Large African elephant bulls such as these occasionally group together, especially when they share foraging areas. Bull groups tend to be smaller than those of female elephants, although some large all-male groups of over 25 individuals have been observed.

bulls that have strong long-term associations with other bulls, but most bull groups are fluid in composition. Bulls establish residence in specific 'bull' areas. Those that share the same residence area are more likely to associate than those from distant areas. Occasionally, young males from the same family unit will maintain a strong friendly association and share the same bull area, but this may not be universal. Indeed, it may be advantageous for brothers or cousins to disperse, because bulls that share an area could come into direct competition for access to oestrous females.

Within bull groups, or when several bull elephants aggregate with female herds, the bulls may assess each other through sparring or play fighting, as do the juveniles. The relative dominance of bulls is related to their size, and hence to their power or weight. Since these increase with age, older bulls tend to be dominant, and young bulls will often avoid a larger, older male. This avoidance of dominant bulls may be one factor promoting the instability of male-male associations. Musth bulls are particularly

dominant, and are avoided even by larger, non-musth bulls. The reproductively active bulls are typically found with cow-calf groups, or searching for females. During their non-musth period, the old large bulls are usually solitary, or with bulls from their area. Interestingly, the large, older non-musth bulls are infrequently found with females and their bull areas tend to be away from the cow-calf core areas. Large bulls may feed more efficiently in the absence of females, or they may require different qualities and quantities of food, leading to a separation in the areas utilized by males and female. This separation tends to reduce the probability and frequency of social contact between the sexes.

For elephant bulls, their social organization revolves around finding adequate amounts of food to maintain their growth and fuel their large bodies while minimizing feeding competition from other bulls and cow-calf groups. However, a degree of sociality is maintained between bulls in order to monitor the size and strength, i.e. the relative dominance, of their potential rivals for

mates. Social links with individual females are weak or non-existent; reproductive activities during the musth period require active searching and only temporary affiliation with females. During musth periods, bulls are aggressive and willing to engage in severe and damaging fights with each other. Non-musth bulls tend to avoid costly and dangerous associations with other bulls

Right: Two African elephant bulls engage in a face-to-face contest as part of a fight to establish dominance. Large bulls are often aggressive towards each other. Such a contest can escalate into dramatic and serious aggression, with long chases and body contact, perhaps resulting in wounds or permanent damage. The tusks are frequently brought into play during such fights.

Below: When bulls meet they often exchange mild greetings and appear to test the identity and strength of potential rivals. Much of a bull's adult life is spent assessing his dominance relative to other bulls, so complex social interactions are needed. Despite being solitary, bulls are still social animals.

and are frequently solitary. Younger bulls that have not yet begun to exhibit musth maintain strong relations with females and with other males, but defer to musth bulls. Long-term social knowledge and the ability to make complex assessments of the capacities of other bulls and the reproductive status of females structure bull social organization. Despite the initial appearance of a solitary mode of life, elephant bull sociality is just as complex as that of females. Bulls interact and associate in response to female sociality and reproductive status, as well as the reproductive status of other bulls and their own condition, history and possibly kinship relations.

Elephant societies

Elephant society as described above is based primarily on cooperation between relatives within the female core family unit. Their interactions, systems of communication and communal rearing of calves serve to perpetuate these cooperative bonds. The cooperative structure may extend to bond groups, either as more distant relatives or as unrelated families that have formed some specific patterns of affiliation. These relationships may persist for several generations (possibly for the lifespans of mothers and daughters or even for hundreds of years). These are further imbedded in the context of the more competitive relationships between animals seeking food in the same areas, which also join together and interact in larger herds. The multi-tiered society of elephant females may be unique among the grazing or browsing mammals, and rivals the complexity of societies seen among the non-human primates in terms of the diversity of interactions, the duration of relationships and the ability to recognize and discriminate between individuals.

Bulls appear to lead a somewhat less complicated social life than do females, and spend large amounts of time on their own. But they too need social skills to assess each other and compete effectively for mates, to locate and guard reproductive females, and to maintain their relationships with non-reproductive bulls in the bull areas. The basis for establishing the social skills of males may lie in their early experiences within the complex female units, but we have little information as yet. Since the lifespan of an elephant is over 60 years, it will be some time before we can fully understand their social dynamics. Meanwhile we have only begun to unravel the complexities of elephant social organization over our own human lifespan.

Right: Elephants are long-lived and highly social animals that maintain relationships over many generations. Families are the core of elephant society, providing the focus for interaction, knowledge and raising offspring.

REPRODUCTION

A tiny newborn African elephant calf leans against its mother for support while she forages. Its older sibling is close by the calf and mother, ready to help the newborn. First-year calves can easily fit under their mothers and will stay close for milk and protection.

Some elements of the reproductive biology and behaviour of elephants have been known for centuries. Others have only recently come to light with attention paid to captive breeding and through the results of studies on wild animals. Due to their large size, elephants reproduce slowly and their reproductive behaviour sheds fascinating insights on the problems of being a large, slowly growing animal. Both sexes have a lifespan of 60 years or more, only a part of which can be devoted to producing the next generation. The problems facing bulls and cows in terms of physiology, behaviour and ecology are different and greatly influence the patterns of reproduction we observe. Elephant cows begin their reproductive careers at about the age of 10, and produce a single calf at four- to five-year intervals, ending up with a range of one to eight surviving calves. Bulls, although capable of mating at about 10 years, become active in seeking mates some time after they reach 30 years of age.

For most mammals, reproduction is a fairly complicated affair, involving the coordination of biology and behaviour within a short period between males and females. The sexes often have different goals. The male with few paternal demands, ideally attempts to fertilize as many females as possible. The female, on the other hand, needs a mate that will either provide care for her offspring, or will transmit to her sons those characteristics that will in turn make them successful mates. Bull elephants play almost no role in the rearing of their sons and daughters. This is left to the cows within a family unit. However, bulls do face competition from other males in their natural environment, and many characteristics of their reproductive biology and behaviour are directly related to this competition. Elephant cows, on the other hand, face the problems of producing enough milk for a hungry and rapidly growing calf, protecting it from environmental and social stresses, and defending it against possible predators. Thus the characteristics of reproduction among elephant females are associated with the problems of obtaining sufficient food at critical times, and with preventing calf death.

In comparison with other mammals, elephants face several unique problems in their reproduction. The first of these is that they can reproduce only infrequently as a consequence of their large body size. Being large slows down all the crucial processes; it lengthens pregnancy, increases the time between births, and delays the onset of reproductive age, which makes for a long period of infancy and adolescence. A further problem for elephants is that they often range over relatively large areas, and the bulls live separately from the cows and calves. Bringing the sexes together in order to mate requires specific behaviours associated with searching, communication of reproductive state and changes in typical patterns of association.

Among both Asian and African elephants, the patterns of reproduction and mating behaviour thus differ dramatically between males and females. These sex differences are in part due to the nature of elephant social organization, but also result from the general effects of large body size. Obviously, there must be coordination of mating between the sexes, but the priorities of each sex for reproduction, the timing of reproductive events and the social context of reproduction, are essentially different for bulls and cows. Therefore, this chapter will discuss the general reproductive patterns of each sex separately.

Female reproductive patterns

Elephant cows are sexually active during a relatively short period called an oestrous cycle, associated with changes in circulating reproductive hormones. These hormones control the development and release of the egg, indepen-

Below: A large African elephant bull stands alert at the edge of a swamp, perhaps on the lookout for oestrous females. Bulls of this size are reproductively active during specific musth periods in each year. Older bulls tend to be solitary for much of the time.

dently of any act of mating. The spontaneous shedding of an egg ready for fertilization is called ovulation. Examination of the uterus of African elephant cows has revealed that anywhere from 2 to 26 eggs are released during an oestrous cycle, in several separate ovulations, before the female becomes pregnant.

Females mate during the period of ovulation, although they sometimes remain attractive to bulls after this time. The interval between successive ovulations during an oestrous cycle, should the cow fail to be mated or to conceive, appears to be about 16 weeks. Since it is difficult to assess physiological oestrus accurately in wild elephants, these figures come from captive or zoo females. In the wild, oestrus may be signalled by a change in general female behaviour. African elephant cows sometimes exhibit a specific

oestrous walk, with head held high while looking back over their shoulders. Oestrous females may be more active, and show greater interest and enthusiasm at the approach of a large sexually active bull. The conspicuous walk is visible over a long distance, providing clues to the female's reproductive state to distant bulls. Vocalizations by the female during oestrus, and especially when she is mated, appear to travel long distances as well, and may allow bulls to locate a receptive female in the large areas over which elephants range.

Once a bull has found a female, he will test her urine or vulva, using his trunk to carry scents to a specialized gland (called the Jacobson's organ) on the roof of his mouth . By testing a female's secretions, the bull appears to assay the hormonal state of the cow. If she is in oestrus, he

will respond with excitement and interest in the cow, and will remain with her, testing her urine and vulva frequently. This interest on the part of the bulls is one of the best signals of the female's state. Among Asian elephants, the oestrous female and the bull show pre-copulatory manoeuvres, including face-to-face orientation and mouth-to-mouth contacts while twining trunks. Among African elephants, most oestrous cows respond to the testing of a bull by urinating and defecating, backing into the bull, and spinning around dramatically. She will then walk quickly away from the bull. If he is sexually active, he will follow her. This can lead to an oestrous chase, with the bull running to catch up with the female and laying his trunk on her head or back. The reaching over a female's shoulder with the trunk also signals the

Above: *A herd of female African elephants and their calves cluster at the edge of a waterhole, enjoying cooling mud baths and a drink. A large bull in musth, secreting from the temporal glands on the side of his head and dribbling urine, is approaching the group ready to assess the cows for their reproductive status. Several of the herd are investigating his approach with trunks outstretched*

Left: *A bull Asian elephant engages in courtship contact with a cow, gently laying his trunk on her head and body as the two elephants face each other. An oestrous cow should respond by twining her trunk with the bull, which will then lead to copulation. An older juvenile calf is taking a particular interest in the bull during these courtship proceedings.*

Above: A young African elephant bull has joined a group of females and is investigating the reproductive status of an older cow. He reaches out to touch the female's vulva with his trunk, and will sample her state by smelling and tasting her urine and secretions.

Right: A large African elephant bull has successfully mounted a cow and is proceeding to mate. He supports his vast weight on his hind legs, balancing on the cow's back. His independently mobile penis is manoeuvring into the female's downward-pointing vulva.

onset of a mount among Asian elephants. The cow then chooses either to cooperate with the bull by stopping and allowing him to mount, or to continue to run away quickly. The success of a bull seems to be strongly influenced by the female's cooperation. If she continues to move away, she can outrun the larger, slower bull. In combination with the specific oestrous vocalizations that solicit male attentions from long distances, the courtship running is one of the main ways in which elephant cows appear to exert some degree of choice over their mates.

If the bull is successful in mounting, he will then attempt to manoeuvre his penis into the downward-pointing vulva of the female. Again, there must be coordination between bull and cow for this to be successful, and ejaculation can take place. A bull may mount a female several times before he achieves intromission.

The length and specialized muscles of the elephant's penis permit penetration of the cow's 'backward' pointing reproductive tract, and the male deposits his sperm closer to the egg. A bull produces as much as a litre of ejaculate, which also increases the chances of some sperm reaching the distant egg. A typical mount lasts only about a minute, even with ejaculation, before the bull dismounts and remains beside the cow, guarding her from other mating attempts by different bulls.

This consortship, consisting of a bull and an oestrous female staying together and the bull guarding the female against the approach of other males while he occasionally mates with her, lasts between a few hours and four days. After this time, the cow is no longer likely to conceive and the bull loses interest in her. She may remain attractive to younger bulls for some days, but finally she is able to continue her normal daily pursuits without the attentions of bulls.

The production of calves

Once the cow has been successfully mated and conception has occurred, she has a long wait before the calf is born. The length of pregnancy, or gestation time, is almost two years among elephants. Among both African and Asian elephants, pregnancy lasts for about 22 months (630-660 days). Foetal development is relatively rapid, and by the third month of pregnancy some of the features of an elephant, such as ears, trunk and tail, are present. Most of the growth, however, takes place in the second half of gestation. Male African elephant calves may weigh up to 165kg(364lb) at birth, but both male and female newborn calves typically weigh about 120kg(264lb). Among Asian elephants, the weight at birth is about 91kg(200lb), possibly associated with a slightly shorter gestation.

Birth takes place with the female squatting or occasionally lying, and cows appear somewhat restless during the hour or so of the birth process. The delivery of the calf is relatively quick, lasting only about half a minute. The newborn is helped onto its feet by its mother and other females and guided to the nipple for its first suck. Within one to two hours, the calf is capable of walking – somewhat shakily – alongside its mother.

When the calf is very young the mother is essential to its survival, since she provides milk and defends it. Calves begin

Right: This captive Asian cow elephant is shown with her calf, born only a few hours earlier. Clean-up operations are in progress. The calf is very hairy and has rather red eyes at birth. In the wild, small, weak Asian elephant calves are especially vulnerable to tigers, and if separated from their mothers will usually starve. Young calves stay close by mothers, depending on them for milk and protection during the first years of life.

Male and female reproductive organs

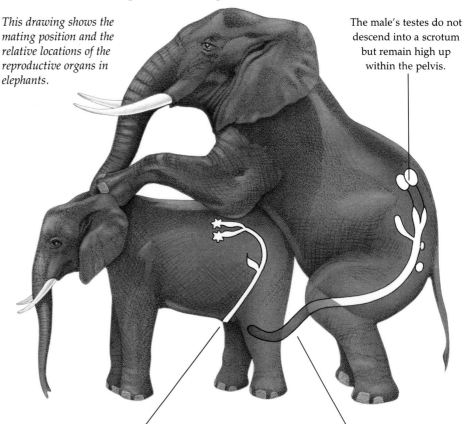

This drawing shows the mating position and the relative locations of the reproductive organs in elephants.

The male's testes do not descend into a scrotum but remain high up within the pelvis.

The ovaries and uterus are located high in the pelvic region, and the long, backwardly pointing vagina emerges via the vulva between her hind legs.

The long muscular penis is mobile enough to penetrate the vulva of the female.

Right: Calves suck through their mouths from breasts between the mother's front legs, curling their trunk and resting it on the mother's body.

Below: A young African elephant calf close to its mother, tests its ability to use its trunk. Small calves are often hairy to reduce heat loss.

trying food other than milk at about four months, but are not capable of feeding themselves on solid foods until well into their second year. Calves suckle several times an hour for an average of two to three minutes during the first year. After this time the rate declines to about once an hour, although they stay on the nipple for about two minutes. Calves often continue to suckle for a further several years. In the African elephant, suckling carries on until the birth of the next calf, sometimes for as long as eight years! Weaning (the cessation of suckling) is a gradual process, with little conflict between mother and calf. Its timing depends on when the next calf is born, and it is thus highly variable between individuals.

Calves can be weaned as young as two and a half years, but a calf that loses its mother before the age of two is unlikely to survive, even if protected and cared for by other members of its family unit. Among Asian elephants, calves can survive the removal of the mother at a younger age, about 18 months. During the suckling period, calves grow rapidly, and may weigh 850-900kg (1,874-1,984lb) by the time they are weaned. Males grow more rapidly than females throughout the months of lactation, and continue to grow more rapidly and for longer during their lifespan.

Influences on female reproduction

The time between successive births is called the interbirth interval and is close to four years among many populations. The interbirth interval varies between individuals, between years and between populations. Among female African elephants, we now know that there are two critical influences on female reproductive performance. The first of these is whether the cow has a suckling calf. The second is the general body condition of the cow, which is related to her food supply. There is a further variable, that of the size and age of the cow, which is important for the younger, growing cows and for the very old females.

If a cow is suckling a calf, she is unlikely to resume her oestrous cycles until the calf is at least nine months old, and typically this period appears to last 12-24 months. One interesting phenomenon associated with the rapid growth of male calves is that they suckle more frequently than do their female counterparts. In consequence, they tend to delay their mother's resumption of oestrus by about six months. Thus, mothers of sons tend to have slightly longer interbirth intervals than do mothers of daughters. Cows have been observed being mated, or with sexually active males showing interest in them, shortly after a birth. However, it is uncertain yet if elephant cows have some form of postpartum oestrus, or if the bulls are simply responding to the high levels of circulating hormones associated

Interbirth intervals in elephant populations

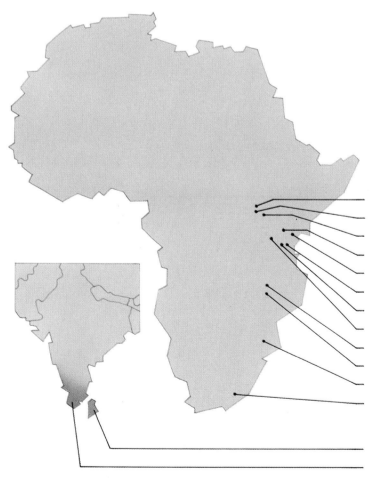

Below: The number of years between births for a variety of African and Asian elephant populations. The range is from three to nine years (average four years), depending on local environmental conditions.

Above: A nonchalant mother feeds on a plentiful supply of grass while both her youngest and older calves suck at her breasts. Elephant mothers are extremely tolerant of their calves' attempts to suckle and seldom reject them from the nipple, but such a sight is rare. Juveniles of 4-5 years are capable of feeding for themselves, and this older sibling is depriving his younger sister of much needed milk. The younger calf may starve in the face of such sibling competition.

LOCATION   Number of years

AFRICA	0 1 2 3 4 5 6 7 8 9 10
Murchison North	
Murchison South	
Budongo Forest	
Amboseli	
Tsavo	
Mkomasi East	
Mkomasi Central	
Manyara	
Kasungu	
Luangwa	
Kruger	
Addo	

ASIA	0 1 2 3 4 5 6 7 8 9 10
Sri Lanka	
Southern India	

with the birth process, which may make the cow appear interesting.

By far the most important influence on the frequency and timing of elephant reproduction is the nature and quality of the food supply. Under conditions of poor nutrition, African elephant cows are unlikely to come into oestrus, whether or not they have a suckling calf. Drought years can dramatically reduce the number of females conceiving, whereas during wet years – when foods of higher quality are more plentiful – many cows are likely to become pregnant. Within a single year, changes in food supply associated with seasonal rainfall also influence the time when female elephants will conceive (see also *Ecology*, page 94).

Elephants are not physiologically forced to breed seasonally; it would be impossible to give birth in a specific season with a gestation length that lasts just under two years. Thus, oestrous females can in theory be observed in any month of the year. However, in some populations of African and Asian elephants, there is a distinct birth peak. Optimal months for conception, and hence for giving birth almost two years later, are defined by the rainfall prior to conception (as the graph on this page shows). Most females tend to come into oestrus soon after rainy periods, with a delay of several weeks to several months from the onset of the rains. Rainfall triggers the growth of grass, and increases the availability of shrubs and leaves. Once this growth of plant foods is under way, plentiful food with high-quality protein and other nutrients becomes available to the cows. Their body condition improves, and they gain weight, put on fat and spend less time foraging during the day.

All these factors tend to increase the probability of a cow coming into oestrus. Thus, most conceptions among elephants living in seasonal environments tend to occur during the rainy periods. A further advantage of conceiving

Conceptions in relation to rainfall

Right: The number of cows conceiving in a month is strongly influenced by rainfall in the previous months. High rain produces abundant food for elephants, and cows are more likely to become pregnant when well fed. This graph represents the pattern for one population in Kenya. The exact timing varies between populations.

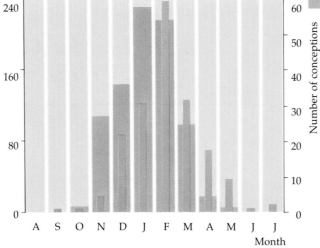

Below: An African elephant cow and her juvenile feed on abundant grasses. Elephant cows need large quantities of food to reproduce. When a juvenile is able to feed on its own, its mother is likely to become pregnant again – if the environmental conditions are favourable.

Age-specific reproduction

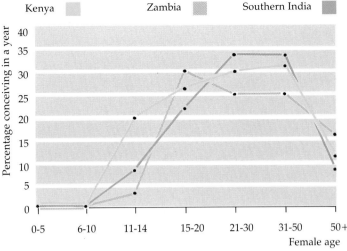

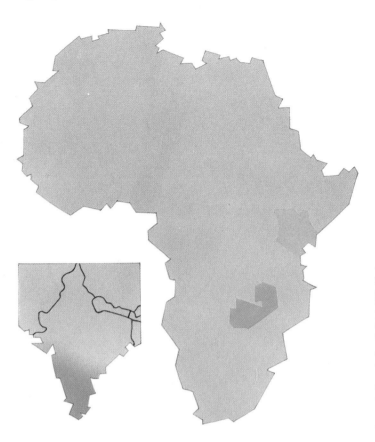

Above: *Cows begin reproducing after 10 years of age. Those of 15-50 years are most likely to conceive, while younger cows and the oldest show reduced fertility. This graph shows the age-specific reproductive rates for Asian cows and two populations of African elephants.*

several months into a yearly rainy season is that when the calf is born, 22 months later, the rains are likely to have started again. Abundant high-quality food should again be available for the mother, who needs extra food to meet the additional energetic burden of providing milk for her hungry, rapidly growing calf.

There are also differences in reproduction as a result of the age of the cow. Elephant cows become reproductively mature at about the age of 12-14 years. There is considerable variation in the age of first oestrus, and females may mature sexually as young as eight or as old as 18 years. In good environments, the age of maturity tends to be younger than in those environments where food is limited. A cow that reaches the age of 12 during a succession of dry years might be delayed in achieving sexual maturity and will not begin ovulating until she is older. As yet, we know little of what controls the age of first reproduction. Elephants could be similar to humans in having to attain some critical weight or threshold of body fat, and thus differences between the ages of sexual maturity would be expected for female elephants with different rates of growth or nutritionally related body condition. Research continues on this topic.

As is typical among many mammals, the younger and oldest females give birth less frequently than do the prime or middle-aged cows. Cows under the age of 10 may be capable of ovulation, but they appear to be less likely to become pregnant. Very old cows (over 50-55) also come into oestrus infrequently. The precise hormonal mechanisms controlling these differences between elephant cows of varying ages are still poorly known. We can only speculate that young cows between 10 and 18 years have frequent infertile cycles because of hormonal variation, or alternatively that they are still having to grow relatively rapidly and thus are unable to maintain the extra energy costs of pregnancy and lactation. Older cows may be in poorer condition, or have less fat reserves than do the middle-aged cows, and again their reproductive performance will be limited.

In at least one population of African elephants, cows over the age of 55 ceased reproducing. This suggested that elephants experience a form of 'menopause'. Data from captive Asian elephants and from other populations of wild African elephants contradict this finding: the oldest females are still capable of reproduction, although they do show a decline in fertility. As with so many aspects of elephant reproduction, this issue of whether or not elephants, like humans, cease reproducing well before they die remains to be resolved.

Reproductive rates
All these factors – food supply, the presence of a suckling calf, its sex and the age of the cow – interact and produce considerable variation in reproductive rates within one population over time, and between different populations. Some popu-

lations show a decline in reproductive rate as the population size increases, possibly due to increasing numbers of animals eating limited food. The highest recorded rate of population growth is 11 percent per year among one small population of elephants in Addo in South Africa. There, the average interbirth interval of three years is short, and is unlikely to be maintained over the long term or to be found in other, larger populations. Once many females in any population have a suckling calf, their reproductive rates would necessarily decline. But such a high rate of increase under excellent conditions implies that elephant populations can recover relatively rapidly from short-term mortality stress. The reproductive biology of elephant cows is thus of extreme importance to the current problem of a marked decline in numbers (see *Conservation*, page 180).

Reproductive patterns of bulls
Unusually for mammals, the testes of elephants are located within the body, close to the kidneys. These organs produce sperm and the hormones regulating reproductive functions. Elephant bulls begin producing sperm between 10 and 15 years of age. Among both African and Asian elephants, such young bulls are unlikely to father many calves in practice. Only the older bulls successfully mate in the wild, but young fathers are known in captivity at various places.

One of the main determinants of the mating success of a bull is if he comes into a specific reproductive condition called 'musth'. Musth, a corruption of the Urdu word 'mast', is translated as 'intoxicated' or 'angry'. It was originally described in the scientific literature over 100 years ago and was discussed by Darwin in the mid-19th century. It has probably been known for as long as Asian elephants have been kept in captivity. In recent years, this phenomenon has been recognized among African elephant bulls as well. It took many years to establish the occurrence of musth in African elephants, because one of the distinguishing characteristics is a copious secretion from the temporal glands on the sides of the head. In Asian elephants, only bulls show such discharges, but in African elephants both males and females secrete from the temporal glands during times of stress or excitement. However, detailed long-term observations of individual bulls and analysis of the secretions has determined that the secretions are different between musth bulls and excited male or female elephants, and many of the other distinguishing characters of musth in Asian elephants are indeed present among bull African elephants.

Musth among bulls

Musth is a period of behavioural, physical and physiological changes. During musth, bulls become more aggressive towards each other and towards humans; they actively seeking out and copulate with females, feeding infrequently. Musth bulls can be recognized by the copious discharge of thick secretions from the temporal glands, which become swollen and easily visible. Many bulls also have a continual discharge or dribble of urine, and show damp patches on their hind legs. This phenomenon is associated with changes in the hormonal state of Asian and African bulls, specifically an increase in the levels of the sex hormones testosterone and androstenedione (a testosterone precursor). High levels of testosterone increase sperm production, making frequent copulation possible, as well as making it more likely that large numbers of sperm will be present in each ejaculation. This increases the chances of fertilization. Testosterone also suppresses the appetite, and, in humans, increases the persistence with which difficult tasks are carried out. Testosterone *per se* does not necessarily increase aggressiveness, but it may enhance the ability of a male to challenge others or to follow through with a fight should it become necessary.

The phenomenon of musth in Asian and African elephant bulls is associated with specific behaviours and vocalizations. Musth bulls will wave their ears one at a time, either when threatening another bull or when giving a distinct musth rumble. This ear-waving may waft the temporal gland scent to others and indicate the musth status of the bull. Bulls rub their secretions onto trees and bushes, and the urine dribbling also may play a role in scent marking. When walking, musth bulls hold their head and ears high above their shoulders. A large musth bull can be recognized from a considerable distance through his posture while moving. The musth rumble is another of the elephant's repertoire of very low-frequency vocalizations. Females often respond to a musth rumble with a loud call of their own. The most conspicuous behaviour is the irascibility

Above: A large, older musth African bull with swollen temporal glands and damp hind legs where urine has dribbled. The curved trunk and ears held high are also characteristic of African musth bulls.

Right: An Asian bull in full musth, with swollen, secreting temporal glands and an extended penis.

Below: A close view showing the temporal gland located between the eye and ear. It discharges a copious secretion of hormones and various volatile compounds.

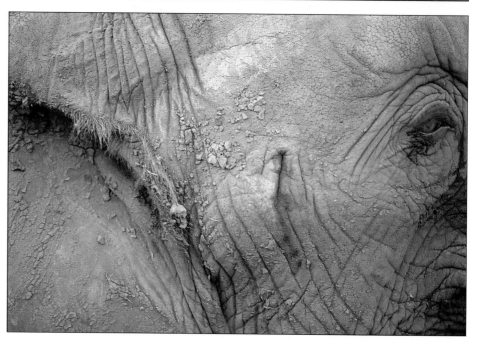

Musth periods for two African elephant bulls

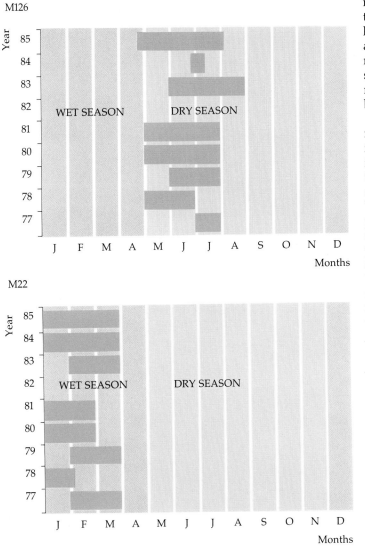

M126

M22

Right: Two bulls were observed by Joyce Poole in Amboseli, Kenya over a period of 10 years. The bull designated M126 comes into musth during dry months, and stays in musth for up to three months. During drought years, he either had a shorter musth, or skipped the year. M22, one of the largest bulls, also has a musth period of about three months, but he occupies the wet months, when more oestrous females are present. Signs of musth become more pronounced when a bull is with females or encounters other bulls, when he will chase or fight with the bulls and attempt to guard an oestrous female. In Asian elephants only bulls secrete during musth; in African elephants all animals produce some discharge when aroused or stressed.

Although younger bulls are likely to back down in the face of a larger, older opponent and thus be the losers in any contest, they tend to have relatively high levels of testosterone, at least while they are in association with females. The hormone controls of the onset of musth are still poorly known. And the difficulties of monitoring reproductive hormones in bulls are considerable!

Each bull elephant usually comes into musth once a year, for a period lasting from several days to several months. Different bulls come into musth at different times during the year, so there is no strictly seasonal pattern to musth. Younger bulls starting out on their reproductive career have a shorter musth duration than do the older bulls. These young bulls may go in and out of musth for short periods several times in a year. With increasing age, however, a bull settles down into a regular cycle of musth. In one population of African elephants, some individual bulls came into musth from year to year close to the same date over a period of 10 years. Despite this consistency in the date of the onset of musth, bulls can also change their musth periods dramatically. If a large bull dies, his musth period becomes available to other bulls. If he came into musth during the peak months of female oestrus, then other bulls will shift their musth periods into that vacant, and desirable, time. Thus, the musth period is not fixed for any bull, and depends on both experience and the number of other bulls. However, for the average, older bull elephant there is a predictable period to his musth from year to year.

The average duration of musth is also dependent on the age and condition of a bull. Younger bulls (in the reproductive context, those under 35 years) have short musth durations of one to 10 days, but older bulls can remain in musth for up to 120 days or even longer. Bulls under 35

of the musth bull. Aggression towards objects, tusking the ground or bushes, charges, threats and fights with other bulls all make the musth bull a formidable opponent. Indeed, the dangers posed by musth bulls mean that few older male elephants can be kept in captivity. Many elephant handlers are injured or killed by musth bulls. At least some of the references to rogue bulls among African elephants may stem from contacts with bulls in musth, before the phenomenon was recognized.

What factors influence reproduction for bulls?

There is a marked effect of age on the probability of bulls coming into musth. Among captive Asian elephants, bulls as young as 11 to 14 years old exhibit the classic signs of musth. In the wild, the incidence of musth increases with age and bulls over 20 show regular musth. Captive African elephants also exhibit musth at the relatively young ages of 15 to 18, but in the wild, bulls under 25 years are unlikely to come into musth. It has been suggested that young bulls are physiologically capable of musth, but when they live in contact with older bulls, some

form of reproductive suppression takes place. For many animals, an aggressive encounter between two males results in a drop in the level of testosterone in the loser. A reduction in the hormone level may eliminate musth; old bulls out of musth show low levels of testosterone.

Left: Two medium-sized bulls clash in a head-to-head fight. Such fights can be intense and long-lasting, resulting in severe wounds to the face, legs or body and causing lasting damage or even death. The tusks are important offensive and defensive weapons for bulls, and many bulls break their tusks during severe fights. Bulls use these sparring fights to assess relative dominance and determine access to oestrous females.

years old also remain in musth only while associating with cow-calf groups; when they return to their bulls areas or associate with males, they drop out of musth. Old bulls remain in musth when they are alone, with bulls, or with females. Bulls in poor condition may skip a year, or come into musth for a shorter period than expected. Poor condition can result from droughts and reduced food availability and quality, from a loss of condition associated with a long previous year's musth, or from severe fights between bulls during musth. In captivity, Asian elephant bulls can be starved out of musth. Because bulls spend little time feeding during musth, it must cause a huge draining of energy, especially over a period of three or four months.

Musth bulls are highly aggressive towards other bulls, and they are frequently involved in fights; these can last for up to six hours, and constitute a further enormous energy drain. Searching for oestrous cows over large distances is yet another energy cost. It is not surprising that only the larger, older bulls are able to sustain such high energy costs and come into musth on a regular yearly basis. In captivity, bulls may be able to sustain musth at a much younger age, because they are well fed and have few other energy demands for travel, fighting or chasing females.

The presence of oestrous females can stimulate the onset of musth, but only among the younger bulls. Alternatively, during years when few oestrous females are available – for example, during droughts – bulls tend to have shorter than expected musth periods or to skip a year entirely. The bulls themselves may be in poor condition and unable to sustain musth during these times. There appears to be a relationship between the timing of musth and the distribution of oestrous females during a year. A larger number of bulls come into musth during the peak breeding months for females, especially in those elephant populations living in areas with a strong seasonal pattern of rainfall and conception. However, musth bulls can be found throughout the year, and they may be responding to past experience of peak oestrous months rather than directly or immediately responding to numbers of oestrous females at a given moment.

The mating success of a bull does not depend solely on getting his timing right. Although it is essential to have reproductive females around at the same time as the male is sexually active, the presence of other musth bulls also contributes to his success or lack of it. Outside the musth period, larger bulls have priority over smaller bulls during contests. Once a bull is in musth, his relative success during fights is much greater and non-musth bulls will defer to a musth bull, irrespective of size. Musth bulls, which

are highly aggressive, will threaten or chase other bulls, especially when they are in the presence of an oestrous female. This heightened aggressiveness of musth bulls can be critical to their mating success. The most serious fights between bulls, leading to severe injury and even death, occur when two musth bulls of similar size and strength meet. The victorious bull is likely to be the one that ends up mating.

All bulls over 10 years old can be sexually active, in that they will investigate, chase and attempt to mount females. However, young, small bulls seldom have the opportunity to successfully mate, both because they are avoided by the cows and they receive aggression

from older bulls. The younger, smaller bulls invariably defer to a musth bull, and thus will have few chances to get close enough to a female to mate. Older bulls which are not currently in musth also occasionally mate. Again, if a musth bull is around, they will avoid that bull and his oestrous female. Since bulls out of musth spend most of their time alone or with other bulls in areas removed from those of the cows and calves, they have relatively few opportunities to mate outside their musth periods.

During musth, the loss of appetite may help the bull reduce the time he would spend feeding, freeing him for the task of searching for females. Persistence in searching, combined with the visual,

olfactory and vocal signals associated with musth may bring the reproductively active males and females together. Females prefer musth bulls, and will cooperate with them in mating, but they avoid or run away from non-musth bulls. Musth bulls are also persistent and effective at guarding an oestrous female during the period of a consortship. Thus, the musth phenomenon increases the male elephant's ability to compete with other bulls and enhances his attractiveness to females, leading to greater reproductive success.

As the musth period progresses, the bull loses weight and condition. While spending time and energy searching for oestrus females and fighting with other bulls, as well as feeding very little, he exhausts his body reserves. After a while his condition declines, he can no longer sustain musth and he 'retires' to his bull area to feed up for the next year's cycle.

The critical elements of reproduction for elephant bulls are three-fold. These elements are physiological (musth and its underlying hormonal controls, and the bull's physical condition, size and age), and behavioural (the number, age and status of other competitor bulls), and they also interact with the environmental and social factors that influence the timing and frequency of female reproduction, making more or fewer females available at any one time. The females also influence male success directly through their cooperation with some bulls and their rejection of others – a form of mate choice on the cows' part. All these elements must be integrated in a complex sequence of physiological changes and behaviour between the sexes to produce the next generation.

Below: A matriarch surrounded by her calves of all ages. The youngest calf is beginning to feed himself, while her adolescent (at extreme left) forages further away but still within contact of the family group. The juvenile (second from left) remains close to both the mother and youngest sibling. This cow has clearly produced her calves at relatively short intervals and has been successful at keeping them alive; the goal of every elephant mother.

ECOLOGY

Elephants need enormous quantities of food, which they get from many trees, shrubs and herbs. The acacias are favourite foods, both in Africa and in Asia. They consume not only the leaves – including these vicious-looking spines – but also the bark of acacias.

As individuals, elephants are the largest consumers of plants among the terrestrial animals. They are very adaptable creatures, inhabiting a range of habitats from the hot and dry Kalahari Desert to the humid and wet tropical forests of Malaysia. The menu they can choose from, even within any one region, would be the envy of a chef in most restaurants, so varied can it be. Wherever the feeding habits of elephants have been studied, in Africa or in Asia, it has been found that they may consume anywhere from 100 to 500 plant species. This has been made possible by the organ that, more than any other feature, distinguishes elephants from other mammals – the trunk. The trunk is an elongation of the nose and the upper lip. It has no hard tissue such as bone, but is made up of thousands of tiny muscles that give it incredible flexibility. The amazing versatility of the elephant, to feed on tiny herbs from the ground as well as to rear up on its hind legs and bring down a branch, is unmatched among land animals.

Elephants need a lot of food and cannot afford to be too choosy about what they eat. We begin our exploration of the ecology of elephants, therefore, with a close look at their diet and how they obtain it.

Diet and feeding habits

The elephant's diet comes from a variety of plants – grasses, broadleaved herbaceous plants, shrubs, palms, vines and trees – and from many plant parts – leaves, twigs, bark, fruits and even flowers. However, the bulk of their food may consist of only a few plants, such as grasses and some shrubs and trees. The components of the diet vary with habitat and also change with the seasons. Obviously, the consumption of fruit is seasonal. Elephants are known to gorge themselves with fruits when these are plentiful. For hours on end they may selectively pick up fruits of palm, *Balanites*, tamarind, wood apple or acacia. If the fruits happen to be somewhat overripe and slightly fermenting, as the fallen fruits of the *Borassus* palm often are, an elephant may get quite drunk!

In drier forests and grasslands the grasses predominate in the diet of elephants. In savannas and woodlands the tall grasses are coarse and unpalatable during the dry season, and fires may have reduced them to ashes. Elephants now prefer to feed on the bark, fruits and leaves of many shrubs and trees. If they have access to swamps, they may still be able to get hold of relatively succulent grasses. With the onset of the rains the new flush of grass is both tender and very nutritious. Especially in areas burnt during the dry season, elephants now switch over largely to eating grasses, which give them an adequate supply of protein to make up for whatever weight they may have lost earlier. In the forests of Asia the bamboos are a very important component of the diet of elephants. The bamboos belong to the grass family, although they resemble trees in appearance and are hence known as 'tree-grasses'. They maintain a high level of protein in their leaves even during the dry season, when good-quality food is otherwise scarce.

Studies in African savanna-woodland and in the drier forests of Asia have shown that seasonal dietary patterns in the two regions are remarkably similar. C.R.Field and I.C.Ross found in Kidepo Valley in Uganda that browse constituted 71 percent of the diet of elephants during the dry season, and grasses formed 57 percent of the diet during the rainy months. In southern India I made similar observations on the Asian elephant's dietary habits. Up to 70 percent of the diet was browse during the dry months, and grasses were consumed to the tune of 54 percent during the early wet season. In rain forests the diet is very different. It is very difficult or impossible to observe elephants directly in these dense forests, and therefore one has to rely on indirect methods, such as analyzing the contents of dung or looking for signs of feeding on plants. Jeff Short found that 93 percent of the elephant dung he examined in the rain forests of Ghana contained remains of fruits. Robert Olivier observed that palms are by far the most commonly eaten plants in the rain forests of Malaysia. In addition, elephants feed on a variety of other plants – including

Above: A bull Asian elephant reaches out for a trunkful of bamboo stems and leaves, standing in water to reach the most succulent growths. Bamboos belong to the grass family and maintain a relatively constant protein value throughout the year. Dozens of bamboo species in Asia are a mainstay of elephants.

Right: The grasses are staple food for elephants in all but the dense tropical rain forests. They are nutritious only during the wet season. In areas burnt during the dry spell, the new flush of tender grass that emerges with the rains attracts elephants. Here, an elephant is clearly enjoying the rich crop of new grass after rains in the Yala National Park, Sri Lanka.

Above: Elephants are fond of eating soils rich in certain minerals such as sodium, but they will also seek other sources. This cave has been created by elephants eating rocks in the Ngorongoro Conservation Area, Tanzania.

Below: In the same cave the tusk marks left by elephants can be clearly seen. The tusks have been used to dig out and remove portions of the mineral-rich rocks. Elephants will even enter dark caves in search of minerals.

climbers, lianas, herbs and succulents.

The last word has not yet been said on the matter of the elephant's strong liking for the bark of many trees and shrubs. Chemical analyses of the kinds of bark consumed by elephants indicate that these may be a significant source of minerals such as calcium, manganese, iron, boron and copper. However, not everyone agrees that elephants feed on bark for the sake of its minerals. The fibre in bark may be important for elephants to avoid constipation. One of the more interesting explanations for bark eating was given by K.G. McCullagh, who found that African elephants were prone to deficiency in certain essential fatty acids and that bark could satisfy this need.

Whether bark is consumed for its nutrients or not, minerals are so important to elephants that they even eat soils rich in them. Rain forest soils and plant parts are particularly deficient in minerals such as sodium, which elephants need. In these regions elephants may frequent natural salt licks. These are small patches of soil that have a high content of various minerals. Some wildlife parks

have taken advantage of this behaviour by artificially supplying common salt at specific locations to attract mammals such as elephants for the benefit of tourists. In the Mount Elgon region along the Kenya-Uganda border, elephants even enter a cave in total darkness to search for rocks that are rich in salts!

Apart from their long-distance seasonal movements, elephants also search for the best possible items on their daily rounds. Where the tall grasses are not very appealing they may search for more tender short grasses that grow in the shade of the coarse swards. They may spend 12-18 hours in feeding each day. The exact time may depend on the availability of suitable forage, the type of plants eaten and the weather. They do not feed at the same rate throughout. There are periods of intense feeding (during the morning and in the late afternoon and evening) and other times when they feed at a more leisurely pace.

Elephants consume a great deal of food. The fresh weight of plants that an elephant consumes each day totals about 6-8 percent of its own body weight. For a

Above: An elephant uses its tusks to scoop out mineral-rich soil, which it will then consume. The power and leverage exerted by the tusks is very apparent here. The strength and flexibility of the trunk also make this excavation possible.

big bull elephant weighing about 5 tonnes(10,125lb) this would amount to 400kg(882lb). A full-grown cow elephant would need about 60 percent of this amount, and an average elephant, weighing about 2 tonnes(4,450lb) may need only 160kg(353lb). This may seem an enormous amount, but when we compare elephants with other animals it turns out that elephants eat less food in relation to their body weight than other animals do. The smaller an animal, the more it consumes in proportion to its body weight. For instance, a rat may consume 40 percent of its body weight as food in a day.

A large animal such as the elephant can also tolerate a diet of poorer quality than does a smaller animal; hence its consumption of coarse grasses or even dry twigs at times. To chew the coarse plant material the teeth of elephants have evolved special and complex adaptations. The molar teeth are large and have high crowns (a characteristic known as *hypsodonty*). The grinding surface of the tooth has a complex pattern of transverse ridges, which are diamond- or lozenge-shaped in the African elephant but nearly parallel in the Asian elephant. As the animal chews its food the jaws move from front to back, with hardly any sideways action. The rasplike surface of the molars and the manner in which the upper and lower molars move against each other cause even the toughest plant material to be well sheared.

Digestion and defecation

The elephant is not very efficient at digesting its food. Experiments with captive elephants indicate that the digestive effi-

ciency of protein may be as low as 22 percent of its amount in food. To make up for this lack of efficiency, a large herbivore usually has a greater rate of passage of food, so that more food can be eaten to obtain the required amount of nutrients. The time taken for food to pass through the gut of an elephant may be anywhere from 11 to 46 hours, but an average time of 24 hours seems usual.

The cud-chewing, or ruminant, animals have stomachs designed to extract energy from cellulose, the complex carbohydrate that predominates in plants. The elephant is not a ruminant but all the fibrous forage that it consumes does not necessarily go to waste. It can obtain a fair amount of energy from the breakdown of cellulose by microorganisms, such as protozoa and bacteria, in the caecum and colon situated after the stomach. An elephant calf that is becoming less dependent on its mother for milk has to be infected with the right microbes for digesting cellulose. It acquires the microbes by eating small quantities of the dung of older elephants, an act known as *coprophagy*.

The large quantities of food eaten by elephants are fairly regularly expelled after digestion. Here again there are varying estimates of the number of times an elephant defecates in a day. Observers who have followed wild and captive elephants, both African and Asian, report between seven and 29 defecations each day. Some of the difference could be due to failure to observe elephants at night, or due to seasonal differences and changes in the nature of the diet. The average rate indicated by many observers is about one defecation every two hours, or 12 defecations daily.

The large quantities of dung deposited by elephants play a major role in the recycling of nutrients in areas where they are numerous. Elephants are generally the dominant species in terms of biomass in many savanna-woodland habitats. If we assume that there is one elephant for every square kilometre of land, and that an average elephant deposits 100kg(220lb) of dung each day, then the landscape is manured with 37 tonnes (74,925lb) of dung per square kilometre in a year. This is a considerable amount when we consider that farmers using organic manure for their millet fields may use about 150 tonnes (303,750lb) over the same area in a year. In some regions the dung of elephants and other animals is quickly removed by dung beetles, which play an important role in the recycling of nutrients.

The dietary habits of elephants also have ecological significance in other ways. Seeds of fruits consumed by them are dispersed away from the parent tree. The seeds of certain plants, such as the acacias, are known to germinate much better if they have passed through the gut of an animal such as the elephant. The enzymes the seeds encounter in the animal's gut soften the tough outer coat and facilitate the germination process. Although there is no firm evidence for this, it is possible that the extinction of large mammals such as the mastodons, close relatives of elephants, severely handicapped the capability of certain plants to disperse and regenerate, and perhaps even led to their extinction.

Whether plants suffered or not, many small mammals seem to have been wiped out in the wake of the disappearance of large mammals such as the proboscids in the Americas. Norman Owen-Smith, a South African zoologist, puts the blame for the extinction of smaller mammals squarely on the extinction of large mammals. In the course of satisfying their prodigious appetites, herbivores such as elephants change the landscape drastically. By pushing over trees they create gaps, which are then invaded by weedy plants. Many smaller mammals use such open habitats. Owen-Smith conjectures that the elimination of the megaherbivores (i.e. mammals over 1,000kg/2,200lb in

Above: *A dung beetle rolls along a ball of dung it has neatly compacted for taking to its nest. In some regions, the dung beetles play an important role in the recycling of nutrients by removing the enormous quantities of dung deposited by elephants and other animals. The beetles scurry out quickly to move fresh dung.*

Left: *An Asian elephant calf, showing the typical hairiness of youth, examines dung with its trunk. All juveniles eat small amounts of the dung of adult elephants. By doing this they pick up the beneficial microorganisms that will remain in the gut to enable them to break down the cellulose in the plants they eat.*

Right: *An olive baboon searches for seeds and insects in elephant droppings in Samburu Nature Reserve, Kenya. Seeds are usually passed out intact and, as well as providing an impromptu snack for other animals, they may also germinate better than those that have not passed through the gut of an animal.*

weight) by human hunters during the Pleistocene, 20,000-10,000 years ago, ultimately led to the transformation of habitats and the extinction of a host of smaller mammals as a result.

Plants on the defensive

Although it may be advantageous for some plants to be eaten by elephants, in that their seeds may be effectively dispersed, it would not be in their interest to be completely at the mercy of these bulldozers. Most plants, in any case, do not have any obvious advantage in being eaten. Plants have evolved their own elaborate defence systems to counter animal consumers; but physical structures such as thorns or spines (as in the acacias) do not prevent elephants from feeding on them. Chemical compounds in plants are a more effective deterrent. These chemical defences are of two main types. Chemicals such as tannins found in the bark of many plants reduce the digestibility of protein in food by binding to

it. Yet, elephants still feed on the bark of many acacias that contain fairly high amounts of tannins. The other class of chemical defences are toxins such as alkaloids and cyanogenic compounds. Plants in the evergreen rain forests contain many such chemicals and are consequently avoided by most mammals. (In fact, stinging nettles are reported to give even pachyderms a fright.) The herbivores of such rain forest plants are mostly insects that have evolved mechanisms allowing them to feed on particular plant species. This is the reason why rain forests have very low densities of the large mammalian herbivores, and consequently of carnivores. Even in more hospitable areas the plants contain many toxins. Many perennial grasses can normally afford not to produce chemical defences, because their leaves can regenerate from the base, unlike broadleaved plants; yet even they may produce sufficiently high quantities of cyanogenic compounds, when they are just sprout-

ing, to repel herbivores. Mammals can often deal with these chemical defences of plants, because the liver or microbes in the gut can detoxify many of the chemicals – provided not too much has been consumed. The dietary preference of the elephant is thus a compromise between obtaining sufficient food for its metabolism and growth and avoiding those dangerous chemicals its system cannot deal with.

Below: African elephants digging for sub-soil water on a dry river bed. The front feet and legs are skilfully coordinated in digging the holes, and the tusks and trunk are indispensable tools for gouging out the dry soil to reach the moisture beneath the surface. As water seeps into the holes from the lower levels of the bed, the elephants suck it up into the trunk and then transfer it – trunkful at a time – to the mouth, swallowing as it trickles down the throat. Here, a youngster drinks at the hole pioneered by its mother. Elephants seem to have a good memory for such watering spots.

Above: An Asian bull elephant reaches out for a trunkful of water at a pond in the Biligirirangan Hills, in southern India. Elephants drink daily when water is available, consuming up to 200 litres(52 US gallons) in a day. For drinking and bathing, water is vital for elephants to thrive in all environments.

Drinking

Elephants drink a lot of water. When water is available they usually drink at least once a day, sometimes several times a day. Each time an adult elephant sucks in water with its trunk it may imbibe 5-10 litres(about 1-2.5 US gallons) of fluid. It may sometimes drink up to 100 litres (26 US gallons) at a time and over 200 litres(52 US gallons) during the day. When water is scarce, elephants dig holes in dry stream beds to get at sub-soil water. Typically the sand is excavated with the front feet and the trunk to create a hole, and the water that seeps into the hole is sucked in with the trunk and consumed. Elephants do not necessarily drink from any waterhole in an area. They clearly prefer waterholes that contain relatively high amounts of mineral salts, particularly sodium. The distribution of elephants can even be correlated with the salt content of waterholes within a region.

It is not true, however, that elephants cannot go without water for more than a few days. In 1973 a herd of 34 elephants accidentally entered a small paddock in the Galana Ranch in Kenya where there was no water. Thirty of these elephants broke out on the fourteenth day, without having drunk any water at all. Of the remaining elephants, two escaped, and two juveniles died (on the fifteenth and seventeenth days). This incident revealed the amazing capacity of such a large mammal to endure without water.

While on the subject of drinking it would be appropriate to mention another drinking habit – their fondness for alcohol! Army camps in forests have been deprived of their stocks of scotch by large, trumpeting night visitors (although the bottles could not be opened by the ransackers), distillers of illicit liquor have found their hidden barrels in the jungle emptied, and policemen in search of outlaws in the forest have been confronted by dancing pachyderms!

Seasonal movement and home range of elephants

To ensure that they get the choicest food items available and adequate water, elephants move long distances. These movements become obvious as the seasons change. During the dry season elephants are largely found where water is available, in river valleys and near swamps. When the rains come and water is found everywhere, it is no longer necessary for them to be confined to such places, and they spread out over a larger area. The distance and area that elephants cover vary from one region to another, depending on rainfall and vegetation types. One of the most detailed studies on elephant movement was carried out in the Tsavo National Park of Kenya by Walter Leuthold. He put radio-collars on a number of male and female elephants and tracked their movements, using an aircraft. He also made aerial transects of the Tsavo population to discover the seasonal distribution patterns. This study showed that elephants were largely confined to belts along rivers such as the Tsavo, Galana and Tiva during the dry season, dispersing from there once the rains came. In this relatively dry region the elephants moved considerable distances. The home ranges of some elephants extended over 100km(62miles) and covered an area of over 3,000km^2(1,172 miles^2). Cynthia Moss observed at the Amboseli National Park in southern Kenya that elephants congregate in the swamps during the dry season and disperse from here during the wet months. There is, however, enormous variation from year to year depending on the environmental conditions.

Studies of the Asian elephant have not been so detailed. Robert Olivier, who radio-tracked a few elephant herds in the rain forests of Malaysia, found that the home range was only 59km^2(23 miles^2) in secondary forest, whereas it was 167km^2(65 miles^2) in primary forest where food was less abundant. My studies in the deciduous forests of southern India showed that elephants may move 20-50km(12-31miles) and cover a minimum home range of 100-300km^2(36-118 miles^2). Since these figures were obtained only from re-sightings of identified elephants, the actual movement would probably have been greater. Here again, elephants occupied the gallery forests, swamps and moist forests during the dry season, and dispersed over a larger area once the rains began.

From these and other studies it seems clear that the movement of elephants is governed by the availability of water and forage during a particular season.

Crop raiding by elephants

Elephants have the habit of raiding cultivated fields and gardens, much to the consternation of farmers across Asia and Africa. In elephant country it is not uncommon for a farmer to look out of his hut at night and find large dark shapes gorging themselves on jack fruit or systematically harvesting his maize field. Elephants have developed crop raiding into a fine art and no amount of persuasion to leave, except the gun, seems to work with them.

The elephants' taste for cultivated crops must have evolved together with the development of agriculture. It is certainly not a new phenomenon. The *Gajasastra*, an ancient account of elephants that may be 2,500 years old, talks about wild elephants devastating agricultural fields in what is today the state of Bihar in northern India. As human settlements and agriculture spread through the plains, river valleys and hill forests, the conflict between elephants and people would have intensified, leading to the elimination of elephants from many of these areas.

Nevertheless, the elephant has persisted in being a connoisseur of many cultivated plants. Staple food crops grown over much of the globe, the cereals and millets, are also greatly preferred by elephants. Rice fields in Asia and maize or millet fields in Africa are frequently raided by them. In a single night's foray a herd of 20 elephants can eat and trample down 2 hectares(5 acres) of crops. A bull party of four or five animals can cause half this damage during the same period. In fact, crop-raiding elephants can satisfy their entire food requirement for 24 hours by spending just seven or eight hours in a cultivated field at night.

For many farmers in poor countries this means the loss of an entire year's crop and the risk of starvation. They also face the risk of being killed if they attempt to chase away the elephants, especially the large bulls. Adult bulls are more tenacious raiders than are the herds, and frequent the fields far more often. In many countries, farmers have resorted to the gun to protect their crops. In Asian countries such as India, a combination of cultural traditions and conservation laws generally prevents farmers from shooting down elephants outright.

In some regions where agriculture is more commercial, losses due to elephants may run into millions of dollars every year. Oil palm and rubber are two money spinners that are common in Malaysia and increasingly so in Sumatra, and plantations of these are often the targets of attack by elephants. The succulent central rachis, or growing shoot, of the oil palm and the bark of the rubber tree are too tempting to elephants. The losses to these plantations were so high in Malaysia during the 1970s that the country had the reputation of having created the million dollar white elephant!

In spite of the hostility shown to them by farmers, elephants continue to prefer crops, for many reasons. Elephants increasingly encounter cultivated fields as human habitation spreads through their former range. When a sugar cane plantation appears along a traditional migration route, the temptation is too great to resist. As the habitat becomes fragmented, the giants are left with too little room for their comfort and tend to spill over into human habitation. Added to this, the quality of their habitat may also deteriorate. This scenario is all too familiar over much of Asia, where the elephant has lost enormous ground. Equivalent situations apply in many parts of Africa. In the Tana River Valley in Kenya, for example, elephants damage crops when they have to traverse fields on their way to water.

Finally, the crops are much more tasty and nutritious than any similar plants that elephants encounter in the wild. When ripe paddy crop or sugar cane is like cake to them, why should they settle for the common bread of coarse grasses?

Impact on trees

Not only the elephant's habit of demolishing cultivated plants has been of concern to people, but so also has its propensity to debark and push over trees in the wilderness. In the relatively dry savanna-woodland regions of Africa it is not uncommon to come across a landscape that seems as though an army of bulldozers plus a hurricane have passed through the area. Stately baobab trees are reduced to pulp, mature mopane trees flattened or a stand of acacias stripped naked of their life-sustaining bark.

Such scenes of destruction by elephants have led to disagreement between researchers and administrators over solutions to the problem. Some people consider the damage to wood-

Right: Farmers in the Lampung Province of Sumatra are trying to push out an elephant herd from their maize fields. If they do nothing more than wave their arms, shout and make a noise, there is not much hope that the elephants will depart. A herd can destroy a farmer's entire crop for the season. Raiding of cultivated fields by elephants is a common occurrence in Africa and Asia. Among their favourite crops are rice, maize, millets, sugar cane, palms, banana and many fruit trees. Most of the incursions into crop fields take place at night.

Below: In elephant land, farmers must cope with sleepless nights for at least three months of the year. These two men are keeping a nightly vigil over their millet field. The finger millet plants have flowered and, at this stage, the crop is very nutritious and highly attractive to raiding elephants. Keeping guard from a flimsy thatched hut on the ground puts these farmers in great danger of being attacked by elephant raiders. It would be more prudent for them to sit up in a large tree nearby.

lands and their eventual conversion into grassland by elephants as an unnatural process that is totally unacceptable. In their view the elephant population in such areas has grossly exceeded the carrying capacity of the habitat and therefore elephants have to be killed – or culled, to use a more pleasant euphemism – for the health of both the habitat and the elephants.

Others took a totally different view. Elephants are not destroying the trees or forests, they are merely utilizing them. This is very much a part of nature's inscrutable ways. As the woodlands disappear, the elephants would likewise become reduced in numbers, with a time lag, allowing the trees to regenerate, only to see a resurgence of the elephant population once again. There is no need for man to interfere in nature's affairs by resorting to the culling of elephants.

Before going into the merits or demerits of the different points of view, let us first ask why elephants resort to such destructive feeding, and whether this is indeed a threat to tree populations. As we have seen earlier, feeding on the bark of trees may provide nutrients, chiefly minerals and fatty acids, needed for a balanced diet. Stripping of bark or pushing a tree over is not the only way in which it may be killed. The main stem

Left: African elephants stripping and feeding on the bark of an acacia tree. The bark may be consumed for its fibre content (to prevent constipation), or for the minerals and other nutrients that it contains. Stripping bark may kill such trees and devastate the landscape.

Below: These acacia trees in the Samburu Nature Reserve, Kenya, have died as a result of being ring-barked by elephants. More 'succulent' trees, such as baobabs, may be smashed by elephants seeking much needed moisture in times of drought.

may be broken or all the branches pulled down so that the crown is scanty and distorted in growth. Such trees may never be able to flower and reproduce normally. Even if there is some life left in them, they are as good as dead for practical purposes. Trees damaged by elephants may be susceptible to attack by wood-boring insects or fungi. Such trees fall over more easily when it is windy. A fire may also kill a damaged tree.

Elephants may completely smash up a tree. The wood of the baobab is relatively spongy, and elephants can gouge out the wood with their tusks, or reduce the tree to a pulpy mass. They may feed on the wood in order to obtain some moisture when water is scarce, a possibility that is also true of feeding on sappy bark. Certain trees, such as the mopane, can be pushed over because of their shallow roots; others have weak stems that can be easily broken.

Destruction of woodland has been reported from many semi-arid regions of Africa where elephants are relatively abundant. Early European explorers noticed and commented upon this phenomenon. However, it was not until the 1960s that the particular problem was quantified and scientifically investigated. H.K.Buechner and H.C.Dawkins compared aerial photographs taken in 1932 and 1956 of Murchison (Kabalega) Falls National Park in Uganda. Their study, published in 1961, estimated that during this 24-year period the tree population in the park had roughly halved. Based on later aerial surveys in the park, Richard Laws and his colleagues made the interesting observation that the densities of trees and bushes were low inside the park but much higher outside. Often an abrupt change in vegetation density practically coincided with the park boundary. In areas with the heaviest damage, some 95 percent of *Terminalia glaucescens* trees

were dead, compared with less than 2 percent dead in areas of low usage. Iain Douglas-Hamilton, working in Lake Manyara Park in Tanzania during the late 1960s, predicted that *Acacia tortilis* would disappear from the park within 10 years due to the heavy damage by elephants. Reports of such damage accumulated from other regions too. In the famous Serengeti National Park there was concern over the disappearance of *Acacia xanthophloea* and other trees. Ruaha in Tanzania, Queen Elizabeth and Kidepo in Uganda, Tsavo in Kenya, Chizarira and Gonarezhou in Zimbabwe, Luangwa Valley in Zambia – all these and more seemed to be plagued by the 'elephant problem'. Although the Asian elephant seemed a gentle cousin by comparison, some reports from Sri Lanka were uncomfortably similar.

Not everyone agreed that elephants were to blame in the matter. R.M.Lawton, studying this phenomenon in Zambia during 1966-70, came to the conclusion that there was no evidence that overfeeding by elephants was responsible for destruction of the habitat. Even plants killed by elephants generally regenerated well through root coppices. He blamed fire for the deterioration of the vegetation. Harvey Croze likewise concluded that the potential of *Acacia tortilis* to regenerate and replace dead trees was being suppressed by fire, not by elephants. Douglas-Hamilton's prediction that *Acacia tortilis* would soon disappear from the Lake Manyara Park did not come true; a decade later, the tree population was very much intact. David Western and C.van Praet found something even more interesting at Amboseli in Kenya. A rising water table was increasing the salinity of the soil and making it difficult for the roots to absorb water. *Acacia xanthophloea* trees were adversely affected by this and were dying in large numbers. For once, the elephant was clearly not the villain.

Different management policies were adopted to deal with the elephant problem. Nature was allowed to take its course in the Tsavo National Park. Following a severe drought during 1970-71, the elephant population here crashed, and at least 6,000 of an estimated 20,000 elephants died of starvation and lack of

Right: This scene along the Voi River in Tsavo East National Park, Kenya, shows a landscape devastated by elephants and the effects of a prolonged drought. In these desperate conditions, the elephants are gathering near the last-remaining sources of water. Elephants can completely transform their habitat by their 'destructive' feeding habits. An entire woodland may be turned into grassland by elephants breaking and pushing over trees. There has been considerable debate as to whether such transformation is unnatural or a part of natural elephant-vegetation cycles.

water. Culling programmes were organized in Murchison Falls Park, Luangwa Valley, Chizararia Reserve, Kruger Park (in South Africa) and Hwange Park (in Zimbabwe). In the last two countries mentioned, culling continues as an official management policy. The *status quo* of the original vegetation has been generally maintained in such places. In particular, woodlands have not been converted into grassland.

Judgments on whether to cull or not cannot be made here, but it is pertinent to note that both sides scored points in the debate. In areas where elephants have been virtually eliminated, such as over much of Uganda, the grasslands are in the process of reverting back to woodland. Countries such as Zimbabwe, which regularly cull elephants, have been able to maintain the habitat and the population of elephants in a healthy state of equilibrium. On the other hand, it has not been proved that elephants have caused widespread desertification through destruction of woodland, as feared. Management decisions have to be made by each country's administrators and scientists, based on its own peculiar problems and goals.

Population dynamics

This brings us to the important question of what regulates elephant populations under natural conditions. Is there some self-regulatory mechanism at work that ensures a declining growth rate if there are too many elephants in an area? Otherwise, it is clear that elephant populations

would increase to such an extent that they would destroy their food supply and set the stage for a catastrophic decline like that at Tsavo during the early 1970s.

Some of the earliest work on the population dynamics of elephants was carried out by Irven Buss and his associates in Uganda. They found that the number of calves below one year old varied in different populations depending on the population densities. A population with a higher density had a lower rate of reproduction. These findings raised questions about what could be the mechanism for this decline. Could elephants delay the start of reproduction? Could they be reproducing less frequently? Was the decline in birth rate due to changes in behaviour or nutrition?

Detailed studies on elephant populations were clearly needed before these questions could be answered. Soon Richard Laws and his team swung into action in East Africa. Their studies began in the Ugandan parks, and later shifted to Tsavo in Kenya. At this time, Uganda was culling elephants to control the population. This provided the opportunity for scientists to obtain detailed information on reproduction patterns in elephants that otherwise would have been impossible or difficult without long-term studies.

The age of an elephant can be determined from its dentition. Usually the lower jaw is used for this purpose. By examining the reproductive organs of culled elephants, invaluable data could be collected. When a female gives birth a

considerable amount of maternal tissue from the uterus lining is also shed, along with the placental tissue. This leaves a permanent scar, which can be easily discerned upon examination. The number of scars in the uterus of a cow elephant is thus the same as the number of pregnancies she has undergone. The ovaries can also be examined, to determine whether an animal has sexually matured. This, together with the presence or absence of uterine scars, indicates the age of first calving. The mean interval between successive calving can be calculated from the number of scars and the age of the elephant.

Richard Laws found that the age of sexual maturity varied greatly from one population to another, but that the males and females within a population matured at roughly the same age. The average age at which a cow matured was 11.7 years at Tsavo but as high as 22.3 years in the Budongo forest of Uganda. The interval between two births similarly varied from 2.9 years at Mkomasi East in Tanzania to

Right: A radio-collar being fitted by researchers on an elephant in the Hluhluwe Game Reserve, South Africa. The signal from the radio transmitter will enable the elephant to be traced during the study period. The elephant will have been temporarily immobilized with a chemical delivered in a 'dart' syringe.

Below: Park staff in Samburu Nature Reserve, Kenya, excavate a hole to provide some water to elephants and other wildlife during an extended period of drought.

9.1 years at Kabalega Falls Park (North). Clearly, there was enormous flexibility in reproductive parameters that could influence the dynamics of the population.

The age structures of the culled populations also revealed interesting patterns. When these were statistically analyzed they showed a large series of fluctuations with a wavelength of six to eight years. This suggested that there had been cycles of recruitment to the population corresponding to rainfall cycles of similar period in East Africa. The age structures also brought out some disturbing features. In the Murchison (Kabalega) Falls Park the structure for elephants culled in 1966 showed an abnormally low number of elephants up to 20 years of age, suggesting that the birth rate had fallen since 1946. Models of population dynamics indicated that the number of elephants in the park may have declined from 16,000 in 1946 to 9,400 in 1966. This was the first evidence that elephant populations could be regulated if their densities went too high.

John Hanks carried out similar work on elephant reproduction in the Luangwa Valley of Zambia, and G.L.Smuts did so at the Kruger Park in South Africa. All this generated considerable information on elephant reproductive biology and population dynamics.

Studies on the Asian elephant have not been as comprehensive. My own work in southern India showed that female elephants first gave birth between 15 and 20 years of age, but that they reproduced every 4.7 years on average, a rate that was comparable to the productive African populations. The southern Indian population also showed large annual fluctuations in births, similar to those observed in Africa.

Population ecologist Graeme Caughley came up with an interesting model in 1976 to explain natural regulation in elephant populations. He suggested that elephants and trees do not exist at equilibrium in the East African savannas but that they fluctuate in a manner that is known in mathematical parlance as a 'stable limit cycle'. As the elephant population increases and the tree population declines, the elephants too decline, with a time lag of several decades. This gives a chance for the trees to re-establish and continue the cycle. Based on the age structure of baobab trees in Zambia's Luangwa Valley, Caughley suggested that the interval between successive peaks in the elephant (or tree) population is about 200 years. I argued that in tropical moist forest, elephants and trees would tend to exist at near equilibrium.

If elephant and tree populations were indeed undergoing cycles of such long duration it would be very difficult to prove this with a few years' observation. Elephant populations are usually well buffered against the vicissitudes of the environment. A long-lived mammal such as the elephant has very low mortality rates. Between the ages of 5 and 40 years the annual death rate may be less than 2 percent in most populations. Even juvenile mortality is relatively low and normally does not exceed 10 percent in a year. At the same time, elephants also breed very slowly. With a gestation period of 20-22 months followed by one or two years of anoestrus, an elephant population cannot breed as rapidly as most other mammals could do. (For more information on this, see the chapter on *Reproduction* starting on page 64.)

Computer models have shown that given the best of conditions an elephant population can increase at not more than about 4 percent a year. Real populations probably increase at much lower rates. In regions where they have been known to increase at greater than 4 percent this has been in part due to immigration of elephants from other regions and not solely due to intrinsic increase.

The elephant is adapted to breed slowly but maintain a high population and biomass level. Such species usually live at close to the carrying capacity of the habitat, and are termed *K-selected* (the K signifies carrying capacity, as opposed to *r* signifying rate of increase). The elephant is the best example of an extremely K-selected species.

The population dynamics of a long-lived species such as the elephant can be understood only if long-term studies are carried out on them. The most detailed information on all the individuals in a population is available for the elephants of the Amboseli National Park in Kenya. Research on this population by Cynthia Moss and other biologists has shown how misleading it can be to look at short-term data gathered over a few years. In 1973 the population was estimated to con-

sist of 602 elephants. Over the next six years the numbers declined to 478 in 1978. During one year (1976) alone there was a decline of 49 elephants, or 9 percent of the total population. Seeing this trend, anyone would have concluded that the elephant population was doomed to decline further.

From 1979, however, the Amboseli population began to increase, and reached 674 by 1983. That year witnessed a phenomenal increase of 70 elephants (an 11.6 percent growth), but this should not be seen in isolation. The overall trend was an increasing population between 1973 and 1983. These data showed how year to year fluctuations may occur in births and deaths within an elephant population. This is largely related to the rainfall patterns. The Amboseli study has clearly brought out the need for taking a long-term perspective of elephant population dynamics.

The wave of ivory poaching during the 1970s and 1980s in Africa has, of course, resulted in the total disruption of social structure and population dynamics of its elephants. Large bulls have been shot to a disproportionately greater extent, resulting in unequal sex ratios with fewer males and more females. Shooting of elephants in family herds has caused changes in social behaviour. The impact of these changes on the future dynamics of the populations has yet to be studied.

The Asian elephant has also been poached, but in this species it is only the males that are killed for tusks. In one sense this is a far better situation than in Africa in that the females, which are more important in contributing to future generations, are immune from ivory poaching. In southern India my own studies have shown that a sex ratio of one adult male for every five adult females does not have any negative effect on the fertility of the population. In some regions the sex ratios have since then become even more unequal. It remains to be seen how these populations will respond. One possibility is that the tuskless bulls, which are relatively few in number, could increase in relation to tusked males. Southern India's elephants could then begin to resemble the northeastern population, in which at least half of the males are tuskless or, if poaching is very severe, the Sri Lankan population, where over 90 percent of the males are tuskless.

Below: An elephant herd in Amboseli, Kenya, crosses the plains at the foot of the snow-capped Mount Kilimanjaro, rising majestically 5,895m(19,340ft) above the surrounding countryside. This is a classic – if well-known – image of animals in harmony with their environment. Understanding the ecology of elephants is a vital step in conserving them where they are threatened.

DISTRIBUTION OF THE AFRICAN ELEPHANT

Originally the range of the African elephant extended throughout Africa except for the Sahara. Most of the populations in the north of the continent were exterminated in classical times and all had disappeared by the middle ages. The elephants in southern Africa did not long survive the arrival of the settlers but elsewhere, the elephant was still numerous and widely distributed until well after the Second World War. Nevertheless, numbers had probably started to decline in many regions by the 1920s and 1930s as the human population expanded, under the protection of newly acquired firearms, into the elephant's domain.

The true state of affairs did not become apparent until the early 1970s, when a drastic reduction in numbers was recorded in Uganda, where elephant numbers in one national park crashed by 87 percent within two years. Investigation showed that the decline was not confined to that country but was widespread throughout East Africa. Ivory poaching coupled with a breakdown in law and order, or at least in the means to conduct effective anti-poaching operations, seem to be the likely causes of the decline.

An overall view

The first attempt at a comprehensive census of elephants throughout Africa was made in 1979 by Iain Douglas-Hamilton, who produced a figure of 1,343,340 from 35 countries. The only thing that one can be certain about this total is that it is wrong! This is no reflection on the competence of the compiler, for the information was derived from a number of sources, of varying quality, by observers using a variety of methods, ranging from carefully planned and executed aerial counts in open country to rank guesses for the rain forests. It is probably of the right order of magnitude, however, and a figure of about a million may not be far wrong. A further extensive, but not comprehensive, survey was organized by Douglas-Hamilton some eight years later and this revealed a decline, as the total came to only 410,235 in 32 countries.

Although published in 1979 and 1987 respectively, these figures do not refer to specific points in time since the data for both surveys were collected over extended periods. It is unlikely that the decline in numbers has now levelled off; current counts, particularly in East Africa, continue to reveal reductions in numbers. Most losses occurred in East and West Africa and, to a lesser extent in Central Africa. Populations were stable in most southern African countries.

West Africa

West Africa has seen a progressive reduction in numbers throughout the present century, possibly as a result of over-exploitation for ivory. Loss of habitat has also played a part and continues to be a threat to the remaining populations.

The West African elephants are now split up into a number of scattered, small groupings, none of which contains more than a few hundred animals and most very many less. These populations are not only small but are also declining, and the prospects for their long-term survival seem bleak.

Central Africa

Although West Africa can be considered a disaster area for elephants, the situation in Central Africa is much brighter because of the still extensive rain forests in the Zaire Basin. Although improved techniques are being developed for estimating numbers in forests (mainly from dung counts), it is still impossible to gauge the numbers present with any great degree of precision. Nonetheless, it can safely be assumed that populations comprise tens, if not hundreds, of thousands, and protection of the central African rain forests represents the best chance for the conservation of elephants because, in the main, forest elephants do not come into conflict with man to the same extent as they do in the savannas. Nevertheless, numbers in Central Africa seem to be following the same downward trend as in other parts of the continent, particularly in those populations outside the protection of forests. The Central African elephants may be reduced in number but they are still very plentiful and the prospects for their survival are not necessarily pessimistic.

East Africa

The elephants of East Africa have received considerable research attention over the years and consequently their numbers in certain areas are known with some precision. The country with the most is Tanzania, whose population was estimated to be 130,369 in 1987. This may seem a lot but it is only about 40 percent of the total reported in 1979, and many of the estimates in the 1987 total were made ten or more years previously. Most of the elephants (55,000) are in the Selous Game Reserve, with another sizeable population of 34,725 in the Ruaha/Rungwa/Kizigo region. Neighbouring Kenya still holds a respectable 34,034, according to the survey, but Uganda is well down with only 2,059; the 1979 estimates for these two countries were 65,000 and 6,000 respectively. The figure for Uganda is probably optimistic; a count in 1991 in all the Ugandan national parks came to only 844 animals. Ethiopia, on the other hand, appears to have shown a marked increase, from an estimated 900 in 1979 to 8,650 in 1985. It is unlikely that numbers have increased that quickly and it is more probable that the earlier counts were inaccurate. Of the other East African countries, elephants have been almost eliminated from Somalia and greatly reduced in the Sudan.

Southern Africa

In southern Africa, Zambia (62,009), Zimbabwe (46,977) and Mozambique (27,150) form a block of contiguous countries with large numbers of elephants, which, in Zimbabwe, are still rising from the 30,000 reported in 1979. Mozambique and Zambia, on the other hand, have suffered massive drops from the previous totals of 150,000 and 54,800 respectively. Elephants are increasing in Botswana, where the total is thought to be of the order of 39,000. Over 5,000 elephants are estimated to live in Namibia and although this is not a high number, half of them are found in the Etosha National Park, where they are secure. The small population of 2,350 in Malawi is also now secure and appears to be stable, after suffering some vicissitudes in the early 1980s. Most of the elephants in South Africa are confined to the Kruger National Park, where their numbers are held at around 7,000 by the culling of any excess. With a total population approaching 200,000 and with excellent management policies in many of the countries, southern Africa is perhaps the most important region for elephant conservation.

Prospects for the future

In conclusion, it can be said that with a population totalling several hundred thousand, the African elephant is in no immediate danger of extinction. One cannot be complacent, however, in view of the rapid and comprehensive population crashes that have occurred in so many countries. It is likely that numbers will decline still further until a level is reached that is compatible with the increasing demands for land by the burgeoning human population. The African elephant should, however, be conservable as a species provided enlightened management policies are carried out. In the long run, it is conservation of habitat, rather than protection from hunting, that is likely to ensure the elephant's future.

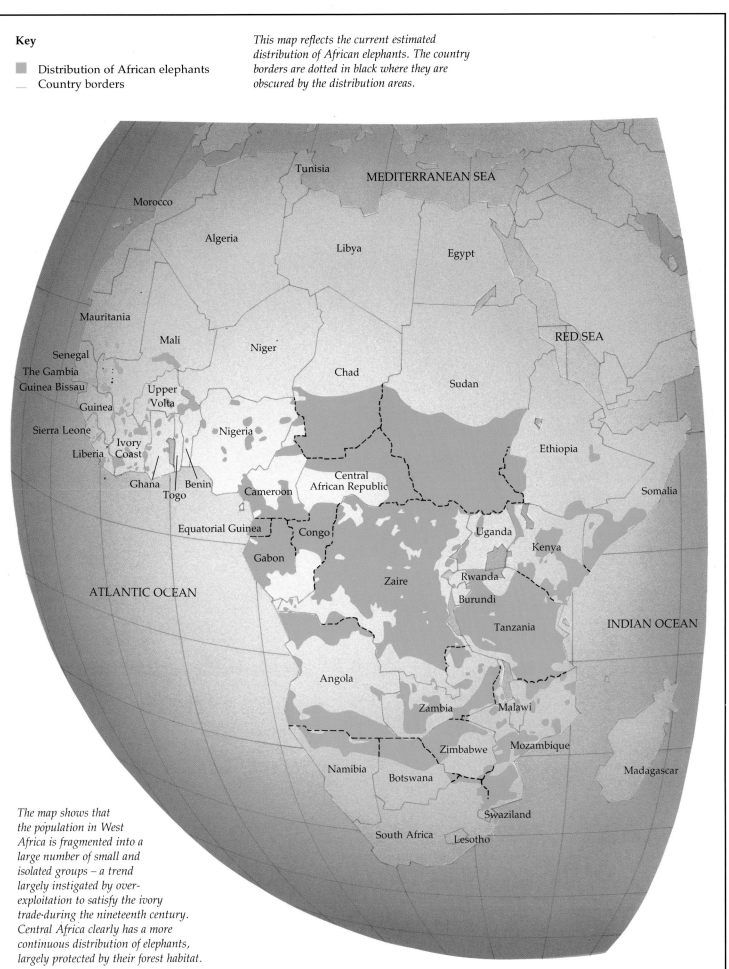

Key

Distribution of African elephants
Country borders

This map reflects the current estimated distribution of African elephants. The country borders are dotted in black where they are obscured by the distribution areas.

The map shows that the population in West Africa is fragmented into a large number of small and isolated groups – a trend largely instigated by over-exploitation to satisfy the ivory trade·during the nineteenth century. Central Africa clearly has a more continuous distribution of elephants, largely protected by their forest habitat.

DISTRIBUTION OF THE ASIAN ELEPHANT

The Asian elephant once had a widespread distribution, from the fertile Tigris-Euphrates crescent in western Asia eastward up to the Yangtze Kiang and perhaps even beyond this in northern China. In the not too distant past *Elephas maximus* may even have met its African cousin in the West Asian/North African cradle of human civilization. Its range covered present-day Iraq and nearby countries, southern Iran, Pakistan, the entire Indian subcontinent and continental Southeast Asia, southern and eastern China, and islands such as Sri Lanka, Sumatra, Borneo and possibly Java. It has been wiped out entirely from western Asia, a major part of the Indian subcontinent, substantial areas of Southeast Asia and almost entirely from China.

The retreat of the Asian elephant can be traced to the spread of human civilization along river valleys and plains. This largely pushed the elephant into the forested hills, which were relatively inaccessible to people. During this century, even these last frontiers have been breached by man in many regions. Hill slopes have been put under the plough and valleys submerged by dams. In Asia, elephants today have their backs to the great wall of human 'progress'.

Estimates of numbers of elephants in forested habitats are largely guesses, sometimes 'educated' guesses, but at other times 'wild' ones. It is extremely difficult to organize a proper census in a forest. It can also be very frustrating, as no elephant may be seen, even after days of wandering in dense rain forest, where elephants are found at very low densities. One does come across elephant dung, however, and the best way of estimating elephant numbers here may be simply by counting dung piles. Objective estimates of Asian elephant numbers are available only from parts of India and Sri Lanka, and from one or two places in Sumatra and Thailand.

The Asian Elephant Specialist Group of the International Union for Conservation of Nature and Natural Resources (IUCN) and World Wide Fund for Nature (WWF) has been mapping the distribution of elephants since the late 1970s. (For more information on the objectives of this group see the text panel on page 177.) With anywhere between 17,000 and 22,000 elephants, India has the largest numbers in the wild among the Asian countries. The elephants are found in four widely separated regions. In southern India, the elephant ranges over the chain of hills known as the Western Ghats and adjoining portions of the Eastern Ghats in the states of Karnataka, Kerala and Tamilnadu. The once continuous distribution has been broken up by developmental projects such as dams, tea and coffee plantations, agriculture, railway lines and roads. About 6,000-8,000 elephants are found here, of which the largest populations inhabit the Nilgiri Hills and Eastern Ghats (4,000-5,000), the Anamalai Hills (800-1,000) and the Periyar

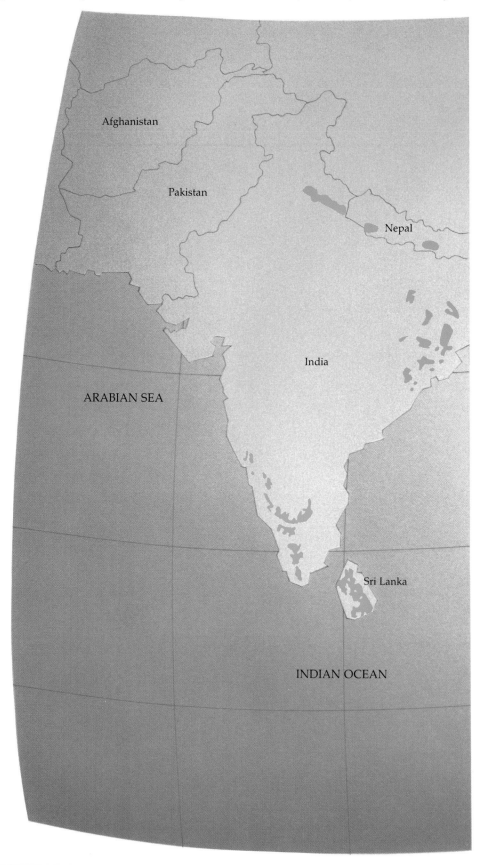

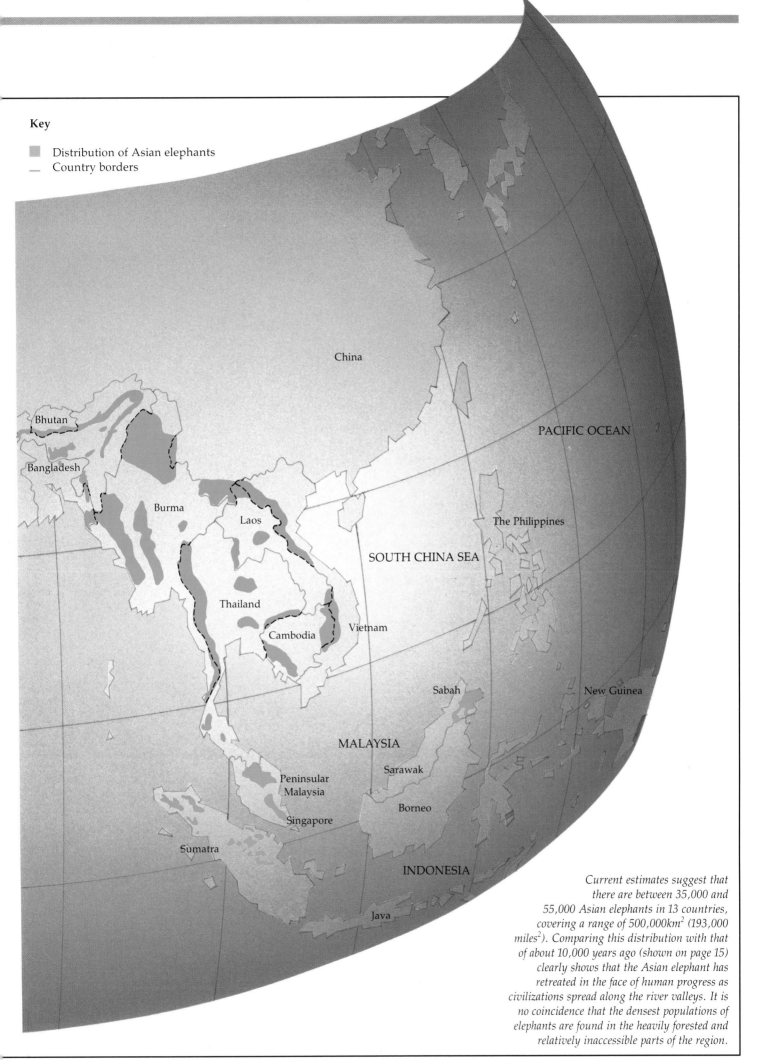

Key

■ Distribution of Asian elephants
— Country borders

China

Bhutan

Bangladesh

Burma

Laos

PACIFIC OCEAN

The Philippines

SOUTH CHINA SEA

Thailand

Cambodia

Vietnam

Sabah

New Guinea

MALAYSIA

Sarawak

Peninsular
Malaysia

Borneo

Singapore

Sumatra

INDONESIA

Java

Current estimates suggest that there are between 35,000 and 55,000 Asian elephants in 13 countries, covering a range of 500,000km^2 (193,000 miles^2). Comparing this distribution with that of about 10,000 years ago (shown on page 15) clearly shows that the Asian elephant has retreated in the face of human progress as civilizations spread along the river valleys. It is no coincidence that the densest populations of elephants are found in the heavily forested and relatively inaccessible parts of the region.

Plateau (700-1,000). Elephant densities in these places are as high as in the well-known African parks. Nagarhole, Bandipur, Mudumalai, and Periyar reserves in southern India are among the best places to see elephants in Asia. The diverse habitats – evergreen forest, deciduous forest and thorn scrub – available to elephants within a relatively small area is no doubt an important factor in supporting these high elephant densities.

Elephants in the east-central states of Bihar and Orissa live in a highly fragmented habitat that is fast degrading under intensive slash-and-burn shifting cultivation. S.P.Shahi and S.Chowdhury estimate that a total of about 1,600 elephants may exist within this region, but these are scattered as numerous small populations. Only the Simlipal Reserve with 375 elephants and the Satkosia Reserve with 300 elephants seem to offer some hope for these beasts.

The narrow belt of moist forest at the foothills of the Himalayas in the northwestern state of Uttar Pradesh is home to about 750 elephants according to an estimate by V.B.Singh. Although their habitat is secured in the Rajaji and Corbett reserves, they still have problems of free movement due to irrigation canals and human settlements.

The largest numbers of elephants in India are to be found in the north east. Our knowledge of the elephants there comes mainly from the work of D.K.Lahiri-Choudhury. Here again they are to be seen in a wide range of habitats, from alluvial floodplains of the Brahmaputra River, through semi-tropical rain forests, to the snow line in the Himalayas. One large population of 3,600-5,600 elephants inhabits the lower hills of the Himalayas from northern West Bengal eastward into Arunachal and Assam. The Manas Reserve in Assam is probably one of the finest places in the region for both elephants and a variety of other endangered animals. Another sizeable population of 1,700 elephants or so is found in the Kaziranga Reserve along the south bank of the Brahmaputra and in the nearby hills. A third large population, estimated at 2,500-3,500 elephants, ranges over the Garo Hills and Khasi Hills in the state of Meghalaya. They lead a precarious existence here because their habitat is subject to uncontrolled slash-and-burn shifting cultivation. Although northeastern India has the largest proportion of India's elephants, it is not the region where they necessarily have the best prospects for survival. Large areas of their habitat are not government-owned reserve lands and are fast degrading. Conservation has also generally taken a back seat due to political problems.

Nepal has very few elephants that are resident. Less than 100 seem to exist here and of these, at least half also move into

the Indian state of Uttar Pradesh. Bhutan's elephants are similarly partly shared with India across the border with the state of Assam. The Bhutan side of the Manas Reserve is the most important habitat for elephants.

Bangladesh has about 300-350 elephants, mainly in the Chittagong Hills bordering India and Burma. Some of these elephants undoubtedly move across the international borders. Two reserves, one in the Chittagong tract and another in Cox's Bazar, are being planned by the government for the protection of elephants.

Burma may still hold some surprises with regard to its elephant population. Historically, large numbers of elephants have been captured from the forests here, and this still continues to some extent. Elephants are widespread in Burma, because a large proportion of the country is still under forest cover. Teak and bamboo forests, favourite haunts of elephants, are plentiful. Although information on distribution and status is very hazy, it is certain that Burma has the largest number of Asian elephants after India. A conservative estimate of 5,000-10,000 elephants can be made for the wild population. These are distributed in the northern hills, the Arakan Yoma in the west bordering Bangladesh and India, the Pegu Yoma in the central region, the eastern Shan states and the Tenasserim Yoma in the southern part of Burma bordering Thailand. The largest populations seem to be in the northern hills and the Irrawaddy and Chindwin valleys.

All this does not mean that the elephant picture in Burma is rosy. Political rebellion in many regions has made it impossible for anyone to take stock of the

true situation. In recent years the Karen people have been poaching elephants on a large scale and smuggling the products, including ivory and skins, into Thailand for sale. Burma is still a closed country to the outside world and, until a proper field assessment can be made, it must be assumed that the elephant is in as much trouble there as elsewhere in Asia.

The last frontier of elephants in China is the southern province of Yunnan along the border with Burma and Laos. Less than 250 elephants seem to survive here, largely in the Xishuangbanna Reserve.

Thailand, the land of the sacred white elephant, has lost its former glory. From a spread covering 80 percent of the country during the 1930s, the forest cover has dwindled to only 30 percent of the land at present. Indiscriminate deforestation for timber and agriculture has been responsible for this attrition. The elephant has also suffered in the process. An estimate of 2,600-4,450 elephants in the wild was made in 1977 by Boonsong Lekagul and Jeff McNeely. Since then, it is certain that the population has been further reduced.

The majority of Thailand's elephants are found in the north and west in the Tennaserim Hill range along its border with Burma. The hills have a diversity of vegetation, including dry forests, which are a favourite habitat of elephants. Two protected area complexes, one in the north comprising Om Koi, Maetuen and Mai Ping reserves, and another in the west including the Huai Kha Khaeng, Thung Yai, Sri Nakarin and Erawan Falls reserves, seem to offer the best hope for elephants here. A significant population also occurs in Peninsular Thailand to the south. The Petchabun Mountains in the north east and the Dangrek Mountains

along the border with Kampuchea (Cambodia) to the south east are other elephant areas. In the Dangreks, the Khao Yai National Park is probably the best place to see elephants in Thailand. Robert Dobias, who has studied the elephant situation in Thailand, estimates that only 500-1,500 elephants are found in the protected area network, which extends over some 25,000km^2(9,655 miles^2).

Laos does not exactly contain a million elephants, as the literal translation of its name implies; in fact, it has only 2,000-3,000 in the wild, according to the most recent estimate. Most of the elephant range occurs along the border with Vietnam to the east. Scattered populations are also found west of the Mekong River in Sayabouri Province and in the highlands along its borders with China to the north and Burma to the west.

Hardly any worthwhile information is available for Kampuchea (Cambodia), where a large proportion of the country is still forested. The stronghold (if one may use this term) of the elephant seems to be along its border with Vietnam to the east, although a considerable number may also be present in the Dangreks to the north west and in the Cardamom and Elephant mountains to the south. Only a 'guesstimate' of 2,000 elephants is available for this country.

With Vietnam gradually recovering from the ravages of war, there is now hope that knowledge about the status of its wildlife will improve. For the present, one has to be content with Le Vu Khoi's recent educated guess of 1,500-2,000 elephants, entirely confined to the east along the border with Laos and Kampuchea. As in the other two neighbouring countries, both elephants and people going in search of them have to contend with unexploded bombs and mines.

Peninsular Malaysia's elephants are confined to its equatorial rain forests, which are now in a fragmented state, largely as a result of the development of rubber and oil-palm plantations. Mohammed Khan bin Momin Khan estimates that less than 1,000 elephants survive in the peninsula. A significant number of these seem to exist as isolated herds that have no hope for the future. A well-organized programme of translocating such small elephant herds to more viable areas is operating here. The most promising area for long-term conservation is Taman Negara (literally 'national park'), with an estimated population of 150-200 elephants.

The island of Sri Lanka has a rich and ancient elephant culture. As in other Asian countries, the elephant population has declined drastically in the wild. Sri Lanka's 3,000 or so elephants, as estimated by A.B.Fernando and more recently by S.K.Kotagama, are found in the drier habitats in the north and the east of the country. Agricultural development has led to the pocketed herd phenomenon in many areas. The Accelerated Mahaweli Development Scheme in the country's largest river basin, involving the construction of numerous dams coupled with agricultural expansion, is expected to make a serious impact on elephants and their habitat. To cope with the anticipated attrition of their habitat, the country has established a network of protected areas linked wherever possible by corridors. (See page 159.) Some of the best-known reserves where elephants can be seen are Wilpattu in the north west, Somawathiya and Maduru Oya in the Mahaweli Basin to the east, and Gal Oya, Ruhuna and Yala in the south east.

The elephant is widespread on the island of Sumatra (Indonesia), the only catch being that it exists as 44 distinct small populations, which have been mapped by Raleigh Blouch and Charles Santiapillai. As in Malaysia, the elephant habitat is almost entirely dense rain forest, often in hilly, inaccessible terrain. Agricultural development, including commercial plantations of rubber and oil-palm, and the transmigration of people from Java have been largely responsible for the reduction in forest cover.

Only 15 populations in Sumatra are believed to consist of over 100 elephants each. The total population on the island is estimated at 2,800-4,800 elephants. The 28 protected areas here have a maximum of 2,500 elephants. According to Charles Santiapillai, the most important of these reserves for elephant conservation are Gunung Leuser, Way Kambas, Kerinci-Seblat and Barisan Selatan.

The origin of elephants on the island of Borneo is not clear. There is fossil evidence that elephants once occurred in Borneo, but no-one is sure whether or not these died out and were replaced by captive elephants brought to the island in 1750 and later set free. Today, elephants are confined to the north east, largely in Sabah (Malaysia) and a small area in Kalimantan (Indonesia). Anywhere from 500 to 2,000 elephants may occur in the dense rain forests in hilly country.

In the final tally, there seem to be between 35,000 and 55,000 Asian elephants left in the wild. Their range covers an area of about 500,000km^2(193,000 miles^2). Even if we consider the 15,000 Asian elephants in captivity, the population numbers and range area of the Asian elephant are less than one tenth of the figures for the African elephant.

DISEASE & MORTALITY

The skull of the largest terrestrial animal, the elephant. Despite their size and seeming invincibility, elephants are still vulnerable to natural causes of mortality, such as disease and malnutrition, and cannot avoid the effects of habitat destruction and mass slaughter by man.

An adult elephant, weighing as much as 7 tonnes(over 15,000lb) and standing up to 4m(13ft) at the shoulder, is a formidable sight silhouetted against the skyline, conjuring up an air of invincibility. It is difficult to imagine that anything could prevent such a magnificent, awe-inspiring beast from achieving its remarkably long lifespan of approximately 65 years. However, such an age is rarely attained. Elephants, like other animals, may be afflicted with diseases of viral, bacterial or parasitic origin, suffer or even die from malnutrition during times of drought or through teeth problems and may sustain injuries following accidents or occasionally through interaction with other members of their own kind. However, the biggest threat to the very existence of elephants is man, primarily through the destruction of habitat in the case of the Asian elephant, but in the African elephant more dramatically as a result of man's insatiable appetite for ivory.

African and Asian elephants may be infested with the same parasites, but many are found in only one of the two species.

Parasites and disease

Our knowledge of parasites infesting wild elephants has been increased by data collected during culling operations, such as the survey between 1967 and 1972 in Zimbabwe, which threw a great deal of light on the internal parasites of the African elephant and the likelihood of their causing disease. The most commonly found parasites were oestrid fly larvae in the stomach of young elephants, flukes (flatworms) in the small intestine, hookworms in the bile duct and a number of nematodes (roundworms) mainly in the caecum and large intestine.

Some internal parasites are found in numbers likely to cause a degree of damage to the structure of the organs they inhabit, but most researchers agree that parasite loads are generally well tolerated, contributing to clinical disease only if the animal is suffering from malnutrition or some concurrent disease. In certain areas of Zimbabwe, notably the Hwange National Park, the concentration of elephants around waterholes in the dry season, and the subsequent contamination of the water with faeces, was the main means by which elephants acquired their parasite burden. There is some concern that with the increasing concentration of large numbers of elephants in national parks, due to the restriction of their former range, the number of parasites picked up from contaminated water is likely to increase, and parasite loads may reach levels likely to cause disease.

Asian elephants have a number of internal parasites not found in their African cousins. The fluke *Fasciola jacksoni* is one such parasite and this species in particular is a known cause of disease and mortality in working Asian elephants and also in zoo and circus elephants. Another type of fluke found in the large intestine has also been observed to cause chronic diarrhoea in captive Asian elephants. Deficiencies in husbandry are known to be responsible for a number of parasitic diseases in working elephants, and such factors, coupled with intensive housing, may also explain their occasional occurrence in zoo and circus elephants.

Blood-borne parasites occur in both African and Asian elephants. Roundworms in the blood, similar to the heartworms found in dogs, are present in both species in large numbers, but are of little clinical significance. A protozoan parasite, *Trypanosoma*, found in both African and Asian elephants, is thought to be responsible for a disease causing anaemia and intermittent fever in Asian elephants. This disease, known as 'thut', occurs particularly around marshy ground where the flies responsible for its transmission flourish.

External parasites are commonly found on elephants. Warble fly larvae, after hatching from eggs laid on the skin and migrating through the body of African elephants, erupt from swellings in the skin over the ears and flanks, causing some bleeding but little irritation or pain. Elephants are also prone to ticks and lice; the former are probably more important as potential carriers of blood-borne disease than as a cause of disease in their own right. Severe infestations with lice have been seen in captive elephants. Finally, oestrid flies may lay their eggs in infected wounds, the hatched larvae causing irritation and discomfort to the elephant. As with internal parasites, external parasites are unlikely to cause ill-health in an elephant unless it is already suffering from malnutrition or disease.

Above: Elephants feeding in a swamp in Amboseli National Park, Kenya. Wetlands and watercourses provide readily available sources of food and water, which become focal points for entire herds, particularly during droughts. Sick and elderly individuals that need readily accessible vegetation and water tend to spend their final days in such locations.

Below: An Asian elephant dust bathing. This activity helps to dislodge external parasites and provide protection against further infestation. Dust bathing, mud wallowing and water bathing are essential parts of the skin care routine. Despite its thickness, the skin requires regular upkeep to maintain its vitality and to keep it free from parasites and disease.

Infectious diseases

The incidence of infectious diseases in both wild African and Asian elephants is relatively low. An outbreak of a pneumonia-like disease that accounted for the death of over a hundred elephants was recorded by Iain Douglas-Hamilton in his well-known study of elephants in the Lake Manyara National Park in Tanzania. Isolated cases of anthrax have been seen in elephants in poor condition in East Africa, but only in wild Asian elephants does this disease ever reach epidemic proportions. Such epidemics largely occur in wet, low-lying regions during the rainy season, causing over 90 percent mortality in affected individuals. Post-mortems of affected animals reveal widespread internal haemorrhage.

Tetanus is occasionally seen in wild Asian elephants; the infection enters through wounds, and often proves fatal. Affected animals suffer from widespread spasm of the muscles, particularly of the

Below: A working elephant in Assam, India, being treated with an extract of ferns to disinfect rope sores. Many such remedies exist for the treatment of a variety of ailments and injuries afflicting working elephants that arise out of their conditions of work and captivity.

limbs and jaw. Rabies has only occasionally been reported in wild Asian elephants, and the source is usually suspected to be a bite from an infected village dog. Foot and mouth disease is also occasionally seen. Here the source is infected cattle, and this disease is rarely fatal.

Captive elephants suffer more frequently than wild ones from bacterial and viral diseases. In addition to those already listed, salmonellosis and tuberculosis have also been observed in captive elephants. Both may be fatal, the former causing persistent diarrhoea and the latter chronic weight loss. Neither has been recorded in wild elephants. The viral disease elephant pox has a greatly increased incidence in the captive elephant population, particularly in European zoos. It causes debility, fever and often lameness, with erosion and ulceration of mucous membranes and skin. In addition, a mycoplasma-related arthritis is now thought to be a relatively common cause of lameness in captive elephants. The increased incidence of disease in the captive population is probably linked to the intensive husbandry of elephants in zoos, circuses and logging camps, and to possible deficiencies in their nutrition and daily care.

The captive elephant and disease

As has already been indicated, parasitic and infectious diseases appear to have a higher incidence in captive elephants than in wild ones. Other conditions also occur more frequently in captivity, again often as a result of intensive housing, inadequate daily care and unsuitable food. In his book about the diseases of the Asian working elephant, G.H.Evans cited the ignorance of mahouts and their tendency to overwork elephants as one of the major reasons for ill-health in the working Asian elephant population. Excessive working of animals in the heat of the day often led to exhaustion, sunstroke and subsequent chilling at night. Improperly balanced and excessive loads led to sores, abscesses and ulceration of the skin, and the housing of elephants in insanitary conditions led to cracking of the soles and heels of the feet and subsequent lameness. In addition, an improperly balanced diet frequently caused colic and indigestion.

Captive elephants in zoos and circuses may also be subjected to insanitary conditions and lack of daily care, leading to foot problems and poor skin quality. Many zoos still provide an unbalanced diet containing large quantities of highly

digestible concentrates, instead of the bulky, fibrous vegetation that an elephant needs. Consequently, obesity is a major problem in zoo elephants, which are essentially sedentary and thus burn off little energy in their daily activities. Deficiency-related diseases may also occur. One example is vitamin E deficiency, where the animal's inability to obtain the natural form of vitamin E from its artificial diet may leave it more susceptible to heart failure and muscular weakness at times of stress.

It is important to emphasize at this point that the captive elephant is not always subjected to poor husbandry, hygiene and nutrition. Many zoos make great efforts to ensure the health and vitality of their charges. This can be achieved only with housing designed to allow efficient cleaning and to hinder the spread of disease. Daily management needs to be of a high standard, with regular foot care and attention to the skin, including bathing, scrubbing and oiling. Veterinary check-ups on a regular basis should involve a general examination and a blood test to pick up the first signs of ill-health. Regular worming and, where necessary, vaccination programmes should be implemented. Finally, but by no means least, care must be taken to provide a well-balanced diet. If these criteria are met, as they are in a number of zoos, there is no reason why elephants cannot be managed successfully in captivity.

Dental problems

Elephants' molars are adapted to masticating a highly fibrous diet. They have large grinding surfaces composed of numerous transverse ridges of dentine covered with enamel, and the grooves in between are filled with cement. The three elements wear at different rates, producing a suitably abrasive surface on the teeth for mastication. (For more details see *Anatomy*, starting on page 30.)

An elephant's molars are replaced continuously during the course of its life. The young African elephant is born with its first molars fully erupted and its second partially erupted. By the time the animal reaches four years of age, both of these have been lost, forced out by the eruption of the third molars, their crowns fragmenting and being spat out and their roots being resorbed. The third, fourth

Right: Inside the mouth of a female Asian elephant. Elephants usually have only one molar fully in wear in each jawbone at any one time. During the animal's lifespan, six progressive sets of molars come into wear, replaced by the next set as they are worn out. The roots are resorbed and the fragmented crowns are spat out. Elephants do not have canines and possess only one pair of extremely modified upper incisors, known in all male elephants and female African elephants as tusks.

How the teeth are formed and replaced

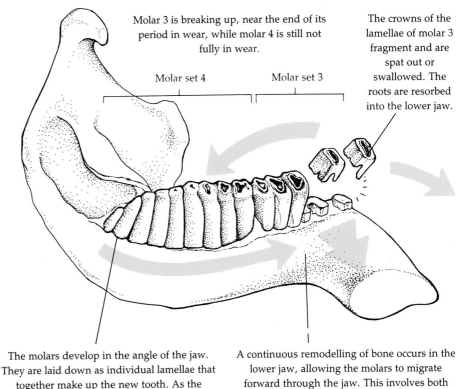

Molar 3 is breaking up, near the end of its period in wear, while molar 4 is still not fully in wear.

The crowns of the lamellae of molar 3 fragment and are spat out or swallowed. The roots are resorbed into the lower jaw.

Molar set 4   Molar set 3

The molars develop in the angle of the jaw. They are laid down as individual lamellae that together make up the new tooth. As the lamellae are produced, they migrate forwards and upwards.

A continuous remodelling of bone occurs in the lower jaw, allowing the molars to migrate forward through the jaw. This involves both the dissolution of old bone and the laying down of new bone.

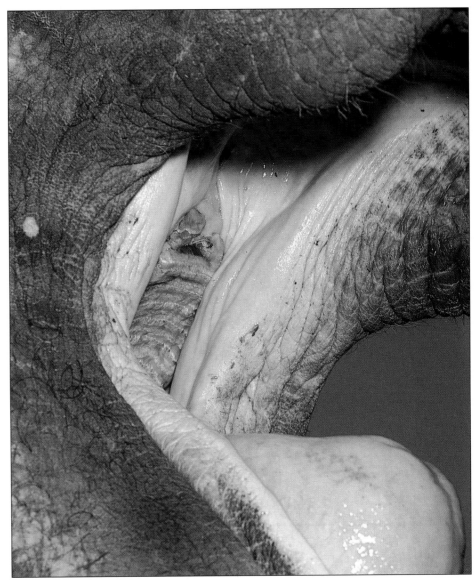

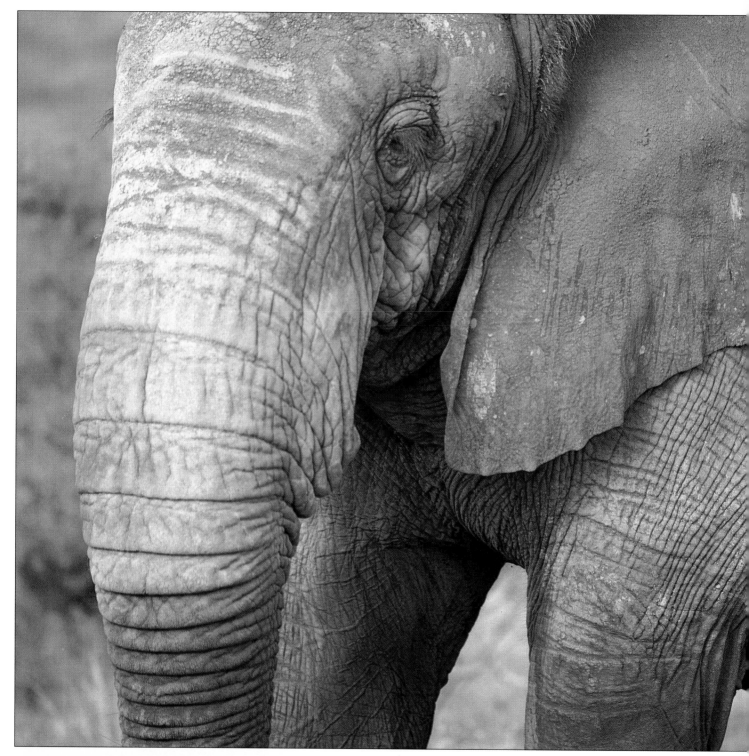

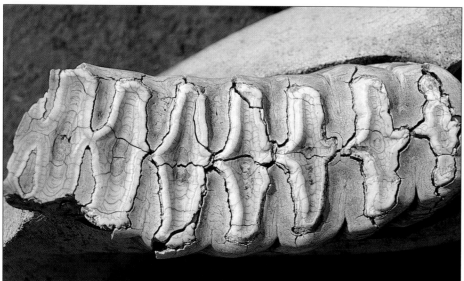

Above: *A tuskless bull African elephant, generally an uncommon sight on the African continent, although an increased frequency of males without tusks has been recorded in South Africa, with the virtual elimination of big tuskers through hunting. In Asian elephants, tusklessness is more frequently observed; in Sri Lanka, males without tusks comprise over 90 percent of the male elephant population.*

Left: *The occlusal, or 'grinding', surface of a molar from an African elephant. The transverse ridges of dentine and overlying enamel are separated by grooves of more rapidly wearing cement. The combination of ridges and grooves provides a suitably abrasive surface capable of dealing with the coarse vegetation – grasses, shrubs and the bark of trees – that make up the elephant's diet.*

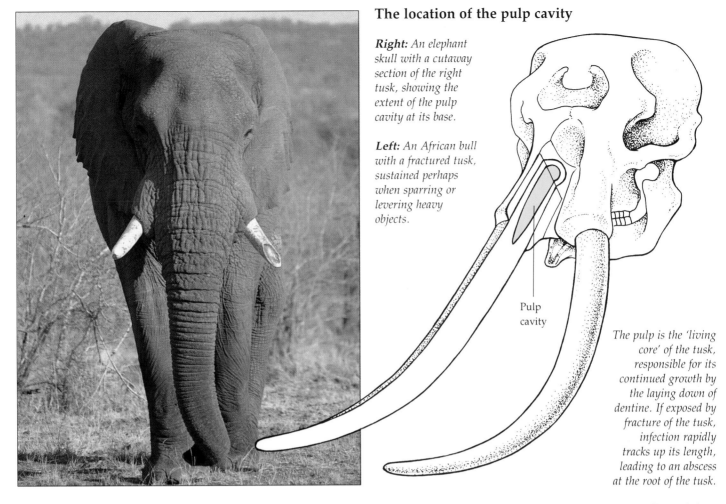

The location of the pulp cavity

Right: *An elephant skull with a cutaway section of the right tusk, showing the extent of the pulp cavity at its base.*

Left: *An African bull with a fractured tusk, sustained perhaps when sparring or levering heavy objects.*

Pulp cavity

The pulp is the 'living core' of the tusk, responsible for its continued growth by the laying down of dentine. If exposed by fracture of the tusk, infection rapidly tracks up its length, leading to an abscess at the root of the tusk.

and fifth molars have all been lost by the time the elephant is in its early forties. The sixth and final molars are now in use, and when these are worn out, by the time the animal has reached its mid-sixties, it will die of starvation.

Any abnormality of the molar, preventing it either from coming into use or from being extruded at the end of its period of wear, will affect its ability to grind the coarse vegetation, impairing subsequent digestion and assimilation of nutrients from the diet. Thus, dental problems are generally associated with a marked loss of condition. In Asian elephants, excessive growth of part of the crown and similar growths on the root causing displacement of the crown may lead to the upper and lower teeth not meeting properly, and this can cause the elephant to keep biting its cheek or tongue accidentally. Both these abnormalities will affect molar function and their rate of wear, with an acceleration of wear on the unaffected side, with which the animal will prefer to chew.

In his book, Evans noted a number of such molar 'tumours' in working Asian elephants and it is therefore likely that the condition is also found in wild Asian elephants. The abnormality appears to be rare in the African elephant, where assessments of the incidence of such conditions rely on the examination of decaying jawbones in the field and the checking of carcasses during culling operations in countries such as Zimbabwe.

Tooth root abscesses appear to be a relatively common problem in wild African elephants in certain locations. Ecologists working in Uganda were able to conduct a survey of tooth root abscesses and accompanying jaw swellings during the elephant cull in Murchison Falls National Park in 1966. Thirty of the 400 elephants examined were affected, and of 309 jawbones examined from elephants presumed to have died of natural causes, 30 were affected. This incidence was much higher than that in jaws examined in a similar survey in Tsavo. It was thought that the high level of stress in the Murchison Falls elephant population at the time was responsible for the marked difference in incidence, because human encroachment had led to greater restriction of the herds, with damage and loss of the forest habitat. The presence of abscesses has an effect similar to growths on the crown and root, interfering with mastication and accelerating wear on the unaffected side. This was the case with Ahmed, the renowned elephant from Marsabit mountain in Kenya, who probably died from malnutrition at the comparatively early age of 55 with a tooth root abscess in one jaw. Dental caries has also been recorded in both captive and wild Asian elephants.

The tusks are continuously growing, modified upper incisor teeth, primarily composed of dentine and tipped with a thin layer of enamel that rapidly wears off. The pulp cavity, responsible for the laying down of ivory internally and thus for the continued growth and development of the tusk, extends along part of its length and may therefore be exposed if a tusk fractures. Once it is exposed, infection rapidly tracks up the pulp cavity and thus many such fractures are associated with infection and abscesses.

Abnormalities of tusk growth may occur either through a congenital defect or through damage and infection. A damaged or infected tusk may become loosened in its socket and often rotates, continuing to grow in an abnormal direction. Such abnormalities may be life-threatening, as in one case encountered by Keith Eltringham, Director of the research station in Queen Elizabeth Park, Uganda. The left tusk of the elephant was growing back into the animal's cheek. Occasionally, damage or infection to a developing tusk may lead to division of the pulp cavity, and the formation of multiple irregular tusklets.

Tusklessness is a congenital abnormality occasionally found in the African elephant. In South Africa, an increased incidence of tuskless elephants has been recorded following the virtual elimination of big tuskers through hunting in the late nineteenth century and the subsequent loss of this particular genotype. In the Asian elephant, only the males have tusks, and in certain localities even most males are without tusks. In Sri Lanka, tusked males make up less than 10 percent of the male population.

Accidents and injuries

A number of accidents and injuries may befall elephants. Individual elephants are known to have died through falling off a precipice, becoming stuck in a swamp, getting caught in a flood or being crushed under a fallen tree. Young calves, weakened in times of drought and often separated from their mothers, are particularly at risk and also vulnerable to predation from lions, hyenas or crocodiles; they may also succumb to snake bites. Plant poisoning may also occur, and this happened to a small herd of elephants that swam out to an island in Lake Edward, Uganda, and died after eating large quantities of a poisonous euphorbia.

Fighting between bulls rarely leads to serious injury or death, except when two musth bulls meet, as disputes are usually settled before any serious clashes occur, the existing hierarchy usually resulting in the subordinate animal backing off. Occasionally, though, fatal injuries may occur, usually following a blow from the tusks. More commonly, a bull may fracture its tusk when sparring. The pulpy cavity is then exposed and infection tracks up the tusk, resulting in the formation of an abscess at its base. This is extremely painful, and may significantly alter an animal's behaviour; he may become a 'rogue' elephant exhibiting heightened aggression against other members of his own species, and also against man. In extreme cases, the abscess may lead to toxaemia (the release of toxins into the blood), resulting in a debilitating illness and eventual death.

Wild elephants may also be afflicted with less serious injuries. When the herd passes through scrubland, ears may be torn, or thorns may penetrate the soles of the feet. Minor wounds and abrasions may occur to the skin. Here, the thickness of an elephant's skin may delay healing, causing the wound to close over. This prevents drainage and leads to the spread of infection under the skin, which can cause great discomfort.

Mortality in the young elephant

The most vulnerable stage in an elephant's life is its first year, when mortality rates may exceed 30 percent. For the first three to four months, the youngster

Below: An elephant trapped in soft mud in Tsavo East National Park, Kenya. Elephants may unwittingly succumb to such accidents. Swamps, precipices, floods and falling trees are all potential hazards and occasionally man-made structures, such as rubbish pits around tourist lodges, may be responsible for injury or even death. Young calves that have strayed from their mothers are particularly at risk.

is totally dependent on its mother's milk for its nutrition. Any lessening of the milk supply, such as may occur when the mother is herself suffering from malnutrition during a drought, will jeopardize the calf's survival. From four months of age the young elephant starts to feed on vegetation and the percentage of its nutrition derived from milk decreases. However, it is still incapable of surviving without its mother's milk for the first two years of its life. Consequently, calves orphaned at less than two years usually die. Only rarely will another female elephant allow it to suck enough of her milk to keep it from starving.

The next vulnerable stage in an elephant's life is at weaning. This usually occurs at four to five years of age, when the calf's mother gives birth to a new calf. This is a period of great stress to the older calf, when its mother suddenly rejects its attempts to suckle. Vegetation now becomes the sole source of nutrition, and if this transition is not successfully made, the youngster will succumb to malnutrition. Again, mortality is increased in years of drought when suitably nutritious vegetation is hard to find; weanlings may wander off on their own to feed in swamps or near river courses, where nutritious food is more readily accessible, and this puts them at risk from predators, such as lions, hyenas and crocodiles.

During the first five years of life, mortality rates differ between the sexes. Males grow at a faster rate than females and have a higher body weight at wean-

Above: *Only young calves are likely to fall prey to predators such as lions, hyenas and crocodiles. They are most vulnerable during times of drought when, weakened through malnutrition, they may become separated from their mothers and the herd; easy pickings for a hungry predator, such as this lioness.*

Below: *A calf that has sustained a broken leg, probably after a fall or heavy blow. Such injuries may heal sufficiently for the animal to adopt a near-normal existence. However, the elephant's incapacity may cause it to fall prey to predators or succumb to malnutrition, and infection of the injury may lead to septicaemia.*

ing. This higher growth rate can be sustained only by a greater intake of milk; males are thus more demanding to feed, and also more susceptible to any decrease in the milk supply. As a result, males die through malnutrition more frequently than females, and this difference is accentuated in times of drought.

Another period of increased mortality in young males occurs in their late teens, when they first leave the herd to embark upon a bachelor existence. Alone and relatively inexperienced, they are more vulnerable to poaching, predation or potentially fatal accidents.

Mortality in the old elephant

Elephants are one of the longest-living animals on earth, although in the wild state they rarely have the chance to realise their potential longevity. If they do, they may attain an age of 65 years or more, and here the usual factor limiting their lifespan is the failure of their teeth. When the sixth and final set of molars is worn down to the gums, the elephant loses the ability to grind up – and thus adequately digest – the large quantities of coarse vegetation that make up the bulk of its diet, mastication becoming a slow and laborious process. By necessity, longer is spent on each feeding bout and the animal tends to lose condition, often becoming thin or even emaciated.

The female elephant may still produce a calf, even when well into her fifties, but its chances of survival are greatly reduced by this stage, either due to genetic defects, or because the mother elephant is unable to provide the milk required for the calf's maintenance and growth.

Old elephants tend to move more slowly and are often a number of paces behind the rest of the herd, which usually slows down to allow the aged animal to stay with them. Finally, the elephant succumbs to the effects of malnutrition, lagging behind the herd and eventually col-

lapsing. At this point, the other members of the herd often vainly attempt to raise it and will usually stay with their dead relative for hours after its death. In the case of a female elephant, her own offspring are often the last to leave her.

Arteriosclerosis: a degenerative disease of old age

Arteriosclerosis is a degenerative condition of the aorta and other major arteries, leading to progressive thickening and calcification of the artery walls with age. This disease is found in long-lived individuals of a wide variety of species. The clinical significance of this disease in elephants is a matter for debate. Some researchers have found little evidence of ill-health or senility in the animals most severely affected with the disease, and one would conclude from their findings that arteriosclerosis is unlikely to affect an elephant's lifespan.

A detailed survey carried out by Sylvia Sikes, who studied elephant diseases in East Africa, reaches a different conclusion. Here, she was able to relate many signs of ill-health to the disease. Lop ears, swollen feet, wasting muscles and poor skin condition were all seen in elephants suffering from arteriosclerosis, and she suggested that the thickening and partial blocking of the supplying arteries leads to oxygen starvation in the affected tissues.

She also postulated that heart attacks in old elephants may be attributable to occlusion of the coronary arteries, which are responsible for supplying oxygen to the heart itself. Sikes also linked degradation of the habitat to the disease, with a higher incidence in grassland habitats degraded by overpopulation with elephants. Here, increased exposure to ultraviolet light from the sun due to lack of shade, together with a lack of certain nutrients in the degraded vegetation, were thought to be predisposing factors in the condition.

Other workers have failed to find any link between overpopulation and increased incidence of the disease. Thus the environmental and clinical significance of arteriosclerosis remains a source of controversy.

Arteriosclerosis in elephants

Right: *These graphs reflect the frequency and severity of arteriosclerotic lesions in the aorta found in a sample of 207 elephants culled in the Luangwa Valley, Zambia in the 1960s.*

Below: *A senile bull elephant in his sixties and approaching the end of his natural lifespan. Ultimately, he will die from starvation when his sixth and final set of molars wears out.*

Light lesions
Medium lesions
Heavy lesions

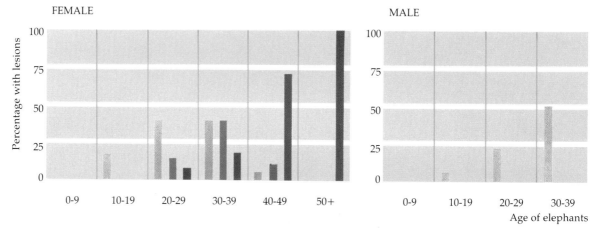

FEMALE

MALE

Percentage with lesions

Age of elephants

Drought

Apart from man, the single greatest cause of death in African elephants is drought. In the dry years of 1970 and 1971, Timothy Corfield, a young British zoologist working in Tsavo, estimated that approximately 5,900 elephants died in the park, with the highest mortality in young, dependent calves. Adult females, particularly in the 15-25 year age group, were also more vulnerable to the effects of drought in these years. Corfield postulated that the strong mother-calf bond restricted the feeding range of adult females to areas that could be covered by their weakened calves. They were forced to feed on the already depleted vegetation around available waterholes, and rapidly succumbed to the effects of malnutrition. Not surprisingly, the highest density of carcasses was around the remaining sources of water.

Cynthia Moss, who since 1973 has carried out a long-term project on the elephants of the Amboseli National Park, Kenya, also recorded high levels of mortality during the dry years of 1972 to 1978, exacerbated by the movement of the Masai and over 10,000 cattle into the park, due to the failure of their own water supply. She recorded the deaths of over 33 percent of the calves less than one year old, and also a high mortality rate in calves at weaning. Again, the elephants congregated on watercourses, primarily swamps, where there was excessive competition for the remaining poor-quality forage. Malnutrition not only affected the ability of adult females to maintain themselves and their calves, but also prevented them from coming on heat. As a result, no births occurred in the population under study from July 1977 to November 1978. It can be seen, therefore, that periods of drought have a pronounced effect not only on the level of mortality, but also on the birth rate.

Mortality due to man

The major cause of death in both the African and the Asian elephant is man.

Indirectly, man may affect their mortality by encroaching on the elephants' range through settlement, livestock grazing, local agriculture and plantations. This is particularly the case in India and other Asian countries, where the rapidly expanding human population has fragmented the elephants' habitat and eliminated traditional routes of migration with the destruction of the forests for agriculture, forestry, hydroelectricity and building. Here, elephants increasingly come into conflict with man when attempting to migrate through agricultural land, inevitably stopping to feed on crops such as rice, and destroying human

settlements that lie in their path. Both men and elephants have been killed in the clashes that result.

In East Africa, confrontation has occurred between the Masai people and the local elephant herds. One such case came about when Amboseli became a National Park in the late seventies. The Masai were persuaded to move from the Amboseli basin and its watercourses. Pipelines were set up to pump water from the park to the areas outside the boundary, but they were inadequate, and additional benefits promised to the Masai following their move were short-lived. At the same time, another import-

ant source of revenue to the Masai was lost when hunting for sport was banned on their land, and the subsequent dispute with the government resulted in a number of protest spearings of elephants in Amboseli. Such spearings still occur, and they tend to increase during periods of drought, when Masai cattle allowed into the park for water come into direct competition with the elephants. The situation was made worse in the past when a fresh group of young men were circumcised and entered the 'Moran', or warrior class, when they had to prove their manhood by killing large dangerous animals, and elephants were an obvious target. Furthermore, the settlement of Masai around the park, with agricultural development sustained by irrigation, has led to conflict similar to that found in Asia, when their crops are trampled and eaten by local elephant herds.

Man affects elephant mortality directly through hunting, poaching and culling. Hunting of elephants primarily for meat is now relatively rare and the numbers killed are negligible in comparison with the slaughter due to poaching. Traditional methods using pitfall traps, weighted spears and foot and trunk snares are still occasionally found in some areas of Africa. In the past, fire was often used to drive the elephants into such traps or onto spears and guns, and virtually the entire carcass was used as food for a whole village. Professional hunting for trophies is responsible for only a limited number of elephant deaths nowadays. Now banned or strictly controlled, the business has largely died out in much of East Africa, with only an occasional rogue elephant being taken in this manner. In Southern Africa, where there is claimed to be an elephant over-population problem, the professional hunting industry is likely to thrive.

Poaching for ivory is now the single largest cause of mortality in the African elephant. Legitimate hunting for ivory in East, West and Southern Africa in the late nineteenth and early twentieth century led to a dramatic decline in elephant numbers and often a marked fragmentation of the remaining herds. With the setting up of national parks and the introduction of strict licences and quotas for hunting in the early twentieth century, ivory hunting – or poaching as it now became – went underground. Initially, poaching occurred at a fairly sustainable level, but all this changed in the 1970s in East Africa, with a massive upsurge in the number of animals poached.

From that time up until the total ban on the ivory trade laid down by the Convention on International Trade in Endangered Species of Wild Fauna and Flora (CITES) in October 1989 in Lausanne, Switzerland, poaching has been responsible for the virtual elimination of the African elephant from countries such as Sudan, Somalia and Chad, and has considerably reduced the numbers in other countries in East and Central Africa. The elephant population in Uganda was drastically reduced during the reign of Idi Amin. In Kenya, following a severe drought in the 1970s and a massive increase in poaching at that time, the elephant population was more than halved, and continued to decline during the 1980s. Zambia's elephant population was also severely affected by poaching, being reduced by 75 percent during the last decade. Substantial losses to poaching also occurred in the war-torn former Portuguese colonies of Mozambique and Angola, where funding for the civil war was being partially obtained from the trade in poached ivory, and army personnel with automatic weapons contributed to the massacre.

What does this mean to the social structure and survival of elephant herds themselves? Poachers select those individuals with the largest tusks, and so solitary bulls and matriarchs are the first to be killed. The loss of a matriarch has a profound effect on the social organization of the herd, disrupting family stability and often leading to the aggregation of survivors from a number of families into a larger herd, which has been interpreted as a response to the increased levels of stress. With the escalation of the ivory trade, elephants with large tusks became scarce, and younger individuals with smaller tusks started being targeted. Thus, the age structure of herds has been considerably altered, with the majority of remaining individuals being young adults and their calves. Calf mortality has been high, as many have lost their mothers because of poaching. Cynthia Moss has predicted that it is likely to rise still further because only inexperienced teenage females are now responsible for

Left: *An elephant with a severed trunk, probably after catching it in a snare. Calves may occasionally lose the tips of their trunks to crocodiles, but they are often able to adapt to drinking and eating solely with their mouths. Adults are less adaptable and may die from starvation if much of the trunk is lost. This female is able to manage with her slightly shortened trunk. Such an injury may lead to the elephant becoming a 'rogue', and if the wound suppurates the animal may suffocate.*

Below: *An elephant poached for its ivory in Kenya. Poaching is the single largest cause of mortality in the African elephant. A massive increase in the number of elephants poached in Kenya in the 1970s, coupled with a drought, led to more than half of the country's elephant population being wiped out. The slaughter continued during the 1980s. The situation was similar elsewhere in East and Central Africa. In Southern Africa, however, a crackdown on poaching has helped to maintain populations.*

calf survival in a herd. In addition, these young, highly stressed females are much less likely to come on heat, and inevitably the birth rate in such herds is likely to fall. Even with the world ban, the enormous impact of poaching on East Africa's elephant herds in the 1970s and 1980s will still be influencing the population dynamics of remaining herds for many years to come.

The situation is considerably different in Southern Africa. Strict enforcement of anti-poaching laws in Zimbabwe and South Africa has led to a steady increase in elephant numbers during the twentieth century. For example, in Zimbabwe, the elephant population increased by 5 percent every year between 1905 and 1965, and by 15 percent every year between 1965 and 1980. At present, the rate of increase is 7 percent. However, with the increasing human population in Zimbabwe and the subsequent restriction of elephant ranges largely to national parks such as Hwange, the elephant population cannot be supported by the land available. Thus, culling, carried out to avoid wholesale destruction of the habitat, is now the major cause of elephant

mortality in Zimbabwe. This is also the case in the Kruger National park in South Africa and in the reserves of Botswana. In order not to disrupt the elephants' social organization, whole family units are culled at a time. This avoids the considerable stress imposed on the surviving individuals as seen in East African herds subjected to indiscriminate poaching.

Assessing mortality in wild elephant populations

The most satisfactory means of assessing mortality is in a closed population, i.e. one that animals are not entering or leaving. If such a population has been studied for a number of years, individual animals can be recognized and all deaths recorded. It is then possible to obtain accurate information on the levels of mortality in different age groups. Such is the case in Amboseli National Park, Kenya, where Cynthia Moss has been studying a closed population of approximately 650 elephants since 1973 and has built up a wealth of data on the subject.

In most locations, however, this ideal cannot be achieved. John Hanks, who studied elephants in Zambia, summar-

Above: When dead, an elephant provides an abundant supply of food for scavengers and predators. Alive, an adult elephant only has one predator: man. Very few other predatory animals would even attempt to tackle an elephant that is more than a few months old.

ized the methods of assessing age-related mortality in elephant populations under such circumstances. Ideally, a large group of the population, born more or less at the same time, would be followed through its period of existence, recording the number of animals dying within the group each year. In this manner, one could obtain an accurate picture of mortality at any given age. Such a survey, however, would take over 60 years to complete, and is therefore impracticable.

Another method of assessing age-related mortality is achieved by estimating the age of all jawbones found at any one time in a given area by studying the pattern of molar wear. If one knows the rate of loss or decay of jawbones in the field, one can then determine the number of animals in different age groups that died over a particular period of time. A third method is to determine the age of in-

Above: A 20-month old elephant carcass, now just a pile of bleached bones. Concentrations of carcasses, often discovered around old watercourses, fired the legend of elephant graveyards. Bones are attractive to passing elephants, which stop to touch and smell them.

dividuals killed during a culling exercise, again by examination of the molars, and then to record how the number of elephants in each different age group decreases with increasing age. The decrease seen then reflects the levels of mortality in the different age groups. Both of the last two methods rely heavily on certain assumptions. With the first, one assumes that the rate of decay of jawbones in the field is the same in all age groups, whereas in fact younger animals' skeletons tend to decay more quickly. With the second method, one assumes that during the cull elephants are shot randomly, irrespective of age, which is not always the case. Finally, in both methods one is assuming that the age structure of the population does not change with time, and that there have been no recent periods when certain age groups have been subjected to greater

than normal mortality, e.g. young calves in drought periods. Thus, using such indirect methods is fraught with difficulties, and any results obtained must be interpreted with caution.

Elephant graveyards: are they fact or imaginative fiction?

The myth of elephant graveyards, to which elephants travel to die, has been in existence for thousands of years. There is no direct evidence to substantiate the claim, only the circumstantial evidence of areas with an unusually high density of elephant skeletons. A number of more feasible explanations have been put forward to explain such gatherings.

Sick and dying elephants tend to migrate to swamps and rivers, where there is a readily accessible supply of water and food. Such migrations are heightened during periods of drought, and the very weak often fail to extract themselves from the muddy pool or river bed. Thus, such an area becomes the site of increased elephant mortality.

In certain areas of Africa, the hunting practices of the past may also have fired the legend. The Nubians in the Sudan,

the ancient Somalians and the local tribes of Uganda and the Atlas Mountains in Algeria used to drive elephant herds into a deep gorge, where adults were slaughtered and calves and adolescents captured for training for use in war. Elsewhere, whole herds were similarly slaughtered after being surrounded by fire, again leading to areas of increased density of elephant skeletons. Thus, the legend of elephant graveyards would appear to be just that. There is little proof that elephants choose to travel to a certain area to die.

The behaviour of elephants that come across elephant remains is very striking, however. They often mill around and become extremely excited, finally approaching the carcass or skeleton and gently exploring it with their trunks. They will even roll bones with their feet and pick up and toss various parts of the skeleton with their trunks, and the jawbone seems to be of particular interest to them. It seems that elephants are capable of recognizing a dead relative and it is often the dead animal's siblings that stay longest with the remains, after the rest of the herd has moved away.

WORKING ELEPHANTS

A working elephant, with its tusks neatly trimmed, carrying fodder across a river in Nepal. The load is supported on a soft cotton quilt that cushions the elephant's backbone. Clearly, this elephant is in harmony with its duties in the service of man.

When did it all begin, this unique condition where a wild animal many times the size of a man, possessing the physical strength to fell him with a flick of its trunk or crush him to death under foot, humbles itself to befriend and serve him, only a few months after its capture? The origins of the human/elephant relationships are lost in antiquity. Did it start with the hunters of old bringing home the young of the mothers they killed for meat? Comparing this with the origins of today's livestock and domestic pets such as dogs and cats, it sounds plausible. Indeed, attempts have been made to reconstruct a scenario of prehistoric man taking the cue from the antics of playful baby elephants, teaching them to push, pull and fetch objects in their primitive compounds, or even to carry children placed on their backs. This may have led to the tame animals being used as decoys during a hunt and perhaps later in the capture of larger ones for domestication.

The earliest historical evidence of elephants being tamed and used by man comes from India from as long ago as 2000 BC. From then on, the elephant occupies a prominent place in the art, literature and religions of Asian countries from Mesopotamia in the west, through India, Sri Lanka and Burma, to China in the east.

The fact that methods of domestication of the African elephant are conspicuously absent from historical records has led to the belief that that species is untameable. But Richard Carrington in his book *Elephants*, disputes this:

"In fact the African elephant was domesticated quite as early as the Asiatic and was the first to make an impact on western European civilization. In Africa there is no certain evidence of domesticated elephants before the Ptolemaic period, but it seems likely that they (African elephants) must have been captured and

Below: At a training school in Thailand, these elephants are learning to pile logs in unison. Note how each elephant uses its tusks to support the log underneath and wraps the trunk over the top to gain a really firm grip.

tamed in the Nile Valley during early dynastic times."

However, when we speak of working elephants today it is understood that we refer to the Asian species.

Applied broadly, the term working elephants could include all the ways in which this remarkable animal has participated in man's social, cultural and development activities. Of the many roles it has played, we are glad that at least two of the unpleasant ones have ended: its use as a war elephant, and as an executioner. Another, in which it was required to carry royal hunters, rulers and other important people in a howdah (wooden enclosure) on its back to shoot animals – including its own kind – has fortunately been replaced by the more economically useful task of ferrying tourists to national parks to observe and photograph wildlife.

Despite the mechanization of the logging industry and the spread of those machines to the East, elephants are still in great demand in countries such as India, Sri Lanka, Burma and Thailand. There, wild elephants still occur in numbers that can supply a reasonable demand for

domestication, and the art of managing and caring for captive elephants is still very much alive. To deliver a wild elephant from the jungle to an owner's stable involves capture, taming and training, in that order. Here we look at the merits and demerits of the different methods used and also make comparisons between the old and the new. This is not only fascinating in its own right, but also provides an insight into the development of the man/elephant relationship.

Capturing wild elephants

There are references to elephant capture in early European literature, e.g. Aristotle's *Historia Animalium*, written in the 4th century BC and Pliny in Book VIII of his *Natural History*. The descriptions are quite misleading because they are based on reports made to writers by travellers. For instance, in Aristotle's account, he refers to the use of tame elephants in capture but does not clarify how the tame ones came to be there. Pliny seems to be alluding to the *keddah* (stockade) technique where elephants are beaten or starved into submission.

But in the East, several techniques

evolved, beginning with the pit trap or pit fall, followed by the use of tame decoys and finally different methods of noosing. As its name suggests, the pit trap was a deep pit dug in the path usually taken by elephants, skilfully camouflaged with leaves on a frame of dried sticks. Usually a smaller pit was also dug close to it and left open. In trying to avoid the visible trap, the unsuspecting animal stepped onto the invisible one. The victims, of course, ran the risk of serious injury during and after the fall, as

Below: A courageous trapper tying the leg of a newly captured Asian elephant to a suitably strong tree. Such traditional methods of elephant capture are being replaced by chemical immobilization, which is a safer method for the trappers and more humane for the elephants.

can be imagined. Due to the possibility of victims being maimed and rendered useless, the pit fall has been abandoned.

In another method, tame elephants were used as decoys to lure selected wild elephants to a spot where tame ones were moving about freely. The victim would be deceived into spending time here. It eventually became accustomed to accepting food and water at a tree selected for tethering it. When the new arrival appeared relatively docile, a band of expert elephant catchers would surprise it from their hiding place and quickly bind it with ropes. This was the method of choice when an impressive tusker considered suitable for the royal stables had been identified by scouts.

Noosing of wild elephants took two different forms. In one form a fearless ele-

phant trapper would follow a wild herd until one elephant happened to stray from the rest. The trapper, armed only with a length of deer-hide rope with a running noose at one end and a deer or sambar antler at the other, would approach it. He would conceal himself behind a large enough tree close to the isolated animal, then with noose at the ready he approached it from behind, prodded one hind leg and, as the animal kicked at the object, swiftly slipped the noose through, tightened the knot and let the rope run. When the enraged animal stampeded along with the rest of the herd, the rope eventually got caught in a root or a sapling and halted the animal's progress. In the meantime, the trapper's companions would have got some more nooses and ropes ready, and now swooped on the animal, slipped more ropes on the other legs and fastened them to other trees. The rest of the herd was then driven away with loud shouts and firecrackers.

The second noosing technique was to conceal the noose on the ground on an elephant trail and set it as a trap. Both methods involving nooses were practised by *panikkians*, a clan of Muslims of Arab origin inhabiting the northwestern and northeastern parts of Sri Lanka. Their craft is now threatened as capture technology changes.

The *mela shikar*, another method which called for skill and daring, is endemic to India and literally means 'a hunt from on top', which refers to the fact that all the trappers are on the backs of tame elephants. These tame elephants, known as *koonkies*, are strong adult bulls not afraid to deal with wild ones their own size or bigger. The hunt begins with a line of beaters advancing on elephant back to investigate the open grassland where elephants were last reported to be. The beaters are followed by another line of koonkies, which carry the trappers armed either with lassoes or with long poles that carry large rope nooses at the end. It is the beaters' task to encircle the herd in open country and keep them there until the trappers arrive. The animals best suited for capture – those below seven years old and young tuskers – are cut off from the herd and worn down. When the trappers know that an animal is sufficiently exhausted, a flurry of lassoes and nooses issues from the tops of the koonkies and with much shouting and whoops of delight, the trappers tighten knots and pull the victims towards them.

All the above methods were employed to capture a restricted number of animals, usually selected for size and sex, and especially tuskers for the royal stables. Elephants were never captured en masse, as with the keddah technique. The *keddah* method of capturing elephants appears to have originated in

India and Sri Lanka, from where it would have spread to Burma. It started as a means of capturing several elephants at a time but appears to have been considerably elaborated by the Portuguese, Dutch and British, who colonized the Asian countries. They saw in it an easy way of capturing elephants for profit. The Europeans coined the phrase 'elephant kraaling', perhaps equating *keddah* (stockade) with a corral for livestock. Whatever the taxonomy, the *keddah* method became highly successful, but it resulted in whole herds being removed from the wild, which would be quite unacceptable today. The figures quoted below from Deraniyagala speak for themselves. Undoubtedly the hundreds captured were exported, tuskers and all.

The following is a record of elephants captured in early kraals from 1666 to 1871 in Sri Lanka:

Dutch
1666: 96 elephants on one kraal
1681: One kraal yielded 13, another 104, yet another 270
1690: 160 taken in Alutkuru Korale
1697: 97 elephants in Matara, of which seven were tuskers

English
1797: 176 in one kraal, 400 in another
1805: 300 elephants at Kotava near Tangalla
1805: 70 elephants at Kotava, of which four were tuskers
1871: 28 captured, one a tusker

The simplest description of a keddah, or kraal, is that it is a stockade, either V-shaped or rectangular, with a funnel at one end into which the herds are driven. The stockade is usually located near a perennial source of water in the dry-weather feeding grounds of known herds of elephants. It is built of 3m(10ft)-long stout poles, about 15cm(6in) in diameter, rammed into the ground. The poles are lashed together with stout ropes and form a wall that will give, but not breach. As the drought continues, the doomed elephants are prevented from watering regularly and are kept thirsty until the stockade is completed.

Thousands of men are employed in the operation, which has three stages: construction of the stockade, beating the jungle to drive the elephants towards the funnel, and the eventual capture of the victims after the door of the stockade closes upon them. The scene inside the stockade after the elephants are trapped and subsequently noosed with the aid of koonkies or monitor elephants is one to cause extreme sadness. Babies are wrenched from their mothers, bulls thrashed by the tame ones if they resist

the nooses, maddened members of the same herd butting each other in a frantic bid to escape, and all the while the heart-rending screams of families being torn apart. In Sri Lanka, the last capture by this means took place in the early 1950s, and perhaps because it ended with the shooting of one of the most beautiful tuskers, kraals have since been abandoned. In India, too, the keddah is virtually extinct.

Elephants are still captured in Asia to replenish domestic stocks, for they form an integral part of the social, cultural and religious life of its peoples. Fortunately a new technology of capture is emerging, which, it is fervently hoped, will spare the animals the frightful ordeals formerly experienced. This method is popularly known as 'chemical immobilization'; a

Above: Newly captured Asian elephants being tied together with rope in a stockade. Tame monitor elephants may be used to help subdue the captives and escort them away for training.

specially devised gun carries a modified hypodermic syringe in place of a cartridge. The syringe is filled with an immobilizing chemical, loaded into a special gun (one of which is known as the capchur gun) and 'fired' into the intended target. The chemical immobilizes the elephant, causing it to lie down. It remains under the influence of the drug for about 30-40 minutes, enabling its captors to manipulate it. First, the recumbent animal must be secured. If there are stout trees at hand, the four legs are tied to them. If reliable trees are not available, the hind legs are hobbled to each other with tensile chains, followed by the fore-legs. For translocation, the services of two trained 'monitor' elephants are required to lead the captive to the transport vehicle. The two monitors are quickly and deftly coupled by rope to either side of the fallen animal's neck. After a final check to see that the captive is ready to be moved, the required antidote is administered to revive the animal, which is then led to the waiting truck, loaded on board and transported to its destination.

Immobilization has become a tool in elephant conservation today; it enables crop-raiding animals or pocketed herds to be captured, led to trucks by the monitor elephants, loaded and transported to the safety of national parks. There is much relief on all sides. This method has also created a new role for domestic elephants, that of partnering man in saving their wild friends from death.

The taming process
Soon after capture comes the taming. This has to be done with much patience and feeling. Unless the elephant is a baby, taming can be a cruel process, for it entails the crushing of the spirit of a highly intelligent, strong and sociable animal. Let us not dwell on the victim's trauma as it is tied with ropes and chains that cut to the bone of fore and hind legs, nor on the sapping of its energy as it

struggles to free itself. Mercifully this primitive practice is being gradually phased out. Instead of the deer-hide or buffalo-hide thongs, now chains encased in soft plastic – which is easier on the skin and causes no lacerations – are increasingly used. In southern India, this securing with ropes of any kind has been superseded by confining new captives in corrals with movable sides. The corral is a strong wooden rectangle built into the ground, its width and length varying with the size of the elephant. The uprights have spaces in them to slot in crossbars both longitudinally and transversely. The size of the corral can thus be adjusted by inserting crossbars into evenly spaced uprights so as to confine the animal at the required width. This highly flexible device has many uses, from taming and training to controlling a bull in musth. Since there is no straining at thongs, the skin is never ruptured, and tame elephants emerging from such confinement are unscarred both physically and mentally. Here, too, the monitor elephants are invaluable as they both calm the nervous new recruit and control it when it takes its daily bath.

All these humane developments save the elephants a great deal of misery following the shock of capture, and reduce the chance of death from suppurating wounds and physical exhaustion. The

elephants themselves seem to accept captivity more quickly and yield to training more willingly. In the skilled hands of experienced elephant keepers – whether they be *mahouts* (India), *oozies* (Burma) or *mos* (Thailand) – taming takes no more than three or four weeks.

Selling tamed elephants
If the capture has been organized by the State for the purpose of selling them, then it is best to sell the elephant at this stage, because would-be owners prefer to train animals in their own way. An auction is the best and fairest way to dispose of the captives. After a suitable date has been fixed, adequate publicity is given at least two weeks in advance. Prospective buyers and trusted mahouts will study the elephants for several days, looking for good signs or bad characteristics, measuring height, judging age and so on. Generally they look out for certain basic features. For instance, an animal that is 'tall, with full face and broad forehead, bright eyes and muscular legs, its back curved with a falling line from the head along its entire length toward the rear' is

Below: A young elephant being trained at the Way Kambas Game Reserve in Sumatra. In experienced hands, and with a great deal of care and understanding, an elephant can be fully trained in the space of just a few weeks.

considered a potentially good worker. Trainers and owners will also look out for animals that have an erect stance, are alert and sway constantly even when tethered. These are good for processions, as they will become majestic animals. In India, Sri Lanka and Burma and probably Thailand, Laos and Cambodia, there are books on the distinctions between good and bad elephants, and these form the basis of a mystic caste system as well.

Although elephant auctions follow the same protocol as, say, real estate or antiques, their atmosphere has changed. Forty years ago it used to be a very calm and dignified affair, for only those to whom hiring an elephant was second to the prestige of owning them would

Above: *This close-up photograph taken in a training camp in Thailand highlights the close relationship between handler and elephant. Note the Thai version of the goad, or ankus, occasionally used to prompt the elephant.*

patronize an auction. On the other hand, for timber merchants wishing to replenish or replace their teams, trained working elephants were freely available at reasonable prices, and the next sale would not be far off. To the former, the patience in training and the expense of it were part of their lifestyle and their standing in the village. To the latter, buying the trained working elephant was cheaper in the long term.

But all this is different now. In many

countries, wild elephant populations have fallen drastically. Habitat destruction goes on unabated and with it all the attendant ills have increased. Poaching for ivory has become so lucrative that every wild tusker appears doomed. Farmers resolve their elephant problems by shooting the marauders, abandoning the old and effective practices of crop protection. As governments tighten laws protecting elephants and captures are banned, prices have risen sharply.

In Sri Lanka today a well-trained female elephant of about 30 years will fetch Rs800,000 (about US$20,000), and a tusker considerably more, as against Rs100,000 two decades ago. A newly captured animal of similar age and size could have been bought for a third of this price 25 years ago. Unfortunately, a new breed of elephant owner has emerged – unscrupulous, mercenary types who have a lot of spare money and who wish to enter the elephant-owning elite. Consequently they dominate every sale or auction, form rings that outbid the genuine lover of elephants and send prices soaring.

Training captive elephants

Now to train the animal. Training an elephant depends on a number of factors: age, whether it was born in captivity or was captured, the purpose of the training and, of course, the keeper's dedication. Ideally, it is simplest to start with babies, either born in captivity or found abandoned when herds have been stampeded for one reason or another. But births of Asian elephants in captivity were never frequent, for two reasons: there was an ample supply of elephants from the wild, and owners had a misplaced dread that a 'romantic' bull elephant could never be trusted again. However, in the timber camps of India, Thailand and Burma, where females were allowed a 'night out' in the forest on the camps' fringes, they invariably consorted with wild paramours. Breeding was a regular feature and thus there were plenty of calves to be trained as successors.

If elephants had to be captured for domestication, it was considered best to go for those under 15 years or less than 2.1m(7ft) in height at the shoulder. In the hands of a good trainer, such an animal will be obeying 20 commands in three to six months' time and ready to serve man with all its versatility.

It is in the process of taming and training elephants that the unique 'elephant language' has evolved. Although the actual words used vary from country to country, the vocabulary develops in proportion to the number of commands that are necessary. When a mahout is on the ground, each command is initially reinforced with a prod from a goad, known as the *ankus* or *hawkus*, which is a wooden pole 1.5-1.8m(5-6ft) long ending in a metal point with an additional hook set about 5cm(2in) back from the tip .

The commands include go, sit, raise foreleg, raise hind leg, reverse, lie down, lower head, give foreleg for mahout to stand on, trumpet, push, pull, etc. At the age of 25 years, a well-trained elephant should recognize and obey 24 different commands. In Sri Lanka, in addition to this range of commands, traditional elephant keepers learn about nerve centres which when pricked with the ankus can produce the desired result with minimum fuss. Some 85 such centres are known but the majority are never used for they can cause great pain, paralysis or even death if pierced too deeply by an inexperienced mahout.

But whatever the words may be, there is a universality in the foot and body language involved. Col. Williams summarizes this clearly in his book *Elephant Bill*: "(they) are taught the simple words of command and the 'aids' of the rider, and by foot control behind the ears. The aids are simply movements of the rider's body by which he translates his wishes almost instinctively to his mount. Thus an intense stiffening of his limbs and leaning back will at once be understood as halt. A pressure on one side will be understood as turn to the left, on the other, as turn to the right. Leaning forward and forcing downwards will mean stoop or kneel. . ."

The training of an elephant is tied up with the dedication of its keeper, for without that devotion to his charge, a mahout can never bring out the best in it or earn its trust and respect. In a sense, mahouts are born with an instinctive affinity towards elephants. They are drawn to elephants as though by a magnet. That is how this man/elephant relationship came to be a great tradition in the East, handed down from father to son. Even in countries where domestic elephants are today rare or 'extinct', such as in Sumatra, Vietnam and China, the traditions live on.

In Sri Lanka an elephant keeper starts life by doing odd jobs in the *panthiya* (camp) where his father is already a fully fledged mahout. He listens, he ask questions. When he is about ten years old, he is allowed to walk by the side of the elephant his father is leading. At the bath, he will talk to the elephant while scrubbing it. After a few weeks he is accepted by the elephants and is allowed to command them. On school holidays he will accompany his father to his workplace to help with the tackle, tying and untying it. Soon he is allowed to ride the elephant seated behind his father. Not until he is about 15 years old does the proud day come when he is allowed to mount the elephant with his father walking beside, ankus in hand.

"When I was ten years old, I could control an elephant from the ground," said D.D. Avis, the head mahout at the Bel-lanwila Buddhist temple in Dehiwala, a suburb of Colombo. We were chatting over a drink about Chandru, the zoo's tusker, now the pride of the temple. "But I was not allowed to ride it, so I ran away from home and joined another owner, to try to satisfy the urge. He told me the same thing – I must first learn everything about elephants, both in captivity and in the wild. We used to visit other elephant camps where logging was done. Only when I was about 15 was I allowed to ride an elephant by myself. My gurus taught me never to lose my temper with an elephant."

Avis was recruited to Bellanwila when Chandru became intractable and was refusing to carry the revered casket con-taining sacred Buddhist relics in the annual *perahera* (procession). Today, 26 years later, he is still with Chandru, which is indeed a regal animal, especially when he is adorned for the well-known Bellanwila perhahera during the full-moon nights of September. "Chandru has never turned on me, even when in musth," Avis elaborated. Recently when the zoo's present tusker broke loose, Avis was summoned. He brought it under control, with deft use of voice and ankus. That is what 40 years in the business can produce.

Elephants at work

An elephant is at its peak between the ages of 20 and 50, although many owners would prefer to delay engaging it in forestry work by another four or five years. Climate has a bearing on the number of hours per day an elephant can be used in productive work. In the cool mountainous districts of India, Burma and Thailand a healthy tusker can work eight hours, but in the lowlands the general rule has been five to six hours

Below: A young elephant being washed in the Mudumalai Wildlife Sanctuary in southern India. Bathing is a necessary and enjoyable part of the daily routine for elephants and usually lasts for at least two or three hours. For captive elephants, the daily bath is an ideal opportunity for man and beast to reinforce their bond of mutual friendship and respect.

with intermittent breaks. In Sri Lanka, the traditional work day ends at around 2pm or earlier on very hot days.

Using the word 'traditional' distinguishes it from a new trend where timber and sawmill merchants have become owners and use elephants solely for commercial purposes. There the timetable is different, and the elephant is a mere mechanical device which is worked from dawn to dusk. Needless to say, the elephants build up a resentment and retaliate when their moment arrives, resulting in many incidents which are new to elephant management. Good mahouts do not work for such owners, who then hire men who get the elephants to work by goading them. There has been an increase in the number of such men being killed. At the same time the incidence of injury to elephants, disease and death has also correspondingly increased. Hopefully, such owners will realize their folly and begin to treat their elephants with the love and respect they deserve.

Today domestic elephants are used for the following main purposes:

1. As a pack animal
2. In the logging industry, and to haul small to medium-sized logs for loading into trucks and trailers for transportation to work sites, sawmills, etc.
3. In ploughing highland rice paddies, harrowing coconut plantations and similar agricultural activities.
4. To add dignity and stature to ceremonials and religious processions and to entertain, notably in village festivities.
5. In nature tourism.

Elephants as pack animals

As a pack animal, a 2.4m(8ft) male or female elephant can carry only up to 500kg(1,100lb) on its back. The pack is placed on a soft cotton quilt spread over the back behind the shoulders. The quilt has a groove down the middle to accommodate the spine, to prevent any abrasion. Walking at a pace of about 6km (4 miles) per hour the elephant transports its load up to 24km(15 miles) in a day. Today its use is restricted to hilly terrain, because four-wheel-drive vehicles are preferred for speed and capacity.

Elephants in logging camps

When elephants were put to work in the large-scale logging concerns in Asia during colonial rule, it was the first time that their economic potential was exploited to the full. The British in particular encouraged the setting up of huge logging camps in the dense forests of India, Burma and Siam (Thailand).

Using the trained elephants already available, these logging companies, invariably under British management, organized timber extraction on an enormous scale. In the latter half of the 19th century and in the early years of the 20th century, when mechanized transport was unavailable, it was the elephants that dragged the massive tree trunks – sometimes weighing over 4 tonnes (almost 9,000lb) – to the nearest river whose waters then carried the logs to their destination near the sea ports.

The gear used in these varied from country to country. For instance, in Sri Lanka the only tackle used was the twisted fibre of palm fronds that an elephant held in its jaws and used in drag-

Above: Two working elephants in Thailand are learning to combine their efforts to drag a particularly heavy log. The harness each is wearing is of a traditional design and still used in India, Burma and Thailand for hauling logs and in other types of heavy work. The calves at the left of the photograph are trying to get in on the act and are not helping matters at all.

ging or lifting logs not exceeding 350kg(770lb). Sri Lankan elephants were never harnessed for dragging the 4-tonne logs so common in Burma. A harness is used today in India, Burma and Thailand. Often these harnesses are used to couple two elephants in parallel to drag logs weighing more than 5 tonnes (over 11,000lb). The management of elephants in logging camps was developed to a fine art, and books by Sanderson, Williams (*Elephant Bill*), Evans (on disease and treatment), Ferrier and Stacey serve as standard texts on the subject. They still provide guidelines to those engaged in the much watered-down logging enterprises of today.

With timber-jacks, bulldozers and four-wheel-drive vehicles now freely available, the elephant has been relegated to a lower position in the industry. However, there may be as many as 12,000 elephants still employed in Thailand.

In Sumatra, Malaysia and Indochina, where until the arrival of colonial rulers there were plenty of domestic elephants, there has been a recent revival of the art. Some of these countries wish to re-establish the practice of using elephants in logging plantation forests, others are looking at their potential in the tourist industry.

Malaysia, which has adopted and further developed the science of chemical immobilization, is capturing elephants for domestication. In Sumatra, two elephant training camps have been estab-lished in the south and east with the help of Thai expertise. China lost its elephant stables many centuries ago, but has also turned to Thailand now for trained elephants. At the present moment the Thai authorities have planned to send three females and one male to Jing Hong for use in nature tourism in the Xishuang-banna National Park. Others may follow to form a nucleus of a team for use in hauling timber in production forests.

Elephants in agriculture

The use of elephants as helpers in agricultural activities is not widely known, but in villages where owners do not hire their elephants, they are often employed in the less strenuous tasks of ploughing, harrowing or drawing water carts. The yokes used are merely massive editions of the ones used by oxen. But the yokes hardly last a season and have to be made anew the next time round.

The ceremonial elephant

The elephant really comes into its own when called upon to participate at any one of the innumerable ceremonies, festivals and rituals that pervade the social life of Asian people. From an elephant's enthusiasm at these events has arisen the mystique that surrounds this remarkable animal. No one will deny that a trained elephant plays its required role as each occasion demands, with a conscious understanding. How else does one explain its patience as it stands still while a score of mothers with babes in arms creep under its belly in order to endow the child with good health, intelligence and strength? Or as it conveys a bridegroom to his wedding ceremony with apparent pride and ostentation?

As the drumming rehearsals commence in Buddhist temples, heralding the approach of the full-moon proces-sions, the elephants know they will soon be the centre of attention of the thousands of devotees who will line the streets. They know they will be required to walk with the dignity and poise deserved by the sacred relics they carry. The resplendent bejewelled casket must not tilt or jolt, so their walk becomes a stately march. They learn to tolerate the bright lights, the fire-dancers, the deafening drums and the hysterical shouts of 'Sadhu' (peace) from the frenetic bystanders.

But they are not averse to a little enjoyment. During festivities such as the New Year, harvest-time and important sporting events, they love to go along with their human friends. Tug-of-war is a favourite, where they can tease the village's twenty strongest men. Almost with a sense of humour, an elephant will first behave as though the men have won, then suddenly with a mighty heave send them sprawling. Running in a race is also part of their fun, causing much hilarity.

Asian monarchies were the trendsetters in the art of keeping elephants, helped by their having first choice in tuskers. In Sri Lanka, scouts were sent out into the jungles to study wild herds and pick elephants thought worthy of a place in the royal stables. The strongest, most regal and fearless tusker would be the one that carried the monarch onto the battlefield when the need arose. From the royal court also came the practice of elephants being used in the various social and religious events described above. Although royalty itself survives in only a handful of Asian countries, such as Nepal, Bhutan and Thailand, elephants continue to serve and entertain in the grand manner.

There are three annual events that must be mentioned here because they illustrate the esteem in which elephants are still held. In Sri Lanka, during the week before the full moon in August, the sacred Tooth Relic of the Lord Buddha is taken around the streets of the hill capital, Kandy. For the past 500 years or more the ornate and brightly illuminated casket containing the relic has been carried by the country's finest tusker, gaily dressed in colourful trappings of traditional design. Accompanying this colossus among tuskers – always aptly named Raja (King) – are up to 200 other elephants (including many more tuskers of lesser calibre) also sporting clothes of intricate design. This incredibly beautiful and world-famous Kandy Perahera symbolizes man's esteem for this unique animal as well as the animal's respect for man.

The Trichur Poornam, an annual religious festival in Kerala, South India, connected with the Hindu deity Shiva, is another event where the most spectacular tuskers take centre-stage. It is actually a competition carried out on the backs of massive tuskers ranged as two teams. The competition itself is to decide which team displays the most striking and colourful umbrellas. The two teams of 25 tuskers face each other, carrying excited riders. At a signal from one of the judges, the riders unfold umbrellas, each one a bigger surprise than the last, from paniers on either side of each tusker. Points are given for the effectiveness of display, size and colour. Each umbrella is greeted by great shouts and loud hand claps, the intensity of which certainly sway the judges too. The elephants join in, trumpeting and blowing to magnify the applause. It is a hilarious affair! "At the end of the evening," says Mr Vijaya Kumar, the Singapore Zoo's 'elephant man', whose antecedents hail from Kerala, "I was amazed to see how these huge animals walked so calmly through streets teeming with people. These people 'worship' their elephants and no mishap occurs."

Another annual elephant spectacle takes place each November in Surin, east of Bangkok in Thailand. It is a sort of May Day for working elephants, hundreds of which are brought for what is popularly known as the Elephant Round-up. There, a football field takes on the air of a sports festival, except that the players are

Above: *A trunk is certainly useful on the football field! Here at the annual Elephant Round-up in Surin, Thailand, these noble beasts let their hair down and join in all sorts of fun and games, including football and a very unequal tug-of-war. These are working elephants and this is the ideal opportunity for them to enjoy a holiday from their labours.*

Below: *On a more solemn note, these beautifully decorated elephants are at the head of a world-famous procession in Kandy, the hill capital of Sri Lanka. The finest tusker in the land bears the casket containing the sacred Tooth Relic of the Lord Buddha and parades it with pride as part of an annual celebration that has graced these streets for over 500 years.*

working elephants on holiday. They play football, engage in a tug-of-war with selected teams of burly Thais, run races and end the day with a cameo from any one of the wars that Thai kings fought with elephants in ancient times.

Elephants and nature tourism

The utilization of natural reserves, especially national parks, as major tourist attractions in Asian countries has been stepped up in recent times. Taking their cue from the manner in which African countries have turned their parks into foreign exchange earners, Asian governments have prepared their blueprints for what has come to be recognized as 'nature tourism'.

Besides the unusual animals and forest types that national parks in Sri Lanka, India, Nepal, Thailand, Malaysia and Indonesia can offer, the experience of penetrating deep into tropical jungles from a safe and elevated seat on an elephant's back has taken foreign tourists by storm. Suddenly, the age-old practice of hunting animals from elephant back has been replaced by observing and photographing them; the cramped and covered howdahs have been modified into more comfortable ones with no cover, in order to give visitors an all-round view of the surrounding country.

The Royal Chitwan National Park in Nepal is an excellent example of how tourism has developed around the use of elephants as the sole method of transport. In earlier times, Chitwan was a hunting ground of Nepalese royalty and was well protected towards that end. But with the royal hunt becoming an anachronism in today's world, Chitwan inevitably became a national park. Situated in the floodplain of the Rapti and Narayni rivers, the plains of tall grass are most unsuited to be traversed by road in a vehi-

cle. The obvious choice, therefore, was to retain the practice of going in on elephant back. The private company that was given the franchise to develop tourism in the park found that tourists would come from the far corners of the globe to see the great one-horned rhinoceros and the Nepalese tiger from elephant back. The notion spread to other tourist facilities in Chitwan and today the eastern entrance to the park at Sauraha has perhaps the greatest concentration of domestic elephants maintained solely for and by tourists. Chitwan today flourishes, supporting a comparatively large human population who service the tourists. To ensure that there will be an ample supply of elephants for the future in a country that has less than 60 in the wild, the park authorities have established a breeding centre, which has met with success.

The example is being followed in Indian national parks. For instance in the Corbett National Park, where even in former times one traversed the park on elephant back, the authorities have upgraded the facility. Before long, tourists will be lured to it by its well-organized elephant safaris. If more countries were to use elephants seriously in this way and prove that they have tremendous economic value in a non-extractive industry, it might provide another incentive to protect them in the wild.

Right: Tourists clamber up a steep wooden stairway and climb on to the back of a fine male Asian elephant and await with anticipation their stately ride around the Mudumalai Wildlife Sanctuary in southern India.

Below: European tourists on elephant back in the Royal Chitwan National Park in Nepal. What better way to go in search of tigers and the one-horned rhinoceros? In the floodplains and tall grass, elephants offer ideal transport.

AN ENCOUNTER WITH WORKING ELEPHANTS

"This is Jayanthi", said Mr Millangoda, proudly patting the 2.7m(9ft)-tall tusker, which had just carried a 250kg(550lb) mahogany log in his mouth as though it were a gigantic cigar and deposited it on the open truck precisely in the slot provided for it. Knowing that in the Sinhala language Jayanthi is a girl's name, I queried it. "That's because I bought it in 1956, the year of Buddha Jayanthi," was the reply, adding with a smile, "I bought it as a baby from the zoo!", knowing my 30-year association with Sri Lanka's National Zoo. (Buddha Jayanthi marked 2,500 years of Buddhism.)

It's a small world, I thought to myself, that out of some 400 domesticated elephants spread throughout the country, I should meet an old acquaintance on a chance visit. But that is the way with working elephants, you can meet them almost anywhere, for a good worker is in constant demand, even far from its owner's village.

Jayanthi dropped the tackle with which he had dragged the log some distance before hoisting it. The next step was to pack the log inside the truck. He nudged it in – pushed would be an exaggeration – and then positioned it alongside the rest with an incredible delicacy, using only the base of his trunk to do so. What was more amazing was that all this went on in silence; not a command was given, not a word spoken by Punchi Bandara, his *mahout* (keeper), sitting astride the animal's shoulders.

Bandara reversed the great tusker, got its 1.2m(4ft) tusks out of harm's way. The tusker picked up the tackle, which consisted of several strands of palm-frond fibre woven together and tied to a chain. Mahout and elephant moved to the next log, a short distance away. The mahout's assistant fastened the chain and Jayanthi knelt and took the woven fibre in his right jaw, then heaved the log off the ground. What was the command? How did the elephant know what was expected? To the casual observer, it was strange, this noiseless dialogue. Actually, the mahout 'spoke' to his elephant through his bare toes pressing behind its ears and his legs stiffening against the elephant's shoulders. What I was watching was a display of classical elephant/man understanding, preserved in many Asian countries for over 3,000 years.

Earlier that morning Punchi Bandara and his senior colleague Ram Banda had risen early, even though it was cool, misty and overcast, for the preliminaries with ten adult elephants take time and they must be ready for work by 7am. As is

Above: *Jayanthi sizes up each log and decides how best to handle it. Then he uses his jaws as a fulcrum and centres the log for balance.*

the custom, the mahouts made their presence felt from some distance away by clearing their throats, a sound familiar to their charges. One should not startle an elephant, however tame he or she may be. The animals reciprocated with a friendly 'whoosh' and a 'stomach rumble' of pleasure. The other mahouts now joined them and soon the stable (or *panthiya*) was a hive of activity. Mahouts would chide their charges jokingly for stealing food or prodding his neighbour with his tusks during the night, chains would clang as the hobbling was undone, stomach rumbles would increase.

Mr Millangoda, owner, trainer and an undisputed authority on elephants in Sri Lanka's Kegalla district, and his son

Ananda, now made their appearance. One elephant stepped forward to greet them with trunk extended. Mr Millangoda gave her a banana then sidled up to Ram Banda and whispered, "You had better take Patiya today. I hear he was disobedient these last few days. Punchi Bandara can walk Jayanthi to Pinnawela to load the mahogany." Patiya was an 2.6m(8.5ft) tuskless, no-nonsense bull. Two more elephants were despatched to collect the 2 tonnes (4,400lb) of foliage needed for the panthiya every night.

Father and son now moved over to Raja, easily the elephant with the longest pair of tusks in the country, sweeping down 2m(6.5ft) and almost touching the ground. But he was not walking today. He was firmly secured, hand and foot, with high-tensile chains. He was in musth. Only Millangoda senior could talk any sense into him, and admonish

Above: Fresh and willing in the cool morning, Patiya, the tuskless bull, hauls his first jak log along the narrow village road, with a little moral support from his keeper, Ram Banda, walking alongside. He will achieve his target of moving and loading 20 logs by lunchtime.

him for launching missiles at keeper and passer-by. In fact, we had been sent a coconut frond which fell just short of us, before the Millangodas arrived.

Jayanthi and Patiya reached their respective work-sites by 8am. They had both to do the same sort of work in two villages nearby. The troublesome Patiya had a tougher task than the tusker. He had to drag jak (*Artocarpus integrifolia*) logs three times his length a distance of nearly 100m(110yd) along a narrow village road, then lift them into a covered lorry. There were approximately 20 logs, each weighing 250kg(550lb) and an average girth of 1m(39in), but he took them in his stride. Ram Banda handled him expertly, preferring to direct him from the ground, and remembering that Patiya was in a cantankerous mood, he used his voice to give crisp, firm and unambiguous commands. After every log the elephant, with a proprietary air, would pull down

fresh leaves from trees on the way and stuff them into his mouth.

By midday, mahout and elephant were exhausted. In Sri Lanka an elephant is worked only four to five hours a day, before the sun bears down too harshly. Their work was worth Rs1,000, sufficient to maintain them both and to cover the expenses of those not working daily.

By 1.30pm, we started back for the Millangoda elephant 'village', as it is popularly known. We met the two female elephants returning with their loads of coconut palm fronds, kitul (fish-tail palm) logs and sundry edible leaves. At the village four other elephants were already bathing in the swift stream that runs along the northern boundary of the camp. They would soak there until about 4pm, then wend their way to the snack bar for their titbits of sugar cane, bananas and jaggery (palm sugar). Shortly before nightfall they were tethered in their stalls

to feast throughout the night on their allotted 150kg(330lb) of greenstuff.

So ends a day in this typical Sinhalese elephant stable, begun by Millangoda's ancestors in the distant past. Like other old elephant-owning families in Sri Lanka, the Millangodas adhere to the traditions of elephant management. This is especially so when it comes to the work ethic. They treat their animals with both respect and affection, which are automatically reciprocated. They expect their mahouts to do the same. Hours of work should not be extended, and the animals must be scrubbed and bathed for a minimum of two to three hours and allowed to roam free on the grounds before being tethered. But each mahout has his own secret of ensuring that the elephant also fears him. Without this a mahout is never really safe. These are the ingredients of the understanding between man and elephant we saw that morning.

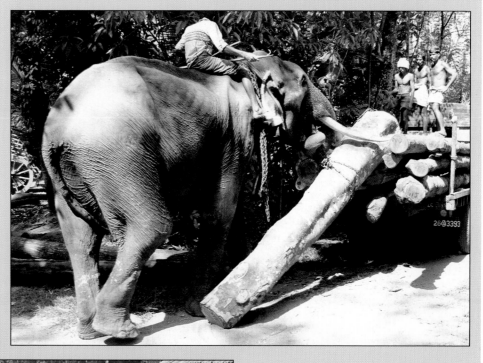

Above: To watch Jayanthi at work is a treat. Sufficient brawn backed by brain tells him how to manipulate the heaviest log. He uses his sturdy tusks like a fork-lift. (If the log is not heavy he will not bring the tusks into play, using only his trunk as support.) Punchi Bandara on top has little to say or do, even when the 250kg(550lb) mahogany log is about to be hoisted onto the open truck.

Left: Equal work, equal pay. Two of Mr. Millangoda's elephants have helped pack dinner for the 'village' and now wend their way along the main Kandy Road. They will get an equal share when the elephant keepers distribute the greenstuff between the animals.

INDIAN MYTHS & HISTORY

*Ganesha, the elephant-headed god of learning
and success (Hoysala, 11th-13th century AD).
Possibly a Brahmanic adaptation of a tribal
deity, Ganesha is nevertheless the most widely
adored – and perhaps the most adorable
– of all the Hindu gods.*

Tracing references to elephants in 5,000 years of Indian history and mythology is a fascinating but – especially for Western readers – somewhat bewildering journey of discovery. This is a vast canvas to explore, stretching in time and space from the Indus Valley civilization (or Harappan civilization) that succumbed to the Aryan invasion in about 1500 BC, through the Vedic Age, the setting up of the Mauryan Empire in about 300 BC, the Gupta Empire in about AD 300 and the Mughal Empire in the early 1500s, with echoes of the British Raj still reverberating, even today. Interweaving these historical events into the rich fabric of Indian society is an immense tradition of religious and epic literature that not only reflects the moral values of the time, but also reveals many practical details about everyday life. Using both these strands, our story follows the domestication of elephants and their integration into all aspects of Indian life, including war and royal patronage.

The evidence of a number of seals seems to indicate that captive elephants could have been known in India as early as the Indus Valley civilization (about 3000-1500 BC); some of them clearly show lines on the body of the elephant that suggest ropes. Recent excavations have unearthed a trove of terracotta and bronze figurines of the late Harappan phase at Daimabad in Maharashtra, including the figure of an elephant on wheels, which could be a child's toy. However, the fact remains that no figurine or seal of elephants from this period shows an elephant with a proper harness on, or carrying a rider. (On the other hand, the rhinoceros is shown as a domesticated animal with a rope around its neck and eating out of a trough.) Thus, the Harappan seals could indicate captivity of elephants, but not necessarily their training. Until the Harappan scripts are deciphered, the most ancient of Indian literatures, the Vedas, will continue to remain the earliest recorded source for Indian history. This is where our historical and cultural journey begins.

Elephants in the Vedas

The Vedas are a series of compositions compiled over a period of about a thousand years, from about 1500 to 600 BC, by the Aryans, fair-skinned nomads from Central Asia, who invaded the north-western region of India. The hymns, prayers, poems, rituals, incantations and magic spells of the Vedas – plus the complex commentaries that were built up about them – form an immensely rich source of information about this important period of India's history.

In the earliest Veda – Rigveda – the words for *elephant* are often used only as similes with reference to the animal's size and strength, such as 'strong/big as an elephant', which indicate a familiarity with elephants but cannot be taken as evidence of their domestication. In Vedic texts of about 800 BC, however, an elephant (*hastin*) is recommended as a gift. Since one cannot make a gift of an elephant without owning it, this seems to refer to elephants in captivity or domestication. A later text of about 650-600 BC refers to a gift of 10,000 elephants, along with, be it noted, 10,000 slave girls. Therefore, gifting elephants seems to have become a well-established practice. The suggestion of domestication of elephants is also reflected in a reference to the practice of accepting the ownership of an elephant as a mark of greatness, a status symbol. There is also a mention of an elephant coming up 'when bidden by the voice', which has been recognized as a clear reference to tame elephants. And the reference to making offerings to 'man or elephant with hand stretched out', apparently as an example of an unusual behaviour, appears to represent offering food to tame elephants, which one would

not try to do to wild ones. There are also mentions of actual field observations of elephants, such as elephants in musth, or an elephant being tormented by flies, indicating considerable familiarity with the animal.

It seems, therefore, that even in the earliest Vedic period, which perhaps overlapped the period of late Harappan culture, elephants were in domesticity. Possibly, an important person such as a king would ride on an elephant. Rich, 'golden' caparisons (ornamental coverings) of elephants were already in use, and the gifting of elephants was a laudable act, though not the acceptance of it. The possession of an elephant was, in fact, a status symbol, and elephant-

Below: A Harappan seal featuring an elephant. This is from the ancient city of Mohenjo Daro, with Harappa, one of the two centres of the Indus Valley civilization. Some Harappan seals show elephants with lines on the body suggesting ropes. This could indicate captivity but not necessarily domestication, because no Harappan seal or artefact shows an elephant carrying a proper harness or a rider.

keepers or owners (*hastipa*) were a people of recognized category. Even so, it seems that horses were still the most important animals in the Vedas, not elephants. The time when the elephant would supplant the place of the horse as the *vahana* (carrier) of Indra – originally the general of the gods, later the king of the gods – had not yet come. It appears that this represents the early years of the contact between the horse-culture of the Indo-Aryans and the elephants of the territory into which they had moved.

The Jataka stories

The Jataka stories, or the stories of Buddha's former births, make up the most complete surviving collection of folklore

Bottom: A Harappan seal (right) plus its 'print' (left) clearly showing the rhinoceros as a domesticated animal eating out of a trough, and with a rope around its neck. In the riverain grasslands of the floodplains of the Indus River and its tributaries, where the Harappan culture flourished from about 3000 BC until 1500 BC, the rhinoceros must have been far more common than the elephant.

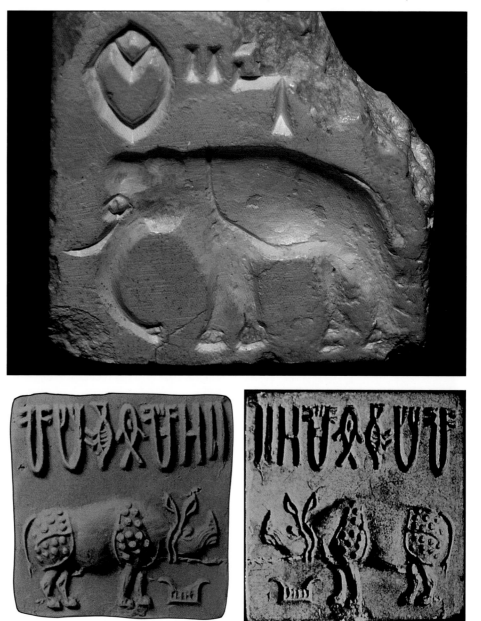

in any literature of the world. Although the prose stories, or commentaries, in the existing version are ascribed to the fifth century AD, the verses they illustrate are recognized to be much older. The stories must have been compiled, although perhaps not in the exact verbal form of the present text, by the second century BC at the latest.

The older Pali Jatakas provide us with an insight into the status of the elephant in eastern India (northern Bihar) during the period of republics and kingdoms before the emergence of the Mauryan Empire with Chandragupta Maurya (about 600-321 BC). One of these stories speaks of the state elephant and elephant trainers, and how the state elephant was tied to a post for training and, unable to bear the strain, broke the post down and ran away to the forest. Trained elephants escaping to the forest is even now a common phenomenon, and posts are still used to stretch out and punish trained but truculent animals to bring them to discipline. In another story, Buddha subdues the wicked Licchavi prince with a single exhortation that was 'like training

Left: *A princely rider and his groom holding an umbrella (recognized as a royal insignia) over his head (Sunga terracotta, 2nd century BC, National Museum, Delhi). The ability to ride elephants and horses and to drive chariots was a desirable princely accomplishment. The heroes of the epic poem the* Mahabharata, *Indra himself (the king of the gods) and Emperor Akbar were all expert elephant riders.*

six rutting elephants at once'. The story goes on to spell out the early stages of an elephant's training, followed to this day: 'The elephant-tamer . . . guides the elephant he is breaking in, making it go to the right or left, backward or forward, according to his will. . . . '

There are references to a white umbrella and an elephant, preferably white, as royal insignia. And on the birthday of Prince Vessantara, a former incarnation of Buddha, 'a female flying elephant brought a young one . . . white all over. . . . '

The Great Being (Bodhisatta) visited his alms-halls mounted upon his magnificent elephant. There is a detailed description of the value of the elephant's caparison, mentioning each part of the body. People resent his giving away this glorious animal, which is also a great asset in war. The elephant which brings back the prince after the period of banishment is ' . . . a fine young elephant, so mighty and strong, which neither spear nor battle-din could fright.'

One of the Jakatas tells of the white state elephant that defeated the king of

Kosala who was attacking Varanasi. Another story features King Kusa riding victorious on an elephant 'trained to stand impassive under attack'. The idea of the state elephant has become firmly established – a king goes into battle riding on his state elephant, not on a chariot. Although there is mention of a 'host of the four arms' – consisting of chariots, cavalry, elephants, and foot soldiers – the actual accounts of battles do not describe large-scale deployment of elephants. Elephants were used most effectively to storm established positions of the enemy and batter down barriers like city gates.

That some elephants are savage by nature and are killers is recognized in the story of Buddha overcoming the savage elephant Nalagiri, made more savage by liquor. That grown-up elephants can be dangerous and should not be treated as pets is recognized, and elephant doctors also emerge in some Jatakas as a specific professional group.

Elephant festivals are mentioned in several Jatakas, a practice which has died out in the north of India but still survives in the south. There was even a master of

ceremonies for such festivals, a valued and highly lucrative hereditary appointment. Elephants were displayed in such festivals, with the highest in the land pointing out individual animals by name. Processions of elephants were also a part of the festivals.

Elephant-trainers' manuals were by now well-established, which an expert was supposed to know along with the 'three Vedas', and elephant-trainers were acknowledged professionals, with keen, no-holds-barred competition among them. In more than one story, Bodhisatta is born in an elephant-trainer's family and adopts the profession himself with great credit.

Rogue elephants are specifically discussed in one of the Jatakas, with Bodhisatta as the King Elephant protecting a quail's family until a rogue elephant following him kills them. Stories also tell of Bodhisatta being born as a white elephant in the Himalayas, the leader of a great number of elephants – 80,000 in one story and 8,000 in another. In a famous Jataka, Bodhisatta is born pure white and with six tusks as the son of the chief of 8,000 elephants, and gives up his tusks to meet the unscrupulous demand for ivory. There are tales of wild elephants being killed with poisoned arrows from pits, and a trade in ivory is established with Varanasi as its centre, an area still active in the ivory trade.

The main concentration of elephants (80,000/8,000) referred to in these stories is in the Himalayas, apparently to the

Below left: The dream of Maya Devi (Gupta, 5th Century AD, National Museum, Delhi), a recurrent motif in Buddhist art. Before the birth of Prince Gautama (later the Buddha), his mother, Maya Devi, dreamt one night that a white elephant was descending toward her from heaven (seen here near the top righthand corner of the picture) – a symbolic vision of the great birth of which she was to be the vehicle.

Below: An illustration of the story of Chhaddanta Jataka *from Bharut (2nd-1st century BC, The Indian Museum, Calcutta). Buddha, born as a six-tusked white king elephant, agreed to sacrifice his tusks to satisfy the greed of man, rather than take the path of bloody conflict. Note the man with the saw, ready to remove the tusks. Clearly, the threat from ivory poachers has a long history.*

north of what is now eastern Uttar Pradesh and northern Bihar, where – ironically – less than a hundred survive today. There is on the whole an unmistakable shift from the earlier horse culture to an elephant culture. Nothing illustrates it better than the bas-reliefs on the railings of the *stupa* (Buddhist memorial) in Bharut, where elephants not only dominate the illustrations of the Jataka stories, but also appear as decorative motifs; horses and chariots are hardly anywhere to be seen.

As evidence of the changing trend, it is

Left: *A floral design with elephant border depicted on a railing medallion from Bharut (2nd-1st century BC, The Indian Museum, Calcutta). In the early Buddhist literature, iconography, art, and even decorative motifs, there is an unmistakable shift from the earlier horse culture of the Vedic people – fair-skinned Aryans from Central Asia who invaded northwestern India – to an elephant culture.*

Below: *An elephant fashioned in the capital (top) of an Ashokan pillar flanked by the wheels of universal law. By Emperor Ashoka's time (reigned about 268-231 BC), the elephant had become an emblem of Buddhism, a religion that Ashoka adopted and promoted during his reign, even sending missionaries to other lands.*

interesting to note that Seleukos, Alexander the Great's general and master of the eastern part of Alexander's conquered domains, failing to regain the control of the provinces east of the River Sind, had to conclude a treaty with Chandragupta Maurya (the founder of India's first great empire – the Mauryan – who reigned in about 321-298 BC), by which he surrendered a large territory, including what is now Kabul, Herat, Qandahar and Baluchistan, in return for 500 elephants. It is not known if Seleukos considered it a good or a bad bargain, but he certainly put them to excellent use in his army, and later Seleucid Bactrian and Indo-Greek potentates used the image of the elephant extensively on their coins.

It is not surprising that during the reign of Chandragupta Maurya's grandson, the emperor Ashoka (reigned about 268-231 BC), the elephant had become a symbol, not only of Ashoka, but also of Buddhism. Ashoka marked his victory in Kalinga by having an elephant carved on the rock surface at Dhauli near Bubaneswar, the capital of modern Orissa. Along with lions, the elephant also occupies a prominent place in the Ashokan capital. (In fact, Ashoka became a powerful supporter of Buddhism and instilled its teachings into his civil administration.)

The ancient epics of the *Ramayana* and the *Mahabharata*

The *Ramayana* and the *Mahabharata* are the two great ancient epics of India, stirring combinations of moral instruction and heroic adventure. Although it is generally believed that the events described in these two epics might have taken place some time between about 1000 and 700 BC, the existing versions are of much later origin. According to one view, the *Ramayana* was probably compiled around the third century BC based on ancient ballads, and the present form was reached towards the end of the second century AD with some later additions. The *Mahabharata* grew from the original 8,800 four-line stanzas, to 24,000 stanzas, and then eventually to 100,000 stanzas by the fourth century AD, and thus became the longest 'single' poem in the world. With both the *Ramayana* and the *Mahabharata* there are several versions of the text representing different local traditions, and so it is necessary to interpret these texts with a good deal of caution.

Elephants in the *Ramayana*

The *Ramayana* abounds in similes of elephants to describe strength. Taraka, by Brahma's blessing (Brahma, the Creator, is the first of the Hindu Trinity), is as strong as 10,000 elephants, and Lakshmana is like an angry King Elephant. Sometimes, comparisons are made with playful elephants in lotus pools, a common motif in the poetry tradition. A flourishing city is conventionally described as full of elephants, horses, bulls, cows and other domesticated animals, which are obviously considered visible signs of wealth. Noblemen and citizens are described as proceeding on gorgeously caparisoned elephants, horses and chariots to receive Rama (the central hero of the *Ramayana*) on his victorious return from exile. To be an expert rider of elephants and horses is clearly a desirable princely attainment. All this indicates perhaps an even closer association with elephants than is found in the Jatakas.

The advice against receiving gifts of elephants referred to in the Vedas is now largely ignored. The sage Vashistha's son receives the gift of Rama's elephant Santrunjaya without qualms when Rama prepares to go into exile, and Bharata receives an excellent elephant as a parting gift when returning from the domain of his maternal grandfather.

The concept of the elephant as a royal mount is also firmly established. Rama and Lakshmana in exile see Bharata's

Right: The silver coin of the Indo-Bactrian King Apollodotos (about 156-40 BC, The Indian Museum, Calcutta). Seleukos I surrendered a sizeable chunk of the easternmost part of his empire to Chandragupta Maurya in return for 500 elephants. The Seleucid Indo-Bactrian kings valued elephants highly, for their image appeared extensively on their coins.

Below: The gold coin of Kumaragupta (AD 413-455, The Indian Museum, Calcutta). Elephants are less common on the coins of the Imperial Guptas, but not totally absent.

retine approaching from afar and conclude that their father, King Dasharatha, is not there because the old royal elephant Satrunjaya, carrying a white umbrella – the royal isignia – is not visible. The description of Bharata returning with Rama's sandals carried ceremoniously on an elephant's head (not on the back) recalls one of the bas-reliefs of Bharut that shows an elephant carrying the precious casket containing the sacred relic of Buddha.

References to *Chaturanga bal* (four-armed forces consisting of elephants, chariots, cavalry and infantry) abound; indeed it is a standard epithet to describe a large host. Actual descriptions of elephants in battles are few. There are descriptions of monkeys being trampled down by elephants and chariot wheels in battle, but there is no special mention of elephants being used in combat. In fact, the heroes still use chariots in war. Indrajit, Ravana's son and the greatest general on the Lankan side, uses a chariot, not an elephant. Although leading a force of, among other things, three million elephants, Ravana (the king of demons) rides on a chariot drawn by eight horses, while Rama, leading his primitive force of monkeys, is on foot.

Considering this an unequal combat, Indra sends his personal chariot and charioteer for Rama's use. The grand finale is played out in the best heroic tradition, with both the main combatants entering into battle on chariots.

Observations on elephant behaviour in the *Ramayana* are more detailed and acute than in the Jataka stories. There are references to Bharata breathing like a goaded elephant and descriptions of elephants dusting themselves after a bath. Elsewhere, there are interesting references to the contemporary mode of capturing elephants. Elephants complain that they do not fear fire, weapons or spears, but they do fear their own selfish relations, presumably because domesticated elephants were used to capture wild ones. If so, this must be among the earliest references to the practice of capturing wild elephants with the help of *koonkies* (elephants trained in capturing operations). This is still the *modus operandi* for capturing elephants in northern and northeastern India. Elephant hunting with arrows at night over a waterhole is not considered unsporting, but estrangement from his dearest son, Rama, is the price King Dasharatha has to pay for killing a young hermit by mistake when on such a hunt.

Above: An elephant carrying the relic of Buddha on its head. (Bharut, 2nd-1st century BC, The Indian Museum, Calcutta). Bharata in the Ramayana *also has the sandals of Rama carried back on an elephant's head to serve as Rama's emblem during his years in exile.*

Below: Temple sculpture (Hoysala, 11th-13th century AD) showing the three 'arms' of the 'four-armed' host that figures so prominently in Indian history. From the top of the picture downwards, these are clearly depicted as infantry, cavalry and elephantry. The fourth 'arm', chariotry, possibly atrophied in India soon after the beginning of the Christian era.

Possession of four-tusked, and even three-tusked white elephants, (not six-tusked as in one of the Jataka stories) signals opulence and grandeur; they adorn Ravana's palace gates. The celestial elephant Airavata, the mount of Indra, is given its traditional description: white and four-tusked. This is a post-Vedic embellishment, possibly derived from Buddhist mythology.

Compare the picture created in the *Ramayana* with that in the Jatakas, where kings have large stables, but elephants with other common domesticated animals are not the marks of a flourishing city. It appears that this could mark the stage when elephants were not mainly in royal possession, but were owned by the citizens along with their bulls, cows, horses, camels, asses and mules. The idea of the elephant as a ceremonial royal mount is certainly confirmed in the *Ramayana*; but in war, heroes and kings still use chariots, not elephants. The idea of the *chaturanga bal* (four-armed host) is now commonplace; but in actual descriptions of battles, the role of the elephant is not well-defined or considered decisive. Gifts of elephants certainly appear to indicate royal munificence.

Ravana's Lanka (traditionally identified with what is now Sri Lanka), situated, very probably, beyond the limits of *Aryavarta* (the land of the Aryans in northern India), has a vast number of elephants in domesticity and they seem to enjoy prominence not afforded them in the description of the towns in *Aryavarta*. Perhaps because the action of the epic moves away from the north, the Himalayas are not mentioned as the chief abode of wild elephants. The forests where Rama spends his period of exile (Dandakaranya) has elephants, but surprisingly, he has no unpleasant encounter with them, nor are large herds reported from the region. It is very much a speculative conclusion; but it seems that elephants in domesticity are now much more a part of the way of life than in the Jatakas. The forces stationed beyond *Aryavarta* appear to have many more of them than the forces in *Aryavarta* proper, despite the rather comical and realistic description of the dung of the vast number of elephants and horses belonging to Bharata's entourage fouling up Rama's camping ground in the forest.

Elephants in the *Mahabharata*

In the *Mahabharata*, the scene shifts to the Kuru-Panchala region, west of Prayag, present-day Allahabad in Uttar Pradesh, and the cultural background seems to be different. Here, they were still using chariots in warfare, however.

The usual elephant similes abound: Duryodhana and Bhima and later Bhima and Jarasandha clash 'roaring like elephants'. Bhima is 'as strong as 10,000 elephants'; Duryodhana slaps his thigh which is 'like the trunk of an elephant'; Krishna in a battle rushes towards Bhishma 'as a lion rushes to kill an elephant in fury/musth. Bhishma, it is reported, is demolishing the Pandava soldiers 'as an elephant demolishes reeds'. Karna asks his fellow warriors to rush to the rescue of Drona as otherwise 'the Pandavas will kill him as a pack of wolves kill a great elephant'. Satyaki and Duryodhana fight like 'elephant and lion'.

Some of the similes reveal considerable knowledge of elephant behaviour, both in the wild and in domesticity. The enemies catch Krishna by his arms, but he kills them by shaking his two arms as 'a bad elephant fells its *mahawat*, or driver'. It is interesting to note that the trunk of an elephant is called 'hand' (*hasta*) in Sanskrit and the Sanskrit term for elephant, *hastin* or *mriga hastin*, means an 'animal with hand'. A really mischievous elephant would try to pull down its driver with its trunk.

Bhima and Duhshasana clash 'as two rutting (musth) elephants clash over a cow elephant' – a pithy simile, as the original cause of the quarrel was Duhshasana's molestation of Draupadi, wife to Bhima and his brothers. Bhima tram-ples on the head of fallen Duryodhana 'as an infuriated elephant'. Crushing the head of the guilty under the foot of an elephant was a common form of capital punishment even in late medieval India. The great hero Abhimanyu moves 'like a furious elephant'. Bhishma states that 'as an elephant goad (*ankus* or *ankush*) controls an elephant, code of royalty (*Rajad-harma*) controls all people'. As all tracks are obliterated by the tracks of the elephant, so all other codes are subsumed in the code of the supreme authority, kingship. The old king Dhritarashtra moves slowly like 'an age-afflicted King Elephant'. Bhima has the gait of a master bull (elephant) in musth, and young Arjuna is like the master bull of a herd of elephants. In the *Kavya* (poetry) tradition, Bhima emerging after a bath in a lake is likened to 'a great elephant sporting in a lotus pool'.

Trade in elephants captured from the

Below: This colourful and dramatic illustration from the manuscript of Harivamsa (Mughal, about AD 1590) shows Krishna on the Bird-God Garuda fighting Indra – the king of gods – mounted on an elephant. This elephant is traditionally shown as white with four tusks, signifying opulence and grandeur.

wild is well established in the *Mahabharata*. According to Bhishma, a king should employ reliable people to collect excise duty on 'minerals, production of salt, captured wild animals etc.'. There is a vivid account of how a merchants' camp in the forest with many elephants, horses and chariots – the merchandise – was visited at night by a group of wild elephants in musth which attacked the domesticated elephants, causing immense damage. (Domesticated elephants in forest camps, especially bulls, are particularly vulnerable to attacks by wild bulls. As recently as 1990, a magnificent *mukna* (tuskless male elephant) belonging to the Tamil Nadu Forest Department was killed by a wild bull. A few years ago, Tamil Nadu Forest Department's magnificent tusker Inspector General was killed by a wild bull, and West Bengal Forest Directorate still bewails the loss of its great tusker Shivji in a similar manner in the 1950s.)

Princely accomplishments include proficiency in riding horses and elephants, driving chariots, wrestling and the use of arms, in which Drona trains the princes under his tutelage. King Dhritarashtra speaks admiringly of his soldiers, employed on appropriate wages after a thorough test of their proficiency in the use of arms, in riding horses and elephants and driving chariots – an indica-

tion of the level of training expected of a professional soldier of the time.

Gifting elephants is widely practised. Bhishma gives gold, jewels, elephants and horses as dowry for Madri, chosen by him as the second wife for Pandu. Whenever King Janmejaya performed a sacrifice, he made an offering of 10,000 elephants, many thousands of girls, and ten million bulls. Karna in battle boastfully offers a prize of one hundred beautiful girls, or elephants, or chariots, or horses, or bulls to any one who would point out Arjuna to him. The list of gifts from various kings to Yudhisthira at Indraprastha includes many elephants, as well as horses, camels, women, and silk and woollen cloth. Especially noteworthy is Krishna's gift of 14,000 fine elephants in honour of Arjuna. Among other things, Yudhisthira loses 1,000 excellent elephants to Shakuni in a fateful game of dice.

The elephant is an integral part of the idea of a *chaturangini sena* (four-armed host). The basic unit of the *Chaturanga* force is the *patti*, consisting of one elephant, one chariot, three mounted soldiers and five foot soldiers. One army corps, or *akhshauhini*, has 21,870 elephants, 21,870 chariots, 65,610 cavalry and 109,350 infantry. The Kauravas had 11 such corps and the Pandavas seven when the war started, making a total of 18

corps. On the Kaurava side, Duryodhana fixed four horses to each chariot, two horse-keepers and two rear guards. Each elephant had two persons with goads (presumably one the driver, or *mahawat*, the other to spur or goad from behind for fast movement), two archers, one spearman and one standard bearer. When the war ended on the 18th day, the Kaurava army had been totally destroyed and the Pandavas were left with only 2,000 chariots, 700 elephants, 5,000 horses and 10,000 infantry. On the third day's battle, Arjuna alone destroyed 10,000 chariots and 700 elephants.

The idea of the 'four-armed' composition of the fighting forces is thus basic to the conception of the war described in the *Mahabharata*. All the four 'arms' are mentioned almost as a matter of form whenever a large formation of soldiery or the large-scale destruction of enemy forces by a hero is described. These are so much a part of the texture of the story, particularly of the central episodes – the battle scenes – that they could not possibly be

Below: A war elephant in action shown in a detail from a temple frieze (Hoysala, 11th-13th century AD). War elephants in India enjoyed an uninterrupted history from the 1st millenium BC to the early 19th century, when improved musketry and mobile cannons pushed them from the front line to the supply line.

Above: Shankara (Shiva) – representing power – dancing inside the slain elephant demon, Gajasura (Hoysala, 11-13th century AD). The terrifying aspects of an elephant were recognized early, including the realization that one elephant could be a rogue and another an incarnation of Buddha – benign and docile.

indiscriminate later additions. Similarly, the episode of Yudhisthira lying to Drona about the death of Ashvatthama, Drona's only son, to make him leave arms, adding *sotto voce* 'iti kunjarah' ('that is, the elephant'), is too central to the main story to be an interpolation.

The fourth day's battle in the story is especially concerned with elephants in war, with Bhima appearing as a great slayer of elephants, and being compared to the god Shankara (another representation of Shiva) dancing after slaying an elephant. The chapter climaxes in the account of Bhagadatta on his mighty elephant flowing with musth fluid attacking the Pandavas, and Ghatotkacha and his demon companions, all on their own elephants, leading the counterattack from the Pandava side. There are graphic descriptions of elephant fighting against elephant.

In spite of the large-scale deployment of elephants in warfare, chariots constitute the main fighting arm in the *Mahabharata*. Great heroes fight on chariots and are graded accordingly as *rathi* (charioteer), *maharath* (great charioteer, a leader of charioteers) and *atirath* (super-charioteer, a leader of many maharaths). Chariot drivers clearly play a crucial role in battle. A few kings, however, do ride on elephants in the *Mahabharata* war, but they are mostly, but not all, from beyond the pale, including Bhagadatta on his enormous and terrifying elephant, who

is represented as a *mlechchha* (impure, i.e. non-Aryan) king.

Experts in elephant warfare are aboriginal hunting/fishing tribes, most of whom come from the fringes of the area of Aryan settlement in northern India, and some are expressly identified as hunters belonging to non-Aryan tribes. This could indicate how the Aryans were absorbing the native culture of elephants as they moved east along the Ganga valley and spread their sphere of influence to the south, learning uses of elephants they had not known or needed before. Alexander had been told (in India 327-325 BC) that east of the Beas, elephants were as numerous as cattle. More than 1,800 years later, Babur, the founder of the Mughal Empire in India (reigned 1526-30) noted that as one moved east, elephants became more numerous. By indirect evidence, the *Mahabharata* provides a confirmation of this account of the distribution of elephants in northern India, and provides some additional information regarding the fringe areas on the south and south east. Bhishma's advice to Yudhisthira perhaps provides a clue to why chariots were favoured in drier western India. In the dry season, says Bhishma, use a force with a predominance of horses and chariots, but in the rainy season use infantry supported by many elephants. (Even in May 1991, after the premonsoon showers during the Indian general elections, elephants had to carry government officials, ballot boxes and papers to inaccessible areas of Tripura in wet northeastern India.)

While the elephant culture had apparently developed considerably in the eastern parts, in the drier western part – despite the reference to *gajashastra* (elephantology) in connection with the elephant ridden by Shalva, which could be a later interpolation – it is the horse culture which continued to dominate. We are told of the good points of a horse, not of the elephant. Nakula and Sahadeva, the younger of the five Pandava brothers, take employment as experts in treating horses, not elephants. Bhima's role is limited to breaking powerful elephants. We do not hear of elephant trainers as a class, nor of elephant festivals or markets of ivory traders and carvers, as in the *Jataka* stories, although crafted ivory is not unknown in the *Mahabharata*. The gifts of Bhagadatta to Yudhisthira at Indraprastha include swords with ivory handles, and the white umbrella held over Yudhisthira's head as a royal emblem has ivory spokes. Yudhisthira's mother, Kunti, sits on a gold-encrusted ivory seat at the time of his ceremonial enthronement after the final victory, and the ceremony of ordaining Karna as the supreme commander of the Kaurava forces involves the use of, among other things, elephant tusks set with jewels.

Significantly, the sage Palakapya, who

Above: Alexander's coin commemorating his victory over Poros (326 BC): Alexander on horseback and Poros on his elephant (The Indian Museum, Calcutta). The elephants of Poros brought Alexander closer to defeat than at any other time during his campaigns. It has been suggested that Alexander's troops refused to march farther east because of their experience with the war elephants of Poros.

founded the discipline of elephantology in his pioneering 'Medication of Elephants', according to tradition, hailed from Anga (present-day eastern Bihar) in the wet eastern part of India.

Revelations from Megasthenes

The writings of Megasthenes, the ambassador of Seleukos to the court of Chandragupta Maurya, provides valuable information about the status and management of the elephant in Mauryan eastern India in the last quarter of the fourth century BC. Ambassador Megasthenes writes: 'The king hunts in enclosures and shoots arrows from a platform. . . . If he hunts in the open grounds he shoots from the back of an elephant.' Apparently, during his years in the city of Taxila (in northern Pakistan) Chandragupta had absorbed some of the West Asian culture; for we find in the British Museum low reliefs showing Assyrian monarchs hunting lions with arrows within enclosures. But the second mode, hunting from an elephant's back, is India's own, and this appears to be one of the earliest accounts of such hunts. It is easy to see how the technique developed, as this is the only feasible way of beating out game in the vast riverain grasslands of eastern and northeastern India. The Mughals took to this, and refined upon the practice, but did not invent it. The British copied it in their attempt to emulate imperial grandeur.

The organization of the 'four-armed' army is confirmed by Megasthenes. He adds: 'The war-elephant carries four men – three shoot arrows, and the driver.' His accounts also tell us that a private person was not allowed to keep either a horse or an elephant, which were held to be the special property of the king. In fact, probably as valuable military intelligence, Megasthenes records the number of ele-

phants kept by some of the more important kings of India, including the king of Andhra (until very recently, there were no wild elephants there), and of the west coast (no elephant in living memory in the northern part of the coast in the state of Maharashtra). The total comes to 13,260, of which 9,000 belonged to Chandragupta alone.

Megasthenes provides the first datable report of using the stockade method to capture elephants. He reports that the enclosure was made of deep and wide trenches and tame female elephants were used to tempt wild elephants into the enclosure. This is followed by a detailed description, probably based on personal observation, of the process of tying up and training. While being tamed, the elephants were soothed by words, songs and music – still the prevailing practice in eastern and northeastern India. Megasthenes' observations on the periods of gestation and nursing in elephants are remarkably close to the facts, and he reports accurately, if rather quaintly, that elephants bathe 'with all the zest of a consummate voluptuary'. He also notes, rightly, that elephants in captivity are vulnerable to sores and inflammation of the eyes. According to Megasthenes, elephants undergoing fatigues of war were given an extra ration of rice-wine – still the favourite tipple of the poorer section of the people in the rice-growing areas of eastern India. The British kept up the tradition but replaced rice-wine with rum.

Alexander's encounter with elephants at war

Although Alexander's encounter with the war elephants of the Paurava king (*Poros* in Greek) of India (in 326 BC) predates Megasthenes' visit to India, the surviving accounts by Western chroniclers such as Arrian, Curtius and Diodorus were actually written several hundred years later. Alexander did not meet elephants at war for the first time at the battle of Hydaspes, but it was here that he learnt the importance of the elephant as a fighting machine. Although his Persian opponent Darius was on a chariot at the battles of Issus (333 BC) and Gaugamela (331 BC), the Indian contingent of Darius' forces from 'this side of the Indus' had some 15 elephants. The elephants had been posted ahead of Darius' royal squadron, presumably to act as linebreakers and to frighten Alexander's cavalry. But in the actual attack Darius used scythe-chariots to penetrate the enemy line, not elephants. After the rout of the Persian army by Alexander, the Persian camp was taken with the baggage trains, elephants and camels, showing where the elephants really belonged. There is no mention of Alexander taking the elephants with him.

On his eastward march, King Taxiles (King of Taxila) and the Indians 'on this

side of the Indus' promised to give him their elephants, 25 in number. As he proceeded eastward, he met a hostile army of tribesmen who had 30 elephants. He met more elephants on his way, and even indulged in the sport of hunting (capturing) elephants from horseback (one wonders how – by noosing perhaps?) and taking them into the army. Gifts from Taxiles to Alexander included 30 elephants. But he, apparently, had none with him at the battle of Hydaspes. According to Arrian, Poros had 200 elephants (Curtius mentions 85, Diodorus 130). That the revolt of his soldiers forced Alexander to turn back from the river Hyphasis (Beas) is allowed by all. Both Arrian and Curtius agree that in the country beyond the Hyphasis elephants were more numerous and larger than elsewhere. Curtius and Diodorus write of King Aggrames (identified as King Mahapadma Nanda) blocking the road beyond with a huge force including 3,000 elephants, a special cause of terror. Curtius records that Alexander chided his soldiers for their fear of these animals. According to this account, the elephants of the easterners were a major cause of Alexander's not pushing farther eastwards in his quest for the eastern sea.

Curtius records that in India the king makes his shorter journeys on horseback, and longer journeys in chariots drawn by elephants (*elephanti vehunt currum*), which should, perhaps, have been rendered as 'chariot/*howdah* carried by elephants'. The huge animals are covered with gold, a further confirmation of the idea of the elephant as royal mount found in the epics and other ancient literature.

Clues from the *Arthashastra*

This account of elephants in northern India in the early years can be appropriately rounded off with a reference to *Arthashastra*, a comprehensive account of Indian politics and governmental organization (300 BC-AD 300). Apart from civil and military administration, the work discusses a land-use strategy as well as rules for the management of elephants, and includes the following edicts. The king shall carry on mining, manufactures, and exploit timber and elephant forests. A special game reserve will be created for the king's sport, protected by ditches all round with only one entrance, filled with harmless animals and 'tigers, beasts of prey, male and female elephants, and bisons [*Bos gaurus*] – all deprived of their claws and teeth.' 'On the edge of the country . . . a game

Right: Prince Salim, Akbar's son, surprised by a lion while hunting (about AD 1595-1600). The custom of hunting from the back of an elephant was reported by Megasthenes in the fourth century BC. An essentially Indian mode of hunting, this was adopted by the Mughals and later emulated by the British .

reserve open to all shall be made, [i.e. safely away from human habitation where, presumably, dangerous animals would be allowed to retain their claws and teeth]. In the extreme limit of the country, elephant forests, separated from wild tracts, shall be formed, maintained by the superintendent of elephant forests.' 'Whoever kills an elephant shall be put to death.' 'Whoever brings in the pair of tusks of an elephant, dead from natural causes, shall receive a reward of four-and-a-half panas.'

Guards of the elephant forests, with assistance from trainers and keepers of elephants, trackers and local villagers, shall keep precise information regarding movement of elephants: herds, a loner, a stray one, a leader of herds, a tusker, a rogue, one in musth, or one which has escaped from captivity.

Experts in catching elephants, as per instructions of the elephant doctor, shall catch elephants with auspicious characteristics and good character.

'The victory of kings [in battle] depends mainly on elephants; for elephants, being of large bodily frame, are capable not only to destroy the arrayed army of an enemy, his fortifications and encampments, but also to undertake works that are dangerous to life.'

'Elephants bred in countries such as Kalinga, Anga, Karusa and the East are the best; those of the Dasarna and Western countries are of middle quality; and those of Saurashtra and Panchajana countries are of low quality.'

The *Arthashastra* lays down the duties of the superintendent of elephants, covering not only every aspect of their management in captivity, but also of elephant forests. Exact measurements for the construction of elephant stables are given. Detailed instructions are given regarding elephants that may be captured and those which may not, with summer being given as the prescribed time to capture elephants. A diet chart for different categories of elephants is given, and elephants are classified according to physical features as well as temper. The *bhadra* and *mandra* classification of elephant types, so much a part of later Indian elephant lore, also appears here.

Part of the *Arthashastra* is devoted to the training of elephants, including seven kinds of military training. Elephant ornaments and armour are detailed, and the duties of men attending to elephants are specified, with a particular mention of elephant doctors. Precise instructions are also given for periodic sawing off of tusks. Many of these rules are still operative, and survive even in official or government manuals.

Teasing an elephant is set down as a legal offence, and a man grievously hurt by an elephant (presumably because of teasing it) will be fined. Even death caused by an elephant should not be a reason for complaint; 'for death caused by an elephant is as meritorious as the sacred bath taken at the end of a horse-sacrifice'.(The logic here is that you should not make too much fuss if you are injured by an elephant; indeed, it would have been an honour if the elephant had killed you. This fine will teach you to be more careful next time.) But if the negligence of the driver or the owner of an animal causes death this is a capital offence.

The work of elephants in the army is also set down in great detail, including the placement of elephants in a four-armed battle formation. The best army is considered to be that which consists of a strong infantry and the best-quality elephants and horses. Chariots, significantly, are not singled out here for their importance.

Tamil writings of the 1st-3rd century AD

Most of the sources discussed so far concern northern India. For the early years of the Christian era the ancient Tamil literature of the Sangam period (1st-3rd century AD) offers a wealth of information and shows that elephants were a part of the culture and the way of life of the ancient Tamils. *Nigandu*, the old poetical lexicon, has 44 names for the elephant species, four separate names for female elephants and five for calves. There are also separate names for each part of the elephant's body.

Elephants are woven into the texture of many of the poems, and many minor chieftains are praised by the poets for owning very large numbers of elephants and making lavish gifts of elephants. There are also references to big chariots drawn by elephants. Similes based on elephants' strength and other qualities abound. The period of gestation is noted as 16 to 18 months, never exceeding 18. Deadly fighting qualities of elephants are much admired. We also know of Kurava hill men killing elephants with arrows. Along with other evidence already cited, this seems to indicate that the domestication of elephants was indigenous to India, and the Aryans picked it up in the course of their assimilation.

The 'Classical' period onwards

Strangely, the coins of the Imperial Guptas (about AD 319 to 454), in what is considered to be the golden or classical age of Indian art, show the dominance of the horse rather than of elephants. The account of the Chinese pilgrim Fa-Hsien (AD 405-11) does not add much to our knowledge of the status, distribution and management of elephants under the Guptas. For King Harsha-vardhana of Kanauj in northern India (AD 606-47), our chief source is the account of the Chinese traveller Hsuan-Tsang (in India AD 630-44), which gives us a detailed picture of the organization of the government, but not much on elephants. Bana's *Harshacharita* (seventh century AD), even allowing for the poet's habitual rhetorical exuberance, records a description of the royal camp of Harsha. The royal entrance is described as being 'dark with congregation of elephants: some for tying up with silk [for royal use?]; some for carrying trumpets; some freshly captured; some received as revenue; some received gratis; some to satisfy the emperor's curiosity to have the first look; some sent by the chiefs of Nagabana [*naga* = elephant; *bana* = forest, thus 'elephant forests' of Kautilya?]; some by the chieftains of Shabar Bustee (settlement of the Shabar, a hunting tribe); some borrowed for elephant-fights and games; some as gifts for sending with ambassadors; some given gratis; some seized by force; some free from chains kept for guarding, etc.' The passage offers a remarkable overview of various uses elephants were put to during the period, and their general importance. Even in Mughal times some of the chiefs of northeastern India – the chief of Gauripore in Assam, for example – paid their annual tribute to the emperor in pairs of elephants. We also learn from Bana that ivory craft was an established industry.

We have to turn to the south, however, for the most impressive visual account of elephants during this period in the rock-cut works of the Pallavas (AD 600 to 740), and later in the temple sculpture and bas-reliefs of the Hoysala period (about AD 1110-1318), as well as in the temple sculptures of Orissa.

In our quest for knowledge of elephants during the period (AD 300-1200) a cursory reference to Kalidasa (about AD 400), perhaps the greatest poet of this golden age of Sanskrit literature, must suffice for the occasion. In the *Kumara-sambhavam*, which is replete with similes of and references to elephants (including hunters killing them), Parvati, the daughter of the King of Mountains, Himalaya, observing severe rites to attain Mahadeva as her husband, is asked to consider if the silk dress of a newly wedded young girl is compatible with a blood-smeared elephant skin. This is a reference to Mahadeva's costume and to the myth of Shankara dancing after destroying Gajasura, the elephant demon. Attempts to dissuade her from marrying Mahadeva include the argument that if she rides a bull (the *vahana*, or carrier of Mahadeva, also called Shiva or Shankara) instead of an elephant while journeying to her husband's house, she will be ridiculed by all respectable people. This emphasizes the aspect of social status involved in being carried on an elephant. After all, Parvati was a princess.

Raghuvamsham, another of Kalidasa's poems, has a very interesting observation of wild elephants debarking trees, a continuing problem of elephant management that has engaged the serious attention of recent ecologists. Raghu fighting Indra, the king of the gods, lets fly an arrow that pierces Indra's hand, the fingers of which had become caloused by striking the celestial elephant Airavata, his *vahana*. As seen earlier, royalty not only rides on but also rides elephants. On its victorious march, Raghu's army crosses the river Kapisa by a sort of pontoon bridge made by elephants. The King of Kalinga opposes him with his elephant force and the hillsides become scarred with tusk marks of Raghu's elephants. In this story, Pragjyotishpura (Bhagadatta's kingdom in *Mahabharata*) is identified with Kamrup in Assam, and its king is noted for owning warlike elephants that are presented to Raghu. Significantly, Assam and the surrounding region is still the most important elephant-bearing area in India.

Act I of Kalidasa's play *Abhijnanashakuntalam* describes the appearance of a wild tusker with a broken tusk in the groves of prayer (*ashrama*) of the sage Kanva. The elephant is described as causing general alarm and scattering herds of tame deer, 'disturbance incarnate'. Wild elephants entering such secluded human settlements in the forest were obviously a regular source of danger; for as early as one of the *Dharmashastras* (about 3rd-2nd century BC) a week's respite from studies was prescribed if wild elephants entered a *tapovana* (grove of meditation), presumably because of the disruption, destruction and chaos that was caused.

The Islamic Period

With the beginning of the Islamic period, we once again enter the era of historical records of the use of elephants, particularly in war, with the supreme commander leading his army into battle on an elephant as the standard practice. In the first battle of Taraori (Thaneswar, AD 1190) Govind Rai, the Governor of Delhi and the brother of King Prithviraj, won the day against the invading Shihabuddin Ghori, at one stage driving his elephant towards Shihabuddin. Towards the end of the second battle of Taraori (AD 1192), Prithviraj changed his elephant for a horse and the battle was lost. Thus began the Turkish Empire in India (AD 1192-1526). This was to be a recurring pattern in most of the important battles that determined the subsequent course of history in medieval India.

When Timur invaded Delhi (AD 1398), the main fear of the Turkish soldiers was from the reputation for ferocity and power of the Indian war elephants, which were said to twine their trunk around an armour-clad trooper and fling him and his horse into the air. Timur took extraordinary precautions to counter this threat, encircling his camp with elephant-proof barriers, consisting of

ditches wherever possible. This may have been the first use of elephant-proof barriers in war, and his was also perhaps the first attempt to use elephant-repellents – hundreds of buffaloes and camels, trussed up and placed along the barriers – 'the most effective steps in breaking any charge of the elephants'. Elephants terrified horses and were a serious threat to cavalry attack; here, the table was being turned on elephants by using other animals to terrify them. The Delhi Sultan's forces had only 120 elephants, on which they relied totally. Unfortunately, they were not of much avail in the face of waves of determined attack by Timur's ironclad cavalry and long-distance bows.

Ibrahim Lodi's army facing Babur at the first battle of Panipat (1526) reportedly had 1,000 war elephants – probably an exaggeration. The Indians relied chiefly on their elephants, which were of little use. Their drivers were regularly picked off by gunshot or arrows, and the injured beasts, forced to turn back, trampling down their own men (a weakness noted by Alexander and reported in the *Mahabharata*). In war, the *mahawat* sitting in front astride the neck of an elephant was a particularly vulnerable target. Terracotta figurines from the Maurya (4th-3rd century BC) and Satavahana period (1st century BC) show that elephants were trained to keep their heads unnaturally high to protect the *mahawat* behind, who held joined shields before him for added protection. *Mahawats* drive elephants by prodding them behind the ears with their toes; so their hands are relatively free. Its origin quite forgotten, the tradition of this special training still

Above: *A war elephant (terracotta, Satavahana Period, about 1st century BC, National Museum, Delhi). Besides being armoured, war elephants were trained to keep their heads unnaturally high to protect the driver* (mahawat) *sitting behind from missiles. Notice the twin shields carried by the driver as an additional form of protection.*

continues at the annual animal fair at Sonepur in Bihar, where the animals for sale are paraded with their *mahawats* making them hold their heads as high as possible. No doubt this was a quality that the warlike kings and chieftains of yore looked for in their elephants when making a choice at this ancient animal fair. But, to come back to 1526, Babur also used firearms in the battle, a first in India, which eventually forced the elephant off the field of action. Superior arms and tactics earned Babur his victory. Thus ended the Turkish Empire in India and began the Mughal.

Babur's victory against Rana Sanga at the battle of Khanua in 1527 consolidated the gains of Panipat. When Sanga was seriously injured in the battle, a chieftain was put on the royal elephant to impersonate him, lest the soldiers, seeing the *howdah* empty, panicked and deserted. This was a perpetual problem with using an elephant as the royal or supreme commander's mount in a battle; a visible presence inspired, but a sudden lack of it caused general panic, often leading to the loss of the battle.

Sher Shah the Afghan, who became the master of Hindustan after putting Babur's son Humayun to flight, had an army of 150,000 horses, 25,000 foot soldiers and a total of 5,000 elephants.

The second battle of Panipat in 1556 established Akbar, then only 13, on the Mughal throne and led him back to Delhi. His adversary was Himu, the minister of the Afghan chief, Adil Shah. At the first encounter in October, Himu's elephants carried the day. In the first assault the Mughal army captured 400 elephants and slew 3,000 men of the Afghan army. But Himu eventually won the round by deploying his reserve of 300 choice elephants and a force of select horsemen. As a modern historian notes, 'at the impetuous advance of the huge beasts and the dense cavalry behind them, many of the Mughal officers fled away in terror without waiting to offer a defence'. But the second encounter in November, again at Panipat, resulted in a decisive victory for the Mughals. Himu had 500 elephants protected by plate armour, with Himu himself on a tall elephant. Again, the elephants were most effectively deployed, but eventually the day was won by superior Mughal cavalry, after Himu had been hit in the eye by an arrow. The Mughal conquest of Bengal from the Afghans was almost thwarted at the battle of Tukaroi in south Bengal in 1575. The furious charge of Afghan elephants, their tusks and necks covered with black yak tails and skins of the animals, succeeded in stampeding the Mughal cavalry. The Afghan side lost only when their general, Gujar Kahn, fell and his battalion broke.

At the famous battle of Haldighat in 1576 between the army of Akbar and the Rajput prince Rana Pratap, both sides had elephants, but while the Mughals had firearms, the Rajputs had none. Raja Man Singh leading the Mughal forces was on an elephant. When the two centres were locked in combat, Pratap sent in his famous 'rank-breaking' elephant, Lona. The Mughals countered with their equally famous Gajmukta. Pratap put forward his chief elephant, Ram Prasad, which was countered by Gajraj and Ran-mada of the Mughals. All this must have been a spectacular elephant fight. When Ram Prasad's *mahawat* was hit by an arrow and thrown off his mount, Hussain Khan, the commander of the imperial elephants, leapt from the back of his own elephant on to Ram Prasad and made a prize of the great animal, much admired in Akbar's court. The contemporary account of this battle by Akbar's court historian makes fascinating reading, as Muslim chroniclers seldom mention individual animals by name when recording military events. A Mughal painting of Gajraj, the favourite elephant of Emperor Jahangir, son of Akbar, could conceivably be a representation of the hero of Haldighat in mellow retirement.

Elephants again played a vital role in the last Mughal-Pathan battle in eastern Bengal in 1612, where in wet marshy

grounds the 140 elephants of the Afghans, the best in Bengal, clashed with 100 elephants of the imperial army. Eventually, the imperial mounted archery and elephant-borne swivel guns won the day, despite the acknowledged superiority of the Bengal elephants.

The last Hindu bastion in India fell with the shattering of the great Vijaynagar Empire after the crushing defeat at the battle of Talikota in 1565, 'a natural effect', it has been claimed, of Hindu armies neglecting the cavalry arm and artillery, and their leaders riding on elephants instead of swift horses. In the battle, the allied army of the Deccan Sultanates had 50,000 cavalry, 30,000 infantry and, most important, 600 pieces of fire-arms including large ordnance. The Hindu (Vijaynagar) side, according to what is probably a grossly exaggerated contemporary estimate, had 60,000 cavalry, 100,000 infantry and 1,000 elephants, plus some antique guns and rockets. Superior fire power and archery won the day for the allied forces.

During the war for the Delhi throne in 1658-59 between the sons of the aged

Above: Emperor Jahangir's favourite elephant, Gajraj (king elephant) in camp (Mughal, 17th century, The Indian Museum, Calcutta). Rice-based concentrate is being cooked in the foreground of the painting.

emperor Shah Jahan , elephants played their usual role as mounts for commanders in the field, notably in the battle of Dharmat in 1658. At the battle of Samugarh, also in 1658, where the heir apparent and Shah Jahan's eldest son, Prince Dara, faced his younger brothers, Murad Baksh and Aurangzib, the princes were mounted on elephants and therefore were conspicuous targets. At one stage, Murad's *howdah* was 'stuck full of arrows like a porcupine's back.' At the last stage of the battle, Dara's own elephant became the target and he changed to a horse; immediately, all was over. Seeing his *howdah* empty, his troops concluded that he had fallen and, abandoning the fight, fled. No victory could be more complete. Thus, an elephant determined the course of Indian history once again.

At the battle of Khajwa in 1659, which

eliminated the last opposition to Aurangzib, his surviving brother Shuja, the elephant continued to occupy centre stage. Despite numerical inferiority, Shuja's forces nearly carried the day because of elephants. Shuja's attack was led by three infuriated (musth) elephants, each brandishing a two *maund* (74kg/164lb) chain with its trunk. They smashed their way through Aurangzib's army, everybody fleeing before them. One of them came right up to Emperor Aurangzib's elephant. The Emperor, a man with nerves of steel, had the legs of his own elephant chained to prevent its flight, which would have meant a reenactment of the scenario of the battle of Samugarh, with Aurangzib, rather than Dara, the loser this time. However, a matchlockman picked off the driver of the presumptuous elephant and a brave imperial *mahawat* leapt on its neck and brought it under control. On the other side, Shuja, in imminent danger of being shot down, abandoned his elephant and took a horse. Immediately, his army broke and took flight from the battlefield, believing their leader was dead.

The elephant continued to be the royal/general's mount in battle and a frequent source of embarrassment during the scramble for the imperial throne after Aurangzib's death in 1707. At the battle of Jajau in the same year, one after another of four *mahawats* of the mount of Azam Shah, son of Aurangzib, were shot

Below: An example of elephants being used as the commanders' mounts in battle. This mural in the Summer Palace of Tipu Sultan in Mysore shows the combined forces of the British and the Nizam marching against him.

down. Azam Shah tried to direct the animal himself by pushing his leg out of his *howdah* and pressing the animal's head with his toes, but was killed by a musket ball. The results of improved musketry were making themselves felt, and dramatically changing the age-old pattern of combat.

Though firepower was becoming the main argument in battle, in the three eighteenth-century battles of the Nizam-Ratanpur (1720), Balapur (1720) and Shaker Khera (1724) – the commanders still rode on elephants, which often led to disaster and confusion. These three were possibly the last great battles fought with elephants, before the supremacy of modernized artillery began to displace the role of the elephant. Greatly improved range and accuracy of musket-fire increased the threat to field commanders on elephant back beyond the acceptable level, and mobile cannons brought basic changes to war tactics. The deadly effect of improved cannons had been proved on the battlefield of Jajau (1707), where all the leaders on one side – Prince Muhammad Azam, his son Bidar Bakht and the Rajput general Dalpat Rao Bundela – were shot down from their elephants, which led to a complete rout of the side. At Gheria in 1740, victory came to Alivardi of Bengal when a stray bullet finished off his rival Sarfraz Khan on elephant back. The same luck held in the attack on Patna in 1745, when the rebel general Mustafa Khan changed to a horse after his *mahawat* had been killed by a musket shot and he was in imminent danger of being carried away by his own runaway elephant.

At the battle of Manihari in 1756, as

soon as Shaukat Jang, the Nawab of Purnia, was shot down from his elephant, all opposition ceased at the sight, and the Bengal army had a walkover up to the enemy's capital. This could very well be the last important battle fought with the commander on an elephant. Although elephants accompanied Nawab Sirajuddaulah when he marched on the British settlement in Calcutta in 1756 – the place where they were camped is still called *Hathibagan* (elephant grove) – they played no part in the actual assault on the fort. At the fateful battle of Plassey in 1757, neither Siraj nor Mir Jaffar nor Clive of India was on an elephant, though an elephant looms in the background in the painting showing Mir Jaffar's meeting with Clive after the victory. It was treachery and wet gunpowder that secured the day for the British forces, not a runaway elephant.

Things were changing fast as foot soldiers with swords, staffs and spears were being replaced by soldiers with muskets and handguns. From the middle of the eighteenth century onwards, elephants were gradually being pushed back to the commissariat – being used to supply food and equipment for the troops – the position they had occupied at the battle of Gaugamela more than two thousand years ago. Curiously, in the Mughal army, gun carriages were drawn by bullocks, with an occasional push from an elephant in difficult terrain, a practice which the East India Company continued.

Before we come to the end of the Mughal era, it should be recorded that the Mughals set a great store by elephants in war and state pomp. Akbar (reigned 1556-1605) was a connoisseur of elephants, and so was his son and successor, Emperor Jahangir (reigned 1605-1627). Abu'l Fazl, Akbar's friend and court historian, has recorded Akbar's love for the animal, its place at court and in the military administration of the Great Mughal. An elaborate system was devised for the management of the royal elephant stable, which, reportedly, had 32,000 elephants, and in Jahangir's time, 113,000. People holding offices of state (*mansabdar*) had to maintain and command at the time of war a specified number of elephants, in addition to soldiers, cavalry, etc. An elephant was valued because it added to royal pomp and because of its use in the army; a good elephant was considered to be equal to 500 horses. The price of an elephant varied from a hundred to a hundred thousand rupees. During the reign of Jahangir, the price of a well-trained war elephant rose much higher. It was during the reign of Shajahan that the first white elephant was brought from Pegu to the Mughal court.

Akbar made a sevenfold classification of elephants based on his personal

experience – an obvious refinement of the system of classification of ancient Hindu elephant lore to which Abu'l Fazl refers. Diets for each class of elephant were prescribed, and the number of attendants for each type of elephant and their duties specified. There were superintendents (*Faujdar*) for each company of 10, 20 or 30 elephants, and a hierarchical system of commanders over them. Most of the terms for elephant gear used in the Mughal elephant stables as described by Abu'l Fazl are still in use. One hundred and one selected animals were kept for the emperor's personal use, the emperor personally driving the animals. An elaborate system of fines was introduced to enforce strict discipline among the elephant keepers. Elaborate rules guided the procedure for the muster of elephants, and the keeping of records of each animal. Four methods of capture of wild elephants are described, including the *kheda* (drive) and pit methods, the former being a popular entertainment for the court in Jahangir's time. The distribution of wild elephants given by Abu'l Fazl included areas between longitude 75° and 89°17'E and latitude 25°39' and 19°13'N, where, except for very recent incursions in isolated patches, no elephants are to be found now.

Nineteenth century and the Raj

It is curious that although it was Babur who introduced firearms in war, which eventually pushed elephants out of the battlefield, it was under his successors that the management of elephants for war and other purposes reached its highest level of sophistication, which has influenced systems of elephant management in India ever since. General Sir Sydney Cotton, who disarmed the mutinous Sepoys of Peshawar in the rebellion of 1857, points out the changed status, still very much valued, of elephants in warfare:

'Strange as it may appear, there is no beast of burden in the world that can beat an elephant in traversing precipitous mountains, and the author never went without these mortars [2.5kg/5.5lb mortars conveyed on elephants]. Of all animals of the creation there are none so intelligent and so useful in military operations in mountains as the elephants, and sufficient value and importance is not attached to them in the British [Indian] services. One elephant can transport over long distances six British soldiers, with arms, ammunition and bedding, besides rations.'

Earlier, at the opposite corner of India, Ochterlony had employed elephants to carry stores up the hills in his Nepal campaign (1815).

The main period of strife in the process of consolidation of British power in India was over by the first quarter of the nineteenth century. After that, the main use of elephants was in state pomp, as status symbols by princes and land-holding gentry, and in the great *shikar* meets organized during the period and right up to the late 1930s, when the Second World War put an end to this form of revelry.

Elephants were pressed into active service once again when the Japanese swept through Southeast Asia and Burma, and were knocking on the northeastern borders of India. All elephants in private ownership in northeastern India were requisitioned and put into active military service in the difficult wet terrain of the region's hills and swamps.

The present day

The merger of the princely states with democratic India at the time of independence in 1947, the abolition of the zemindary system (collection of land revenues) in the 1950s, followed by the abolition of princely privileges and privy purse in the 1960s ended the era of feudal pomp with elephants at their centre. And the four-wheel drive vehicles finished off the elephant's role in the commissariat.

Modern bulk demands for elephants come from the logging industry in northeastern India and in the Andaman Islands; for use as status symbols in the southern Indian temples and certain areas of northeastern India, northern Bihar and eastern Uttar Pradesh; religious endowments in various parts of the country; circus companies; and forest and tourism departments of the government. The elephant survives despite all odds: respected, worshipped and loved in captivity; deferentially treated and feared in the wild; still in demand by man, its market price higher than ever before, symbol of eternal India.

Left: Viceroy Lord Curzon making his state entry into Delhi in 1903. Although improved musketry reduced the frontline importance of the elephant in the army, its prestige in state pomp – a legacy of Mughal imperial splendour – remained. It continued to be a coveted status symbol with Indian nobility.

Right: The Jatakas refer to elephant festivals in eastern India, when elephants would be displayed and paraded The tradition has died out in northern India, but survives in Kerala, in the south. Here, in the annual Trichur Poornam festival, the armour of war has become a superb decoration.

THE IVORY TRADE

The male African elephant can grow tusks that are at least 3m (almost 10ft) long, each containing 100kg(220lb) of ivory. They are both an asset and a liability, being just as attractive to man on a dead elephant as they are useful to a living one.

Ivory has been valued as an article of adornment since the dawn of mankind. Neolithic figurines carved from ivory have been found in Europe, and the material features prominently in the ancient Egyptian civilizations. Although correctly restricted to the tusks of elephants, the term 'ivory' is also applied to the teeth of other mammals, such as walrus, narwhal, hippopotamus, and the extinct mammoths. The type of ivory used depended on the raw materials available locally or, later, from trade. The neolithic hunters of Europe used mammoth ivory, the later boreal hunters that of narwhal and walrus, and coastal people used the teeth of sperm whales. The Egyptians had a ready supply of African elephants within their empire. The Indian and Chinese civilizations relied on the smaller tusks of the Asian elephant. The development of international trade enabled civilizations to make use of non-indigenous sources of ivory, which is an ideal commodity for trade, being compact and of high value.

Whole elephant tusks make imposing ornaments, and doubtless adorned ancient palaces as they do the grand residences of today. The principal value of ivory, however, lies in its properties as a medium for carving. It is soft enough to work, yet hard enough to be durable and to take a good polish. Its grain is fine; it does not split readily, and its colour is a pure, creamy white. Unlike bone and most other teeth, the texture is uniform throughout the tusk, imposing fewer constraints on the craftsman. Finally, the tusks of the male African elephant can grow to a prodigious size, allowing substantial carvings to be made without the need for jointing.

In the African elephant, both males and females carry tusks, although those of the latter are much smaller. Tusks continue to grow throughout the life of the animal and can exceptionally reach 100kg(220lb) in an old male, at which time they may measure 3.2m(10.5ft) in length. Tusks of females seldom exceed 20kg(44lb). In the Asian elephant, tusks are borne by some males, and are absent or reduced in females. The percentage of males with tusks varies from region to region; for instance, in Sri Lanka, only 7 percent are tuskers, whereas in southern India the proportion of elephants with tusks may be as high as 90 percent.

The tendency to bear tusks is genetically determined, and the current regional variations in their incidence may be due to past levels of hunting having selectively killed the tusked males.

History of the ivory trade

Early evidence of the nature and effects of the ivory trade can be found in its history in Rome. Pliny remarked in AD 77 that large tusks could no longer be found 'in our part of the world', meaning in the Mediterranean Basin; by the end of the Roman Empire, elephants were extinct in North Africa. This may have been partly due to climatic changes in the region, but

hunting for the ivory trade has also been blamed. Fortunately, the African elephant still flourished south of the Sahara and it was from there that the Europeans obtained their supplies of ivory during the colonial era.

The first wave of European colonization, and therefore the first source of ivory, was in West Africa, conferring the name of 'Ivory Coast' on part of it. This name has been retained, although the neighbouring 'Gold Coast' and 'Slave Coast' (both testifying to the other main motives for colonization) have been renamed. The early ivory trade was intimately associated with the slave trade, not least because slaves provided the main means of transporting the ivory from the interior to the coast. Ivory was often the major incentive for the trade, the slave carrying a large tusk being worth only a fraction of the value of his burden.

Another sixteenth-century source of ivory in Mozambique was exploited by the Portuguese, who made use of the trading network of the Arabs who had preceded them. It is probable that the Arabs had been supplying ivory to India and China for some time before the Euro-

Above: *Ivory was carved in workshops set up in Egypt as early as 8000 BC, long before the dynasties of the pharaohs. This elegant comb is from that so-called Pre-Dynastic period.*

Tusk growth rates in African elephants

The graph compares the rate at which the tusks grow in male and female African elephants. The tusks grow throughout the life of the elephant, but clearly much faster and to a greater maximum size in males than in females. The tusks of male Asian elephants can grow just as large as those of the African elephant.

 Female

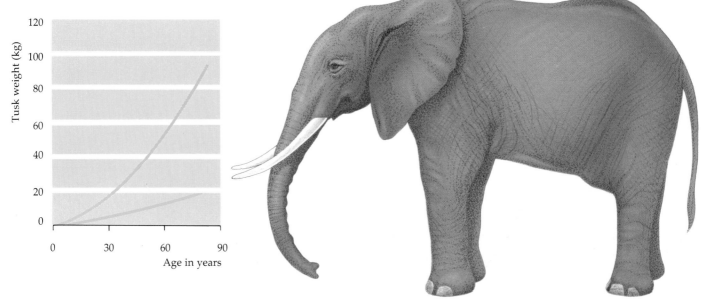

Male

peans arrived. In his major study of the ivory trade, Ian Parker estimated that the trade in the sixteenth and seventeenth centuries amounted to some 200 tonnes(441,000lb) a year, evenly split between the east and west coasts of the continent, with maybe a further 30 tonnes(66,150lb) from the Cape region. Over the next hundred years, the trade swelled to around 500 tonnes(1,102,500lb) a year, extending into the southern Sudan. By the late eighteenth century, the elephant herds of West Africa had been seriously depleted, as had those of South Africa, and ivory was mostly supplied from the colonial trade routes that extended eastwards to Central Africa from the Congo and westwards from the British and German territories in East Africa.

By virtue of the trade routes and the industrial development, most of the ivory passed through Europe: that from the Belgian colonies through Brussels, and that from the British colonies through London. Customs records at the turn of the century can therefore be used to obtain an estimate of the volume of the trade. British imports from 1865-1914 have been added to those of Belgium from

Below: Long trading routes were established to bring ivory from the interior of Africa during the colonial period, which began when the Portuguese discovered the Guinea coast in the 15th century. Often, slaves were used to transport tusks to the coast.

1888-1918 to create the graph on page 152-3, which provides an indication of the trade in raw ivory.

It is clear that ivory was extensively traded as a commodity around Europe and thence to the rest of the world, and so some of the ivory imported to the UK may previously have been imported to Belgium and *vice versa*. However, other ivory was imported directly to Germany, France, the USA and elsewhere, and it is likely that the overall trade was in the region of 1,000 tonnes(2,205,000lb) at the beginning of the twentieth century. The trade declined sharply during the First World War, with British imports virtually ceasing, and it was slow to pick up again thereafter.

A study conducted in 1971 by Ian Parker of Customs export data from the three major East African ivory-producing countries (Kenya, Uganda and Tanganyika/now Tanzania) showed exports rising from 100 tonnes(220,500lb) in 1925 to 600 tonnes(1,323,000lb) in 1960. In 1979, Ian Parker undertook a more extensive analysis of Customs statistics from 1950 onwards, combining those of importing countries with those of the exporting countries to enable an estimation of the world trade. This was later revised and extended to include data up until 1989. It showed a rising level of trade from 1950 until the early 1980s, followed by a sharp decline towards the end of the decade.

It should be noted that, from 1950 until 1960 when the two sets of statistics over-

lapped, the estimate of world trade was actually lower than the estimate of exports from East Africa. This emphasises that the statistics cannot be relied on to give an exact measure of the total trade in ivory but they may, with cautious interpretation, provide an indication of the overall trends. Other calculations of the trade in the early 1980s put the total at around 1,500 tonnes(3,307,500lb) but these were probably excessive, having counted some of the ivory twice.

The growing affluence of Europe in the late Victorian era undoubtedly fuelled a demand for ivory as a luxury item, but it also had some more functional uses. At that time, all billiard balls and most piano keys were made of ivory, the latter being hard-wearing and able to absorb moisture from the perspiring fingers of the virtuoso without becoming slippery. The introduction of plastic substitutes and the economic recession in the 1920s cut the demand substantially.

For the reasons underlying the growth in trade in ivory over the next 50 years, it is necessary to look to the East. The ancient ivory craftsmen in China had mostly relied on Asian ivory, imported from as far afield as India. To this was added a certain amount of African ivory re-exported from India. Most of the ivory was channelled through Hong Kong after its rise as a major trading port, and a number of craftsmen settled there. This trend increased after the 1949 Chinese revolution and ivory carvings began to be

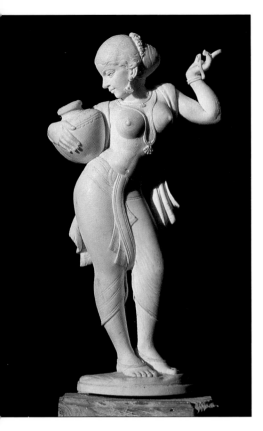

Above: Traditional ivory carving industries have developed in many eastern countries. This figure – 13cm(5in) high – was carved in about 1910 and is from Kerala in southern India.

Below: Tiny figurines like this 19th-century example are typical of the Japanese style of ivory carving. They are called netsuke and are ornamental 'buttons' used in traditional dress.

exported to markets outside China. Japan, too, having been virtually a closed society for centuries, underwent a rapid industrial development and its increasingly affluent population began to buy luxury items. These included carvings from ivory, which Japanese craftsmen had begun to produce, finding ivory a superior medium to wood or stone. By the 1980s, Japan and Hong Kong between them accounted for 80 percent of the world's trade in raw ivory, which totalled over 1,000 tonnes(2,205,000lb) a year. The apparent sudden decline in the late 1980s may have been due to the trade going underground and therefore unreported.

Controlling the ivory trade

So much for the ivory; what about the elephant? In this chapter we have so far regarded ivory as an industrial raw material subject to international trade and, indeed, this is probably how the traders regarded it. There was little consideration given to what level of offtake the wild populations of elephants could stand, principally because this was not a commercially important factor. Although some populations, such as those in West Africa, had been depleted, there were plenty of other sources that could be exploited. Most of the conservation laws in Africa derived from European game laws and were not very effective in controlling international trade in wildlife products.

The environmental consciousness of the 1970s brought an awareness that wildlife populations of the developing countries in Africa, Asia and South America were being depleted to supply luxury products in the developed world. These countries protested that they did not have the resources to devote to controlling the trade and that it was the consumer demand in the rich countries that was the cause of the problem. This led to the drawing up of the Convention on International Trade in Endangered Species of Wild Fauna and Flora (CITES) in Washington in 1973. Once enough countries had ratified the Convention, it came into force in 1975 but, surprisingly, the African elephant was not originally included in the list of protected species. It was only at the instigation of Ghana in 1976 that trade in its local population was controlled, and the species as a whole was not added to the list until 1977.

CITES, also known as the 'Washington Convention', is now the most widely recognized of all international conservation measures, and has been accepted by 110 countries. It establishes one list of species threatened with extinction (Appendix I) that may not be traded internationally for commercial purposes, and another (Appendix II) in which trade is allowed provided that certain conditions have been met and export permits have been duly issued. It does not seek to ban trade in Appendix II species, but merely to ensure that the trade is 'not detrimental to the survival of the species' in the wild. Why, then, did the level of the ivory trade continue to rise from 1977 until 1986, and the population of elephants to fall?

The story is one of repeated, and increasingly cunning, attempts to evade the controls, as exemplified by the trade with Hong Kong. As a Dependent Territory of the UK, Hong Kong has been implementing CITES since 1976; however, during the late 1970s, a large percentage of its ivory came from Burundi, a country that has no elephants. Burundi was issuing export documents that fulfilled the CITES requirements, as far as the authorities who were controlling the imports were concerned. In 1980, however, the Hong Kong Government decided to discontinue allowing imports from Burundi, with the result that the trade shifted to other African countries, notably the Congo (now called Zaire) and the Sudan.

In the same year, Japan joined CITES and immediately Hong Kong's imports from Japan rocketed from virtually nothing in 1979 to 132 tonnes(291,060lb) in 1983. The reason for this was that Japan's import controls were far less strict than those of Hong Kong, and the dealers discovered that, whereas ivory of dubious origin could no longer be imported direct from Africa to Hong Kong, it was allowed into Japan, where it could be issued with re-export certificates that were then acceptable to the Hong Kong authorities.

The focus of enforcement attention shifted to Japan, whose gross imports of raw ivory had risen from 300 tonnes(661,500lb) in 1982 to 500 tonnes(1,102,500lb) in 1984. As a result of international concern, Japan tightened up its import controls in 1985 and officials demanded to see full CITES export documents before any ivory was allowed into the country. Its imports fell sharply to 100 tonnes(220,500lb) in 1986. It can be seen that, as each successive loophole was closed off, the traders found another, and maintained the total annual volume of trade at a level of around 1,000 tonnes(2,205,000lb). CITES was having no effect in stemming the amount of ivory coming out of Africa, and elephant populations continued to decline.

In 1985, the biennial meeting of the Conference of the Parties to CITES took place in Argentina, and delegates agreed to adopt some unprecedented measures to attempt to control the trade. Each tusk coming out of Africa was to have a unique serial number stamped on it, which would be recorded on the export permit, and its progress across the globe tracked on a computer based in the UK. Furthermore, all African countries wishing to export ivory had to apply for a quota at the beginning of the year and were not allowed to export a greater number of tusks than this agreed amount.

The first loophole concerned stockpiles of ivory that were held in numerous countries: these could be registered before a deadline at the end of 1986 and subsequently legally exported. There was a predictable rush to do so. Stockpiles of 51 tonnes(112,455lb) were registered in Somalia, 89 tonnes (196,245lb) in Burundi, 22 tonnes (48,510lb) in Macau, 53 tonnes (116,865lb) in Japan, 178 tonnes (392,490lb) in Hong Kong and a gigantic

Left: A large selection of tusks recovered from poachers and dead elephants being sorted at Tsavo East National Park, Kenya.

Below: Belgian and British Customs import records show a large trade in the late 19th century, collapsing at the outbreak of the First World War. Exports from East Africa (Kenya, Uganda and Tanganyika) grew in the mid-20th century. A compilation of many recent Customs statistics shows the effects of growing affluence, followed by the imposition of CITES controls and the reduction in trade.

International trade in raw ivory

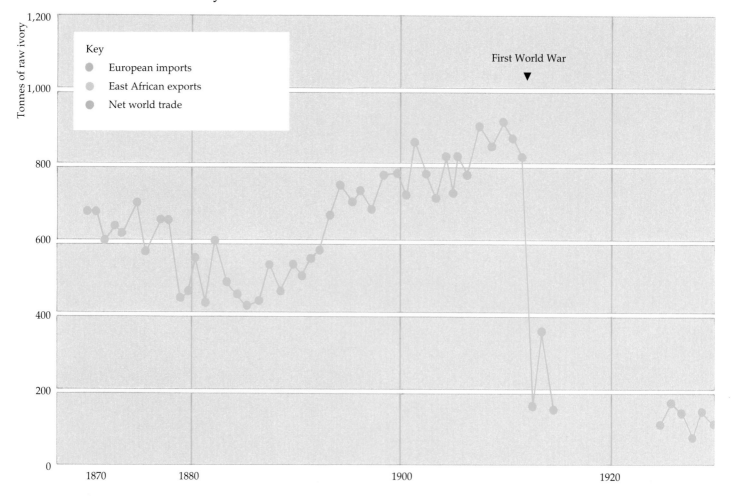

297 tonnes (654,885lb) in Singapore. The latter had been hurriedly bundled into the country, which had at that stage not joined CITES, by Chinese traders who wished to legalize their stocks of dubiously acquired ivory before the deadline. By so doing, the value of their ivory increased enormously and a small number of unscrupulous traders made a fortune.

Further problems were apparent in the African range states, which, under the system, were allowed to apply for quotas to export not only the ivory from elephants legally shot in their countries but also any ivory that had been confiscated from poachers. The ivory authorized under the CITES quota system thus contained a small percentage of legally obtained tusks and a larger percentage from poached elephants. In spite of the many loopholes available for this trade to continue, the reported volume of international trade in raw ivory fell in 1987 and 1988. But had the actual volume of trade fallen?

One further substantial loophole concerned the trade in worked ivory, which was not controlled so strictly under the system. In particular, Hong Kong had no controls over the import of worked ivory and it was merely necessary for the main traders to set up carving factories outside the territory and to fashion the ivory roughly into blanks for later carving,

whereafter they were allowed to be imported freely as worked ivory. During the late 1980s, offshore carving facilities were established in Macau, Singapore, Taiwan and the United Arab Emirates. In this way, large quantities of ivory were laundered into legal circulation until, in mid-1988, Hong Kong introduced a number of measures to control the import of worked ivory.

It was therefore widely believed that the apparent fall in volume of trade in raw ivory did not reflect a reduction in the number of elephants that were being killed to supply the ivory trade, and that the trade was not being fully recorded in the official statistics. As a result, there was a widespread move to ban all trade in ivory by transferring the African elephant to Appendix I of CITES. This measure was proposed by seven governments at the CITES Conference held in Lausanne, Switzerland in late 1989. It was vigorously contested by a consortium of southern African countries whose elephant populations were stable or increasing and who wished to continue to derive economic benefit from them by exporting the ivory. After ten days of heated debate, the proposal was approved and the ivory trade banned.

It is a legitimate concern that, because the partial ban on the ivory trade had been so signally ineffective, the complete ban might likewise be expected to fail.

After all, the rhinoceroses had theoretically received the full protection of CITES since 1975, and yet their populations continued to plummet throughout most of their former range to supply an international demand for their horns. Whereas Hong Kong has undoubtedly played a pivotal role in the ivory trade in recent years, it does not provide the end market. It has merely been an importer and processor of the raw material, re-exporting the finished ivory carvings to markets in Japan, North America and Europe. In these countries, import controls are fairly strict but, more importantly, massive media campaigns have resulted in a public rejection of ivory. Retailers now report that their customers no longer want to buy ivory products, even where legitimate old stocks are available. Even the use of ivory for piano keys – previously thought to be functionally important as opposed to the other, more decorative uses of ivory – has now ceased, the remaining piano manufacturers in Europe and Japan having agreed to use plastic substitutes on all their instruments. As a result, world prices of ivory appear to have fallen, and ivory merchants in Hong Kong have been unable to liquidate their stockpiles, even though they successfully lobbied the British Government for a six-month extension to continue trading.

The saga of the conflicting arguments

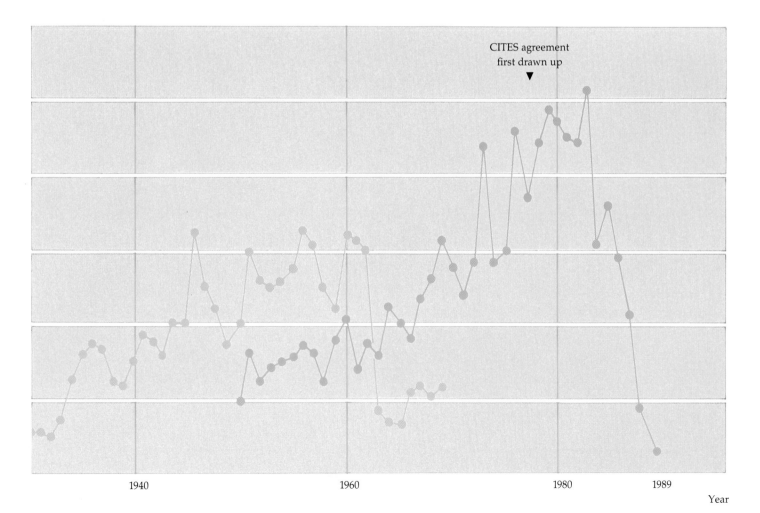

CITES agreement
first drawn up
▼

1940   1960   1980   1989

Year

over the best way of conserving elephants rumbles on and, in mid-1991, South Africa submitted a proposal to re-open trade in its ivory by transferring its population of elephants back to Appendix II of CITES. The outcome of this proposal will not be known until it is discussed by the full Conference of the Parties to CITES, which will be held in Japan in early 1992.

Ivory prices

As would be expected of a luxury item, ivory has always commanded high prices. In 1988, it was worth over US$200 a kilogram in Japan. It is possible to learn much of the fluctuations in price from studying the Customs statistics of the two principal importing countries, Japan and Hong Kong. Obviously, the actual value per kilogram was lower in earlier years but, even when allowance is made for inflation (in the graph on this page the prices have been recalculated to be equivalent to 1988 prices), it can be seen that the real price of ivory rose sharply from the late 1960s onwards. This indicates that the demand in the Far East was increasing faster than the supply. It can be seen that the price in Hong Kong was consistently lower than that in Japan (about half). This is not simply because the Hong Kong Chinese drive a harder bargain, but more because Japanese traders tend to buy larger tusks, which cost more per unit weight. Although many of the carvings made in Japan are of similar size to those made in Hong Kong, there is less wastage from larger tusks, and the fact that the Japanese can afford to pay more is a reflection of the higher retail price of the products in the Japanese market.

The short-term fluctuations in the price are probably attributable to the introduction of controls on international trade. The early peak in 1973 may correspond to the signing of the CITES Convention in Washington and reflects fears about future restrictions rather than actual controls. In 1977, Hong Kong started to implement CITES and this may be responsible for the next peak. The price then rose once more from 1985 onwards as the controls were successively improved.

Of course, the price of ivory in Africa has been very much lower than was seen in the importing countries. Field work suggested that ivory was fetching only about US$50-80 a kilogram in 1987-8 in Zaire, the big profits being retained by the middlemen, who then shipped the ivory to Japan and Hong Kong. Only in Zimbabwe and South Africa were the traders having to pay the real market price for ivory, because the sales were being carried out under strict government control.

The immediate effect of the ban on international trade in ivory imposed in 1989 seems to have been a sharp reduc-

The price of raw ivory

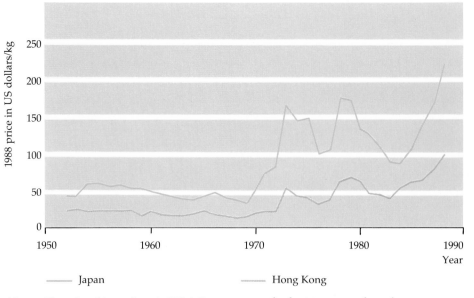

Above: *The price of ivory (here in US dollars adjusted to 1988 values) has increased in real terms since the 1960s. Japan buys larger tusks than the Hong Kong dealers and is prepared to pay proportionately more for them.*

tion in price. Scant evidence from Zaire suggests that ivory is difficult to sell at US$20 a kilogram and the international market appears to have collapsed. This may be because most of the traders in Hong Kong have large stockpiles, which they fear they will be unable to sell. With other commodities, the usual effect of a ban on trade is an increase in price, provided a black market exists. In the short-term it appears that the demand has been cut, although it is too early to say whether the demand for ivory, and therefore the price, will build up again in future.

The ivory trade – the reason for elephant population declines?

Elephant populations have declined throughout much of Africa and ivory trading has undoubtedly increased over the same period, but this fact alone does not explain whether it is the cause or the symptom of the problem. It has been argued that elephant populations will inevitably decline, whether or not their ivory is traded, simply because the expanding human population demands greater area of land for agriculture and thus comes into conflict with the elephants (see the sections on *Ecology* and *Conservation*). The ivory trade could be a by-product of the competition between humans and elephants for land.

Recent research has attempted to relate what is known about the volume of ivory traded to the size of remaining elephant populations. When elephants are abundant, hunters tend to select large males because they produce the largest tusks. However, as these are removed from the population, the average age, and therefore the size of tusks available, declines. An analysis of the size of tusks in trade

over the last ten years has shown a mean weight of around 5kg(11lb), with large numbers in the 1-5kg(2.2-11lb) range and very few in the larger sizes. This is what would be expected if hunters were shooting all the animals available in an already depleted population. Furthermore, this tusk size distribution can be used to calculate the number of elephants that must have been killed to supply the total weight of ivory in trade over the last ten years.

It can be shown that the observed declines in elephant population are attributable to hunting at a rate of about 12-13 percent of the remaining animals per year, and that this almost entirely accounts for the size of the trade. From 1979 until 1986, there was a slight overall decline in the level of trade, which is thought to be due to a decreasing number of elephants in the wild rather than to any reduction in the poaching pressure or any increase in the anti-poaching measures. Under natural conditions, elephant populations are not capable of breeding at a rate sufficient to compensate for this level of mortality, and if hunting continued at this rate, it was predicted that the population would crash.

The volume of trade reported fell still further from 1987 to 1989 but, as explained above, it is thought that this may have been a result of the trade having gone underground and unreported, rather than any true reduction in the number of elephants being killed.

What does the future hold?

Many conservationists, having successfully lobbied to have the international trade in ivory banned, now feel that their task is over and that the future of the elephant is secure. There are a number of reasons why this belief may be misplaced. It is far from certain that banning the trade will prevent it and, although preliminary indications are that the trade has, indeed, declined since the transfer of the African elephant to Appendix I, it may well re-emerge in future. The current effectiveness of the ban seems to be at least partly due to a change in consumer preference in the former markets for ivory. However, the traders have shown themselves adept at seeking new trade routes in the past, and they may be able to develop new markets in other countries in the future. If markets can be found in countries without widespread public conservation ethics, it may prove impossible to prevent ivory from being sold there even if the international trade is theoretically banned.

Furthermore, some have argued that preventing trade in ivory may prove to be an exceptionally bad way of preserving elephants, and may even hasten their demise. The reason for this apparent paradox lies in the interaction between farmers and elephants. Elephants do not coexist easily with agriculture: on the one hand, they tend to damage crops and are persecuted as a result; and, on the other, they require large tracts of natural habitat, which is being destroyed throughout Africa at an increasing rate for conversion to agricultural land. Arguments about the need to preserve elephants for their intrinsic value carry little weight in a rural population faced with widespread famine, or in the corridors of a Ministry of Foreign Trade charged with boosting the production of export crops. Forcing an unwilling populace to refrain from killing elephants requires not only extensive anti-poaching measures, but also considerable political will.

Under these circumstances, the elephants will continue to decline even if there is no international market for ivory. If the people perceive that it is in their best personal interests to preserve elephants, however, then they will do so without coercion. This can be achieved by allowing the local people to benefit financially from elephants in such a way that they derive more income than they would do if the same land was converted for agricultural use.

One country in which elephants generate a great deal of income is Zimbabwe.

There, they are shot on a commercial basis for their tusks, meat and skin, the latter being almost as valuable as the ivory which is sold in Government auctions. They also form the most important component of a large trophy hunting industry in which foreign clients pay exorbitant sums to come to the country to shoot big game, taking the trophies home to hang on their walls. Distasteful though this may seem, it generates a larger amount of income from marginal lands than can be produced by conventional agriculture and it provides a potent argument to prevent landowners replacing wildlife with cattle. A major programme is under way in the country to find ways of bringing this financial benefit to the inhabitants of traditional tribal lands as well as to the large landowners who have already discovered the benefits for themselves.

Another economic benefit of elephants, though less obvious, may be of even more value than the consumptive uses practised in Zimbabwe. Many African countries have large tourist industries that attract visitors from overseas and, with them, foreign exchange. It is difficult to determine why tourists choose to visit a particular country but in Africa one of the chief attractions is the possibility of seeing wild animals, elephants being top of the list. If all the elephants were killed, it is to be feared that many tourists would go elsewhere; or, to look at it another way, preserving elephants is worth a proportion of the overall tourist budget to the exchequer. In Kenya, it has been calculated that elephants are worth US$25 million a year to the tourist industry. Although this argument is obviously not lost on the Government, which has recently devoted considerable resources to anti-poaching measures, it is more difficult to ensure that the financial benefits go to the people who have to put up with the elephants on their land and who might otherwise be tempted to shoot them. However, if the income can be channelled in this way, then the anti-poaching expenditure can be reduced.

Above: Hong Kong is not only the 'shop window' but also the centre of the world ivory trade, importing raw tusks and exporting the carved products all over the world.

In order to be effective as an argument for halting agricultural conversion, it has to be demonstrated that wildlife is more valuable than the alternative forms of land use. Conventional agriculture is usually bolstered by numerous hidden subsidies, and the quantification of its financial benefits is routine. The new science of evaluating the wildlife resources therefore faces an uphill battle, and it is necessary to consider all possible forms of economic use to maximize the total value. Returns from tourism, trophy hunting and the sale of products such as ivory and leather may have to be summed in order to produce a total which exceeds that of agricultural land use. It has been argued that the loss of an international market for ivory would fatally undermine the economic basis for elephant conservation.

Conducting anti-poaching measures is expensive – as much as US$200/km^2 a year – and few African governments are able or willing to support this level of expenditure. One of the chief reasons is that they have been receiving only a very small percentage of the total value of the ivory of the elephants killed within their country. Although the final sale price of ivory in Japan may have been as high as US$200/kg, most of this profit has been taken by foreign traders, with very little returning to the producer country. Only in Zimbabwe is a reasonable price paid for ivory, and it is no coincidence that Zimbabwe is one of the few countries to support an effective anti-poaching campaign. If the ivory trade is to start once more, it would be essential to redress this balance in other African countries. One reason why they may have been reluctant

Left: The growth of the market for ivory objets d'art has resulted in the training of many craftsmen around the world. This carver works in a factory in Thailand and depends on ivory for his livelihood. Thai carving traditionally used Asian elephant ivory, but recently large quantities of African ivory have been imported.

to do so in the past is that they fear international condemnation if they are seen to profit from killing elephants, and prefer instead to accept a lower price and to have the killing done by proxy – illegally by poachers.

The elevation of the African elephant to Appendix I of CITES has predictably been opposed by the ivory carvers, many of whom fear not only that they will lose their livelihood but also that an ancient traditional skill will die out. This has caused a resurgence of interest in other materials for carving, such as mammoth, hippo and walrus ivory, but, apart from being functionally inferior, they can never be available in the same volume as elephant ivory.

The fact that the trade would collapse if the elephant were to be hunted to extinction is not lost on the carvers, but is of less impact because its effects are more remote. However, one country, South Africa, has already proposed that its population of elephants be retransferred to Appendix II and it is anticipated that in future attempts will be made also by those charged with conserving elephant populations in other countries to reopen a legal trade in ivory as a means of ensuring that elephants finance their own protection. Under the current regime, with the species on Appendix I of CITES, the only legitimate economic activities are tourism, trophy hunting and domestic sales of meat and ivory. The lucrative exports of ivory and hides are prohibited, and funds for elephant protection must be augmented by public donation or by government expenditure prompted by public concern. It remains to be seen whether this will be sufficient to prevent the elephant populations from continuing to decline. (This theme is further explored in *Conservation*, page 172.)

Furthermore, even if poaching were to stop tomorrow, ivory would still be produced by elephants. Indeed, because ivory continues to grow throughout the life of the elephant, unlike almost all other bodily organs, it has been calculated that the best harvesting strategy for producing the maximum amount of ivory in a given period is to collect the ivory from elephants that die naturally. If such 'found ivory' is added to that which inevitably will be confiscated from poachers and smugglers, large stockpiles will accumulate without any trade outlets. Are these to be burnt? Kenya has set a precedent with a large ivory bonfire in 1989, but it remains to be seen whether any other African governments will be prepared to follow suit.

Right: These poachers risk their lives for the small percentage of the final price of ivory that they receive for their activities. Will banning the international trade bring the price of ivory down sufficiently to make it not worth their while to continue poaching?

CONSERVATION

Park staff feed baby elephants at the elephant orphanage in the Nairobi National Park, Kenya. Young elephants need specially constituted milk as they cannot digest the fat in cow's milk. They would normally rely on their mother's milk for about two years

The future of elephants is threatened by a variety of factors. In Asia, loss of habitat to human settlements is the greatest threat to elephants. Formerly extensive habitats become fragmented, splitting elephant populations into small ones that face a bleak future. In Africa, the rush for ivory has greatly reduced many elephant populations. Certain African countries, such as Kenya, have some of the world's highest human population growth rates. With the compression of elephants into smaller areas, usually protected reserves, the damage to vegetation becomes very obvious. With so many different problems faced by elephants in the two continents, how can their long-term survival be ensured? Obviously solutions may differ for each continent, country and population. The cultural association between elephants and people in Asia, for instance, will have to be taken into consideration in any management plan. Nevertheless, certain basic principles would apply for conserving many elephant populations.

Elephants need a lot of resources and space. Seasonal movements of herds are a striking feature in most elephant populations. An elephant clan may need anywhere from a few hundred to a few thousand square kilometres of habitat as its home range. Unfortunately, this is no longer available to them in many regions, especially in Asian countries. River valleys have been brought under the plough, large dams and canals straddle their former migration routes, entire hills have been stripped for their mineral ores, even roads and railway lines obstruct the elephants' passage.

Schemes to protect the habitat for elephant populations

Corridors linking habitats that would otherwise remain separated become important in such situations. There can be no hard and fast rule in designing corridors. The main thing is to ensure that elephants will use them and that they will not spill over into adjacent human settlements. The viability of corridors naturally depends on the distance separating the two populations. If the distances are relatively small, say less than 5km(3 miles) then the corridor need not be very broad. A corridor about 1km(1,100yd) wide would suffice to see the elephants through. On the other hand, if the distances are considerably more the width of the corridor has to be about 4km(2.5 miles). A corridor need not even be very good habitat. It can be degraded vegetation, for example, or a monoculture plantation that provides some cover for the migrating elephants.

Sometimes a corridor may be simply a bridge across an irrigation canal that cannot otherwise be traversed by elephants. Such a bridge has to be reasonably broad if herds are to use it; only bulls are bold enough to cross narrow bridges. An example of a system of protected areas connected by corridors can be found in

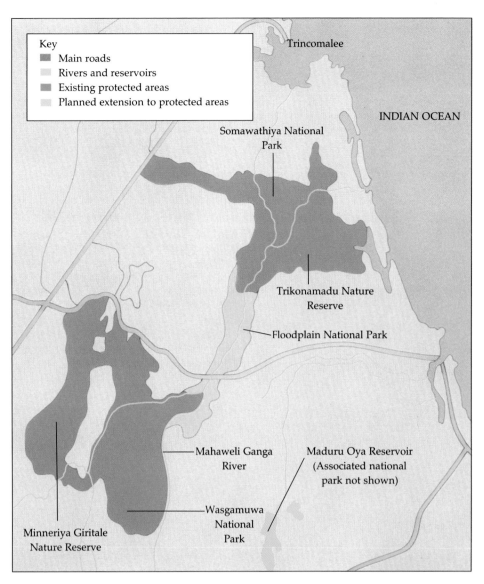

Key
- Main roads
- Rivers and reservoirs
- Existing protected areas
- Planned extension to protected areas

Trincomalee

INDIAN OCEAN

Somawathiya National Park

Trikonamadu Nature Reserve

Floodplain National Park

Mahaweli Ganga River

Maduru Oya Reservoir (Associated national park not shown)

Wasgamuwa National Park

Minneriya Giritale Nature Reserve

Above: *The map shows part of the Mahaweli River Basin in eastern Sri Lanka. A series of dams is planned for the area, followed by agricultural expansion. To help the movement of elephants and other animals, a network of protected areas connected by corridors is being set up – an example of management in action.*

Below:*An elephant herd approaching the reservoir in Periyar Tiger Reserve, India. Although the Periyar Reservoir has not disrupted the movement of elephants, many other dams and canals in India have cut off traditional migration routes, intensifying the conflict between elephants and human interests.*

the Mahaweli Basin of Sri Lanka. Without the corridors, the series of dams and agricultural expansions under the Mahaweli Development Project can be expected to fragment the habitat for elephants. To ensure that elephants can move freely between the surviving habitats, a system of corridors has been designed linking a number of national parks and nature reserves. The network is certainly not perfect – all protected areas in the basin are not connected – but at least the need for habitat contiguity has been recognized.

The area of a complex of reserves for elephant conservation should be large enough to support a viable population. This would also depend on the carrying capacity of the habitat. For instance, if each elephant needs 5km^2(2 miles^2) area and a viable population is 1,000 elephants for long-term conservation, a total contiguous area of 5,000km^2(1,950 miles^2)

should be set aside. The carrying capacity of rain forests may be much lower, about one elephant for every 20km^2(8 miles^2), and thus much larger areas would be needed for ensuring the long-term survival of elephants.

Apart from ensuring that large areas are set apart for conserving elephants, attention must also be paid to the quality of habitat in conservation areas. Elephants are highly adaptable creatures. They can survive in a variety of habitats – grasslands, scrubland, dry forest, rain forest, montane forest. They are most comfortable, however, where this entire range of diversity is available. They can then select the most suitable habitat according to the season and circumstances. When the grasslands are lush with new growth during the rains, the elephants congregate there in large numbers. When the grasses become dry, the

elephants turn to more palatable forage from trees and shrubs. When fires sweep through the grasslands or deciduous forests during the dry season, they seek refuge in forests bordering rivers and lakes or in moist forests that do not burn.

Strategies for maintaining viable populations

All species change as they adapt to changes in their environment, or become extinct if they are unable to cope with change. If we are to maintain the evolu-

Right: This canal leading from a reservoir to a power house in the Anamalai Hills of southern India has proved to be an impediment to elephants. Some elephants have been trapped and have drowned here. Bridges built across such canals and irrigation channels would need to be fairly wide and robust to encourage herds of elephants to cross over.

tionary process we have first to ensure that a species does not disappear before it can adapt to change. Our immediate concern in conservation is usually to prevent extinction over a relatively short period of time, say the next one or two centuries. A small population is highly vulnerable to extinction purely due to bad luck. For a species population there is a critical size below which it is more or less doomed to extinction within a certain time period. The goal, therefore, should be to maintain the size of a population at a level that safeguards it from extinction in the short term. It is impossible to be 100 percent certain that a population, whatever its size, will survive. Therefore, one usually talks in probabilistic terms; the minimum viable population is that which has a 95 percent (or 99 percent) chance of surviving for 100 (or 200 or 500) years.

To determine the minimum viable population, one has to consider the demography and genetic structure of the population, fluctuations in climate and other environmental factors and the probability of a catastrophe. Some of these calculations can be theoretically modelled using computers. For elephants, a population of over 100 individuals is reasonably well buffered against extinction for a century due to chance fluctuations in births and deaths. Such a population is also safe from the genetic problems associated with inbreeding (related individuals will tend to mate in small populations). However, even a population of 100 elephants will continue to lose its genetic variation over the years. How the lack of genetic variation would adversely affect a population is still a controversial matter. It is generally agreed that such populations would not be able to cope with a changing environment and thus would lose their evolutionary potential. From a theoretical viewpoint it has been suggested that a population of 500 breeding individuals is necessary to halt genetic erosion. This would translate into a total population of over 1,000 individual elephants, because less than half the population would be adults capable of breeding. Such a large population would also ensure a measure of safety against epidemics and catastrophes.

What, then, is the prospect for small populations? Should one write them off completely? Fortunately, there are now options available for managing and conserving small populations. If a large

Left: A tranquilized elephant is being loaded onto a trunk with the help of trained captive elephants in Sri Lanka. This elephant is part of a small isolated population being captured and translocated to a more viable habitat. Where the movement of an entire isolated population is not feasible, another strategy is to exchange sexually mature bulls between populations to introduce genetic variety. This is less complicated than moving female elephants.

enough area is available for this population, one option would be to manipulate the habitat so as to increase its carrying capacity for elephants. This may include maintaining some secondary growth forest (which is preferred by elephants) or creating waterholes to sustain them through the dry season.

If the habitat is insufficient or if it is doomed to be replaced with sugar cane or other crops, the best course is to translocate the few elephants to a more secure habitat. An excellent example of this kind of management can be seen in Peninsular Malaysia. Many elephant herds here are isolated in forest patches and in conflict with commercial plantations of oil palm and rubber. The first capture of elephants took place in 1974. Since then the technique of capture by chemical immobilization has been perfected. About 150 elephants have been translocated so far to more viable habitats.

If wholesale translocation of a herd to another area is not feasible, small populations can be managed through exchange of individuals between populations in order to maintain genetic variation. In theory the 'migration' and breeding of even one individual per generation (about 15-20 years) is sufficient to halt the erosion of genetic variation in a small population. To take care of unpredictable events, in practice it would be wise to translocate a few individuals every generation. As male elephants naturally disperse from their families when they mature sexually, the easiest option would be for populations to exchange bulls. If females are translocated it may be necessary to move entire families so that the social bonding crucial to their survival is not disrupted.

In order to manage small populations successfully through exchange of individuals between them, it is important to obtain genetic profiles of elephant populations. Such information is not yet available. Research on elephant genetics can begin with the large numbers of captive elephants whose origins are known.

Strategies for managing over-abundant populations

While many Asian elephant populations face the problem of too few individuals, many African elephant populations face the problem of too many, at least on a localized scale. The problem of destruction of woodland and its conversion to grassland by over-abundant elephant populations is well known. Uganda, Kenya, Tanzania, Zambia, Zimbabwe and South Africa are some of the countries that have faced this problem and have tackled it in different ways. With the exception of Kenya and Tanzania, these countries have experimented with culling elephants in a big way since the 1960s. The tide of ivory poaching during the 1970s and 1980s

Above: Elephants being shot by skilled professionals in Zimbabwe to keep the elephant populations in various parks below arbitrarily determined carrying capacity levels. The issue of whether or not to cull elephants has been fiercely debated in Africa.

Left: Culled elephants in Zimbabwe being examined by the team. All elephants in a herd are dropped within a minute or two to minimize trauma and prevent them communicating distress to other herds in the same area.

largely obliterated the need for any further legal culling in many African countries. Zimbabwe and South Africa are two exceptions that still continue to have organized culling programmes.

When the fierce debate over whether or not to cull elephants erupted in East Africa during the 1960s, Kenya deliberately chose to let nature take its course. Some elephants had been culled in the Tsavo National Park but this was stopped. Then came the drought of 1970-71, when about 6,000 out of 20,000 elephants in Tsavo died of starvation. There was widespread criticism of Kenya's handling of the situation. Many felt that Tsavo's elephant population could have been trimmed by humane culling rather than let the elephants die a painful death. Nevertheless, Kenya stuck to its hands-off policy. One of the first instances of cropping an elephant population for reasons of preventing damage to habitat was in Uganda's Murchison Falls National Park. About 2,000 elephants were killed between 1965 and 1967. This was carried out by professional teams that shot down entire elephant families in order to prevent any survivors with traumatic memories of the event. All members of a family were usually shot within a two-minute time span. On the other hand, many elephants that the Ugandan Game Department attempted to kill as part of their control measures escaped with wounds. Political events in Uganda subsequently overwhelmed any

rational management plans that had been made. During the infamous rule of Idi Amin and the civil war in the wake of his overthrow, Uganda's elephant population crashed by 90 percent.

Zambia organized a major elephant cull between 1965 and 1969 in the Luangwa Valley. Combined with the cull was a scheme for processing elephant meat in an abattoir built specially for this purpose. Elephants were shot with darts containing succinyl-choline chloride, a drug that kills by paralyzing the respiratory muscles. Carcasses were transported to the abattoir for hygienic processing of the meat. The drug used breaks down upon heating and thus the meat is safe for human consumption. After less than 1,500 elephants were culled in this way, the operations were stopped due to a campaign of protests made by conservationists.

Most of South Africa's elephants are in the Kruger National Park to the northeast along the border with Mozambique. At the turn of the century there were very few elephants in this region. Subsequent immigration from Mozambique and Zimbabwe, combined with natural growth, increased the population to about 8,000 elephants by the 1960s. This was perceived as a threat to the vegetation and other fauna. A decision was made to keep the population level at 7,000-7,500, which was believed to be the carrying capacity of the 19,485km^2(7,500 miles^2) park. Culling began in 1968 and continues regularly

on the basis of results from annual aerial censuses of the population. From a helicopter the elephants are darted with a massive dose of succinyl-choline chloride. Ground teams located nearby are alerted about the darted animals. They quickly move in and shoot them in the brain. The carcasses are removed to an abattoir for processing. The meat is shared among local staff or sold to shops in the park's vicinity. Tusks are auctioned, and skin is sold to tanneries for making leather goods. Feet, tail and tail hair are sold to curio manufacturers. All this generates revenue for the park. Bulls carrying large tusks are usually spared because they are a special tourist attraction, and the young elephant calves are captured for sale.

Zimbabwe is another example of a country that manages its elephant population through culling and where the species is not currently endangered. The elephant population has increased from an estimated 5,000 in 1900 to about 57,000 at present. This country decided to cull even in areas where there was no percep-

Below: Meat from culled elephants hangs out to dry in Zimbabwe. This is made available to local villagers, and various other products, such as the hide and ivory, are sold to generate revenue for the local economy and to fund the conservation and management programmes. Strict anti-poaching laws are in operation to ensure that the benefits of the elephant culling programme go to the local people.

tible damage to vegetation from elephants. The population level in the cull areas are determined rather arbitrarily. Regions where elephants have been culled include the Wankie (now Hwange), Chizarira and Matusadona national parks, the Sengwa, Chirisa and Gonarezhou reserves, and the Sebungwe region. There are some important differences in the way Zimbabwe's culling programme operates as compared to South

Below: Bull elephants reach out with their trunks into a water tank in the Galana ranch in Kenya. Shortage of water during droughts often forces elephants to seek this precious fluid from human settlements. They are even known to break taps and pipelines to obtain water. Even outside drought periods, human settlements in elephant country are at risk from their incursion in search of food and water.

Africa's. Isolated elephant herds are located and quickly shot by skilled professionals. This minimizes the transmission of trauma to neighbouring elephants. There is a distinct possibility that elephants communicate distress to other elephants through infrasonic vocalization (very low-frequency sounds).

Asian elephant populations have also been culled through the centuries in a different way, by being captured for domestication. The method of driving entire herds into stockades has had a similar effect of keeping wild populations in check. During the past century alone about 100,000 elephants have been captured in Asia, and perhaps a few million since the species was first tamed some 4,000 years ago. In many countries the capture of elephants has been officially banned, except under special circum-

stances. There has been no serious problem of damage to vegetation as in African countries, but it is conceivable that such a situation could arise in future in some regions of high elephant density. The dilemma of whether or not to cull would be as great as it has been in Africa. Religious sentiments in countries such as India, Sri Lanka or Thailand would strongly oppose the outright killing of elephants. Capturing them for domestication would be more acceptable. However, tame elephants are losing their importance in many Asian countries and this would create a fresh dilemma over what to do with captured elephants.

Managing elephant populations in conflict with people

In the words of ecologist Norman Myers, conservation in developing countries has

to sustain not only the spirit but also the stomach. In a world with rapidly changing social values, particularly in the direction of a highly materialistic culture, it would be unrealistic to expect the poorer sections of society to pay the entire price for conservation. One can hardly expect a farmer whose whole food supply for the year has been destroyed by elephants to be an ardent supporter of their protection. Elephants also sometimes kill people, often during their nocturnal incursions into human settlements, and this creates considerable resentment towards them. It is therefore essential that the impact of elephants on people be minimized if conservation is to receive local support. This is easier said than done. The crux of the problem lies in finding cheap methods of keeping elephants away from human settlements. Trenches and high-voltage electric fences along the forest-settlement boundary have been tried in many regions, with varying degrees of success. (The various strategies being used are discussed in a special feature starting on page 166.)

Crop damage can be reduced to a certain extent by persuading farmers to grow crops that yield good economic returns but are not consumed by elephants. However, it is not an easy task to change traditional patterns of agriculture in developing countries. In certain places conflict has to be reduced by capturing, translocating or even shooting elephants. A small isolated herd of elephants in perpetual conflict with people has to be removed. In some Asian countries it may be possible to take them into captivity. In others, such as Malaysia, a decision may be made to capture and translocate them to a more viable habitat. Both traditional methods of capture such as kheddahs or modern methods such as chemical immobilization may be used, depending on the expertise available in a particular country. African countries may choose to shoot the elephants. A decision to cull elephants should be easier to take if these happen to be bulls. Male elephants cause far more damage *per capita* than do female-led herds. Bulls also seem to be responsible for the majority of human killings, particularly within settlements. Eliminating some notorious bulls would be one way of managing the population. This would not adversely affect the population, whose growth would depend more on the number of females in the population. Symbolic culling may also create a more favourable climate among local people for conservation.

KEEPING WILD ELEPHANTS AT BAY

D.K. Lahiri-Choudhury

Elephants and human settlements are generally taken to be incompatible. African elephant conservation policy has been based on this assumption, although of late there has been some rethinking on the subject. In Asia, however, man and elephants have to live together by mutual adjustment. Depredation, therefore, is a way of life in Asia. The problem is not how to stop it altogether, but how to control it. By elephant depredation we mean the damage and destruction caused by wild animals, not aggressiveness by domesticated male elephants in musth.

Elephant depredation has been increasing in recent years. Various reasons have been suggested for this, the chief one being the loss of habitat, leading to increasing man-elephant confrontation. From time immemorial the Asian elephant has been a friend of man; yet wild elephant and human settlements cannot co-exist without some conflict. This was recognized in the *Arthashastra*, an account of Indian political and governmental strategy compiled between about 300 BC and AD 300. (Traditionally, this is attributed to Kautilya, chief minister to Chandragupta, founder of the Mauryan Empire.) At the present time, elephant depredation has become one of the major management problems in many forest areas.

Identifying the problem

The problem of depredation has two major aspects: (a) loss of human life; and (b) loss of property. Loss of property can be further subdivided into three main kinds: (i) loss of a food crop; (ii) loss of a cash crop (oil palm, tea, sugar cane) by trampling or otherwise; (iii) damage to houses and other constructions.

Loss of human life

The annual toll of human life taken by elephants has risen in northern Bengal,

Left: The haunted look in this boy's eyes still remains, even a month after he was picked up and thrown against a fence by a lone tusker emerging from the nearby Buxa Tiger Reserve and entering his village of Noorpur in northern Bengal. Only the fact that the fence was of bamboo and cushioned his fall saved his life.

Right: His father and younger brother were not so fortunate. They were in this straw and bamboo hut when the elephant smashed into it. His mother had just emerged from the hut and saw the male elephant – about 3m(10ft tall) – like a ghostly white shape in the moonlight. She ran for her life and managed to escape.

Below left: An army supply depot in northern Bengal bears the scars of persistent elephant depradation for the last 20 years. The elephants regularly break through 25cm(10in)-thick walls to get at their favourite booty of army rum, flour and other provisions in the building. Keeping them at bay presents many problems.

from about 30 per year in the 1970s to 60 in 1990. Meanwhile, southwestern Bengal has also been badly affected. The human casualty figures for the two halves of Bengal for the years 1987-90 are:

	1987	1988	1989	1990
Northern Bengal	39	58	45	60
Southwestern Bengal	–	11	23	11

In 1989, elephants killed 52 people in Assam. During 1988-89, straying herds killed 24 people in Bihar. Herds of elephants started spreading into Andhra Pradesh from adjoining Tamil Nadu in 1985. Since that time, about 50 people have been killed in Andhra Pradesh. Estimates suggest that 30-50 people are killed by elephants annually in southern India. Loss of habitat may not be the only reason for this, and when planning anti-elephant depredation measures, it is important to examine the problem more analytically.

Field studies indicate that most – but not all – human casualties are caused by adult male elephants. It has been argued that this may be largely attributable to biological reasons, namely, the increased level of testosterone in the animal's blood during musth, when Asian elephants can become very aggressive and unmanageable. Some adult male elephants regularly chase and sometimes kill men and destroy property during their musth period. Thus, there is a predictable cycle in their aggressive behaviour.

There is at present no standard prescription for dealing with such animals, except shooting them as rogues. When periodicity marks such aggressive behaviour of identified animals, experiments can be undertaken to keep them chemically sedated during the musth period; but it has still to be seen how this will affect their breeding behaviour. The culling of adult males has been recommended as an anti-depradation measure. Although all aggressive male elephants are not killers, the aggressive ones will naturally head the list in such a culling programme. Unfortunately, the aggressive individuals are precisely those that are most successful in breeding and passing on their genes. Elimination of such animals might interfere with the process of natural selection, and thus have a long-term deleterious effect on the species. Therefore, one needs to exercise some caution in this regard before recommending the prescription as a general management practice. This means that we are back to square one. The problem of manslaughter by elephants is not as yet amenable to solution except by the elimination of the offending animals.

It is necessary, however, to distinguish between deliberate and accidental manslaughter. Every year quite a few people are killed by elephants in incidents for which the wild animals cannot be held responsible. A common occurrence is that of a local drunk approaching a wild animal to offer worship to 'Ganesh Baba' (the god Ganesh, or Elephant-headed god). Another common type of accident is the pushing over of a hut and the trampling of the people inside by crop-raiding elephants. It is generally agreed, however, that animals that kill men deliberately and without provocation should be eliminated. Despite the vagueness of the phrase 'without provocation', this is perhaps the best that one can do at present.

The situation is further complicated by subadult male animals (generally below 2.1m/7ft in height) turning aggressive towards man. This aggression is behavioural and is unconnected with musth. When subadult male elephants are expelled from the herd, they often become aggressive and become killers. This may be a temporary phase, but we do not know as yet how to deal with such animals, other than to kill them.

Loss of property and crops

Destruction of property is the other aspect of the elephant problem. Analysis of elephant depredation in northern Bengal suggests that before adequate corrective measures are taken, it is necessary to understand the nature of the depredation. Crop raiding is mainly due to the plants being more attractive as food to elephants than wild vegetation, which may be plentiful. Crop plants have a higher food value for elephants, and they may feed on them as a matter of preference. Attempts at driving away unattached males from a crop are more difficult than driving away family groups. Such determined, and often aggressive solitary adult bulls require special treatment; but the compensation paid for actual damage to crops seems to have a

Above: Conflict between elephants and the human population causes problems in both Africa and Asia. Here an elephant explores the grounds of a camp in the Masai Mara Nature Reserve in Kenya, looking for food.

definite correlation with the movement or presence of herds. Further, the damage done by trampling animals in a herd could be much more per head than that caused by the trampling of unattached males; admittedly, though, this is yet to be quantified.

Coming up with solutions

Depredation by family groups or herds is the kind most open to preventive measures. The International Workshop on Management of Elephants in the Wild and in Captivity, held in 1982, devoted a whole session to the demonstration of such measures, many of which have subsequently been incorporated or reported in various publications. In the main, these measures are of two kinds: combat, which deals with elephants actually raiding a crop; and preventive measures, which are designed to prevent elephants from such raiding. Preventive measures can also be divided into two categories: deterrents, i.e. measures such as barriers, which physically prevent elephants from raiding a crop; and repellents such as lights or chemicals, which, though not actual physical barriers, discourage elephants from raiding a crop. Translocation of troublesome animals to 'safer' areas is hardly the solution; experience in Sri Lanka and India has shown that such animals tend to return to the original point of capture.

Combat measures

Among the combative measures used against elephants, powerful car battery-operated spotlights have been found to be very effective, because elephants move away from powerful beams of light, except for some particularly belligerent adult males. Less bright battery-operated torchlights can be dangerous, because elephants sometimes charge at them, perhaps because as crop-raiders they associate such light with the pain from the arrows or guns of the farmers.

Koonkies – domesticated especially trained elephants – are also used to chase away herds in forests, and they were first used in a planned manner in 1980. Koonkies are meant to be used mainly during daytime, but they have also been used sometimes at night, although this is risky because of the danger of attack by large wild bulls.

Experiments with tear-gas were conducted in northern Bengal in 1975, but the evidence was not conclusive. Its worth is dubious because of its dependence on the wind factor. Rockets that end with a bang are effective, particularly with family groups. Crackers and other such devices producing loud bangs are useful until elephants become habituated to them.

Results of controlled experiments with tape-recorded tiger calls have not been conclusive. It seems that there have been no experiments with low- or high-frequency sound waves to deter elephants, and this could be a fruitful line of further experiment.

Preventive measures

The first consideration is to keep elephants away from vulnerable areas; the second is preventing them from entering vulnerable areas. (If these fail then combat measures take over).

The first approach involves changing the human land-use pattern, for example by not planting food crops on the fringe of the elephants' habitat. The human pressure on land being what it is in South and Southeast Asia, the idea looks fine on paper but is rarely practicable. Koonkies play a crucial role here by chasing away wild elephants from forests fringing vulnerable human settlements.

Sometimes elephants use small pockets of forest solely as refuges from which to carry out crop raiding. This can be dealt with by thinning of the forest, to make these pockets non-viable as daytime cover, without any significant loss either to forestry or to the total area of the elephants' home range.

In patchy forest areas in northern Bengal, Madhya Pradesh or western Bihar, elephants moving from one forest area to another can cause serious loss of human life and damage to property. Where such paths are well established, the problem can be contained by removing human settlements away from these corridors, which are often no more than a few hundred metres wide.

Chemical repellents have been used as barriers, but without much effect so far. A multinational chemical company brought out such a repellent in the mid-1970s on an experimental basis, but this did not prove effective in high-rainfall areas such as northeastern India. Experiments with tiger urine, which could be called a form of chemical repellent, have not given conclusive results. Developing chemical repellents is a line of research that seems worth pursuing.

It is also well known that white or glittering objects attract elephants' attention, whereas constructions painted black or dark green enjoy immunity.

Lastly, physical barriers can be used. Many forms have been tried, again with varying degrees of success, including elephant-proof trenches, dry walls of boulders held together with galvanized wire-netting, spikes embedded in concrete slabs, and electrified fences.

Electrified fencing, first used extensively and effectively against elephants in Malaysia, is undoubtedly the cheapest and the most effective form of all physical barriers. Malaysian companies using these fences to safeguard oil-palm and rubber plantations report an 80 percent reduction in elephant depredation. The success or otherwise of the fence depends largely on adherence to proper

Barriers used against elephants

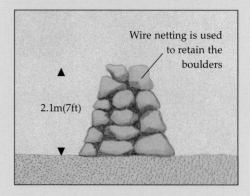

Wire netting is used to retain the boulders

2.1m(7ft)

Above: A dry boulder wall held together with wire mesh provides an effective physical barrier that will keep domestic animals in and wild elephants out. This is a cheap option where suitable boulders are available locally and heavy transport costs are not involved.

design and maintenance. It is not easy to fool elephants. They use their tusks or the soles of their front feet, which are poor conductors of electricity, to break the fence wires. Some elephants even push trees over the fence to break the wires and enter crop fields!

For small areas of permanent vulnerability, such as a tourist complex or forestry department huts in the middle of a forest, permanent physical barriers would seem to be preferable, although they are more expensive. Ditches with non-masonry sides are often useless, particularly in unstable or boggy soil. In hard lateritic soil, however, they can be effective, needing little attention for maintenance. Spikes can be dangerous, for both man and elephants.

The basic idea underlying any experiment in measures to prevent elephant depredation is to try to evolve a *modus vivendi* for man and elephant together. A complete separation of elephant and human habitat is hardly feasible.

Above: High-voltage electrified fences such as this have been quite successful in keeping elephants away from agricultural land. An 'energizer' boosts the current from a 12-volt car battery (which can be charged from the mains or even by a solar panel) to a very high voltage, typically 4,000-5,000 volts. Any animal coming into contact with the fence receives a severe but non-fatal shock in a series of short pulses. One energizer can power 20-50km (12-30 miles) of fencing. These fences are relatively cheap but need careful maintenance.

Left: Forest department elephants waiting to cross the drawbridge over an elephant-proof trench. The recorded history of trenches as barriers against the incursion of elephants goes back to about 315 BC. They are effective but expensive. In wet or unstable soils they must have masonry sides, otherwise they become useless during the rains. Well-built permanent trenches with drawbridges are the best option to protect small vulnerable areas, such as the forest camp featured here.

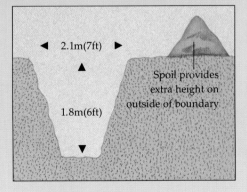

Local plants to disguise stonework

1.8m(6ft)

Above: A variation of the boulder wall with earth infilling. This design requires far less stone and provides the opportunity to create a living hedge that will eventually mask much of the unsightly stonework. It is important to use local plants that will thrive in the conditions.

2.1m(7ft)

Spoil provides extra height on outside of boundary

1.8m(6ft)

Above: A basic design for a deep elephant-proof trench. An elephant cannot stride more than 2.1m(7ft) and so this is the ideal width. Vertical sides are better because they prevent elephants sliding down on their haunches, but they are difficult to maintain in unstable soils.

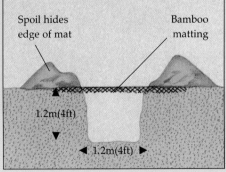

Spoil hides edge of mat

Bamboo matting

1.2m(4ft)

1.2m(4ft)

Above: Shallow trenches covered with a layer of bamboo matting present a psychological rather than a physical barrier. Elephants feeling the mat with their trunks find it unstable and avoid treading on it. They have an instinctive sense about what surface will bear their weight.

Breeding in captivity

Captive elephant populations have historically never been self-sustaining. Chieftains and kings holding elephants in their armies have always had to replenish their stocks with fresh captures from the wild. In more recent times, zoos have generally had a poor record of breeding elephants. Does this mean that captive breeding does not have any place in efforts to save elephants?

The problems with breeding elephants in captivity have been largely sociological. When bulls are in musth and are most likely to mate with cows in oestrus, they are segregated because they are aggressive and do not respond to commands. In most situations captive elephants are kept in surroundings that are a far cry from their natural habitat. Most zoos in western countries do not want to keep bull elephants, because they are difficult to handle and have occasionally killed people.

By contrast, elephants kept under semi-natural conditions, as in many forest camps in India and Burma, have a promising record of breeding. In southern Indian forest camps the captive elephants have regularly bred during this century. The data suggest that these populations could sustain themselves even without any additions from the wild through new captures. Both bulls and cows of all ages are kept together in these forest camps and allowed to mingle. The elephants are also left in the forest during the night so that they can feed. Many of the calves born in captivity are sired by wild bulls that mate with the cows inside the forest. The best record for breeding elephants in zoos seems to be held by the Washington Park Zoo in Portland, USA. Other zoos have not been very successful in captive breeding. Nevertheless, zoos have been important centres for research on reproductive biology in elephants. Modern techniques such as artificial insemination have been tried by some zoos in an attempt to breed elephants, but these have not succeeded so far. Some zoos have plans to create large elephant enclosures that would mimic their natural habitat but such schemes would be very expensive.

Captive breeding certainly has a role in elephant conservation, but this can only be secondary to conserving elephants in the wild. The ecological role of elephants in their natural habitat cannot be duplicated in captivity. There is still plenty of hope for in situ conservation of elephants both in Africa and in Asia. Captive elephants can help their wild relatives through their value in research, educating the public visiting zoos, raising funds for conservation programmes and reinforcing the rich cultural traditions, at least in Asian countries, that would contribute to their conservation.

Right: This famous African elephant, Eleanor, has fostered many orphaned elephants in the Tsavo National Park, Kenya. Raised by David and Daphne Sheldrick from a calf, Eleanor has in turn helped to nurse many orphaned and rejected calves back to full health. Such foster mothers, or allomothers, can make all the difference between life and death for an orphaned calf. (This a theme explored in more detail on page 50 in the chapter on Social Life.) *Here Eleanor waits patiently for a sweet titbit to be unwrapped and offered to her.*

Below: Visitors to the San Diego Zoo in the USA watch a young male Asian elephant, who is clearly interested in the crowd. Zoos can contribute to conservation of elephants through research, public education, fund raising and captive breeding. Most western zoos, however, are reluctant to keep adult bull elephants, which may become aggressive during the musth period and thus difficult to handle.

Fighting the poachers

By far the most important factor contributing to the decline of the African elephant during the past two decades has been poaching for ivory. From an estimated 1,343,340 elephants in 1979 the population fell to less than half this number eight years later. (See page 96 for more information on these population estimates.) Scientists predicted that at this rate the elephant would become virtually extinct in East Africa within five to seven years and perhaps all over the continent in 15 to 20 years. Governments in most countries from Kenya to Zaire were ill-equipped to deal with the large gangs of poachers armed with sophisticated weapons. In some countries there was even a collusion between poachers and the authorities. As ivory prices soared it seemed as though the battle to save the elephant was already lost.

Following the unprecedented international concern over the plight of the African elephant, a number of steps were taken to stem the flow of illegal ivory. Kenya and Tanzania led the way in the fight against poachers. In May 1989, Kenyan President Daniel Arap Moi appointed the well-known palaeontologist Richard Leakey as head of the country's wildlife department. Leakey moved swiftly to reduce inefficiency and corruption, and to equip the department to fight poachers. Since he took charge Kenya has lost relatively few elephants to poachers. On 18th July 1989, President Arap Moi set fire to a stockpile of the country's ivory stock, worth three million dollars, in a spectacular event that was publicized throughout the world. He told the world that "obviously Kenya cannot appeal to the world to stop buying ivory if at the same moment we are selling the very same commodity".

The next step was to try to choke the entire ivory trade and to bring down the high economic pedestal that sustained it. The meeting of the Convention on the International Trade in Endangered Species of Wild Fauna and Flora (CITES)

Below: Kenya President Daniel Arap Moi makes a huge bonfire of ivory on 18th July 1989, in an internationally publicized event. The total ban on the ivory trade has sent ivory prices crashing on the world market.

held at Lausanne in Switzerland in October 1989 was surely a historic one for the African elephant. The 103 member nations of CITES voted overwhelmingly to ban indefinitely the international trade in ivory. Major ivory-importing nations, including Japan, Hong Kong, the United States and the European Community, imposed a total ban on imports of ivory. Following this, the ivory trade seems to be heading towards a collapse. The price of ivory has fallen by 90 percent within Africa and by 60 percent elsewhere. In some East African countries, such as Kenya and Tanzania, and in Central Africa there has certainly been a fall in poaching due to the lack of financial incentive and the effectiveness of anti-poaching efforts by governments.

Some African countries were not happy with the total ban on the ivory trade and voted against this at the CITES meeting. These included Botswana, Burundi, Cameroon, Congo, Gabon, Mozambique, South Africa, Zambia and Zimbabwe. The arguments of some of these countries such as Zimbabwe were simple. They were managing their elephant populations well, with the result that elephants were not declining in their countries. In Botswana and Zimbabwe, the elephant population had actually been increasing. Considerable revenue accrued to the country through the sale of ivory. Why, then, the ban, they asked. These countries made it clear that they would flout the ban. Zimbabwe and Botswana proposed the setting-up of a single auction floor, possibly in Botswana, for selling raw ivory from the southern African nations. The auctions would be controlled by a new body and would include Malawi, Mozambique, Zambia and Angola. Perhaps even South Africa would be asked to join later.

It is true that countries such as Zimbabwe did not face the problem of declining elephant populations. Zimbabwe had been managing its elephant populations on a sustainable basis through its culling programme. Its Communal Area Management Programme for Indigenous Resources (CAMPFIRE) gives the local village councils rights over wildlife in their areas. This has generated considerable economic benefits for the community from the sale of elephants and other animals through culling and hunting. It has been estimated that the elephant populations here are growing at a rate of 5 percent per year. Of this, 2 percent is sold for trophy hunting and the rest is available for culling. From sale proceeds of the trophy hunting or photographic safaris, the village councils get a half share. From culled elephants, the villagers get the meat, and the money from sales of ivory and hide is used for the management of wildlife. As the local people have a stake in protecting the wildlife, they also act as guards against poaching by outsiders. Poachers would find it very difficult to operate without the help of the local people. Zimbabwe also has strict anti-poaching laws under which a poacher could be shot on sight.

Zambia is another country which has a similar wildlife management programme. Local villagers are employed as scouts in the protection of reserves. Hunting and culling schemes generate cash that go to the villagers. The result is a sharp decrease in the poaching of elephants. The South Luangwa National Park, which had lost 40 percent of its elephants between 1979 and 1985, has since maintained a steady population. Zambia and Zimbabwe have shown how important it is to enlist the cooperation and assistance of local people if one is suc-

cessfully to fight the menace of poaching.

In Asian countries, poaching for tusks has not been such a serious problem. Ivory poaching is restricted to male elephants, the females do not carry tusks. Unlike in Africa, this selective poaching of males has generally not affected the population growth. Southern India had one of the highest rates of ivory poaching during the 1970s and 1980s. Even here the incidence has come down sharply since 1987 as a result of increased efforts to catch the poachers. The complete ban on trade in Asian elephant ivory and the more recent ban on African ivory have also helped. Burma, however, seems to have a serious problem of poaching along its borders with Thailand. There are reports of large numbers of elephants, presumably both males and females, being shot for ivory, meat and hide. These elephant products are then smuggled into Thailand for sale.

As we enter the last decade of the twentieth century, there is certainly hope for the elephants in Africa and Asia. The speed with which the international community moved in imposing a total ban on the sale of ivory has choked the trade. As poaching has declined, the elephant populations seem poised for a resurgence. When elephants are below the carrying capacity of their habitats they could potentially increase at a rate of between 3 percent and 5 percent per year. If this trend continues, the elephant populations in Africa could double within 14 to 24 years. It is too early to predict how long the lull in poaching will last. It also remains to be seen what course the southern African countries will chart to manage their elephant populations through sustainable harvest. At present there is no market for their ivory. Japan has stopped buying ivory and even China, a major centre of ivory carving, is considering a ban on the trade.

The survival of the Asian elephant depends on the extent of the habitat it can secure for itself. About a quarter of its range is currently protected in some form of reserves, such as a sanctuary or a national park. The rich cultural association between elephants and people can appeal powerfully in favour of its conservation.

The two living species of elephant are survivors of a spectacular evolutionary history of proboscideans over a period of about 55 million years. These intelligent, sensitive and charismatic animals have the potential of acting as flagship species in the global effort to save the multitude of its living creatures and their habitats from destruction. For this reason alone they are priceless treasures that have to be saved for posterity. As V.S. Pritchett put it, when reviewing *The Roots of Heaven*, "If the elephant vanished the loss to human laughter, wonder and tenderness would be a calamity".

TOURISM AND NATIONAL PARKS

Lyn de Alwis

When the first Duke of Wellington was shown the first railway locomotive, he is said to have exclaimed vehemently 'Progress be damned, this will only mean that people will get about unnecessarily.' His outburst, of course, did nothing to stem the tide of inventions that led to the complex transport industry of modern times. On the contrary, today, over 150 years later, these machines have acted as catalysts in the birth of another industry, namely tourism, which spreads people around the world at a steadily increasing pace.

Some 400 million tourists cross international borders by air, sea, rail and road every year. In doing so they generate huge amounts of money, at times making the industry second only to oil in international trade. Such earnings could mean much to economic development, particularly of the poorer nations if they could attract tourists away from the traditional European and American destinations.

Fortunately, in recent time there has been a tendency for tourism to spread to tropical countries of South and Southeast Asia, South America, the South Pacific and Africa, where most developing countries are located.

This has seen the emergence of a new category of tourist, one that wishes to escape the pollution rampant in their own countries and the traditional resorts. It is back to nature for them, the wilderness for its tranquillity or the thrill of coming face to face with rhinos, elephants, lions and tigers, immortalized in the epics of the hunters of yesteryear.

And with rapid transit systems readily available and western currencies in great demand in developing nations, tourists have a choice of African safaris or Asian shikars at very reasonable prices.

Correspondingly, many third world countries perceiving that a share of the tourism 'cake' is within their grasp have made hefty investments on the infrastructure necessary to attract both the high-spending tourist groups or the free independent traveller. Their governments eager to please their new 'benefactors' were even naive enough to soft-pedal the possible negative effects on the social and cultural make-up of their people. These mostly poor people were mesmerised by the tourist dollar and bartered their simple ways of life, their natural resources and cultural artifacts for it. Almost too late, governments realized that a much longer look at this seemingly benevolent industry was necessary and that a long-term tourism plan was essential.

What did these countries have to offer? Apart from warm seas and clean, wide beaches under a tropical sun – which were compelling enough – the lush vegetation teeming with animal life, archaeological treasures and the mysticism of ancient civilizations that were ravaged by time, beckoned tourists to explore and learn. But all these attractions are very susceptible to over-usage and, unless carefully exploited, suffer irreparable damage. There had to be consensus among planners, sociologists, economists and conservationists before these

highly vulnerable assets could be utilized for the promotion of tourism. One of these assets, namely wildlife and hence national parks, forms the subject of this feature.

The role of national parks

Today, national parks are accessible to the public but 50 years ago their forerunners, the game reserves of Africa and Asia, were the best kept secrets of the colonial rulers. Some purists still believe that national parks, particularly those in Asia and Africa, should not be thrown open to the public but enjoyed only by a coterie of so-called conservationists, researchers and very important people. Fortunately, they have been out-voted and national parks are being recognised as having an important role in tourism.

Actually, national parks have many uses, from affording absolute protection to the animals and plants, through educating visitors on the importance of the natural environment, to recreation derived from observing animals in the peace and quiet of jungle settings.

However, in harnessing a national park as a tourist amenity, both for the indigenous people as well as for foreign tourists, park managers have to tread cautiously lest over-visitation defeats its

Below: *Launching the tourists! Trained elephants from 'Tiger Tops' in Nepal's Chitwan National Park ferry tourists from the airstrip across a river to the lodges from where, later, they will continue into the tall grass on the trail of the great one-horned rhinoceros.*

Above: *"If you want to follow me, you're welcome". The thoughts perhaps of this lone elephant in one of Kenya's national parks. He has other problems on his mind rather than worrying about tourists tagging along.*

very ideals. They must first identify the negative impacts and consciously plan to mitigate them. The biggest danger from too many visitors is the environmental damage that can be caused by construction – of roads, lodges and related infrastructure. These reduce the size of animal habitats significantly and their constant use affects the soil and vegetation, interferes with animal movement and possibly disrupts life cycles and causes air and noise pollution, particularly from the hundreds of vehicles that traverse a park daily. This is bad enough, but if the conduct of visitors does not fall in line with the rules, the park will lose its integrity and become quite meaningless.

Park management strategies

What is the solution to the park manager's dilemma of regulating visitors to a national park? An easy course of action would be to close the park when an arbitrary figure is reached. But limiting numbers in this way would defeat one of the primary objectives, namely, that a national park is created for public appreciation of a country's natural environment. Without valid reason, such a step could also be unacceptable, politically.

Fortunately, through scientific study, trial and error, experience and common sense, an acceptable science of the management of recreation in national parks is available today. This science is based on the application of strategies or a choice of options to avoid damage to the environment. Of course, the manner in which these strategies are applied depends to a large extent on the nature of the park in question. As stated before, there are two distinct types: those that merely form a backdrop for public recreation, and those that preserve an ecological balance.

Four basic strategies emerge from the science of recreation management. Robert E. Manning, in *Parks* magazine Vol 4 Number 1, lists these as:

1. An increase in supply of available space and time. Available space could be increased by physical expansion (which is not always possible) or by using more of the already existing land for visitor use (most national parks keep certain areas undeveloped). By staggering visitor arrivals it is possible to avoid the 'peak-hour' situation and to ensure that there will be a better dispersal of visitors throughout the day. Similarly the week-end rush can be avoided by differential pricing, or by arranging special tours on week-days, or both.

2. Reduce recreation demand by regulating the length of stay or by spacing out activities that have a high impact on the environment (the latter applies more to parks in temperate countries, which may have hillsides for skiing or lakes for motor boats).

3. Reduce the impact of use by zoning the park, i.e. selecting areas most suitable for certain kinds of use e.g. camp-sites, trekking, fishing, bird-watching, etc. and directing only interested groups to those areas.

4. Improve the resources by park management practices such as increasing the size or number of watering places, improving grazing areas, replacing trees that have perished, and thereby increasing the carrying capacity of the park.

For developing countries the most attractive option is the first – to increase the number of national parks. It is indeed an imperative in those countries where the natural forests are disappearing at an alarming rate. Such an increase automatically reduces the other negative impacts by dispersing tourists over a wider geographical area. It would also make it possible to close certain parks while keeping others open, e.g. if one park is in the throes of a severe drought in one part of the country and has to be closed, another, say in the hill country, can be kept open. It is politically acceptable, too, to bring more areas under protection as decision-makers see the economic benefits that can accrue from tourism to both the state and the surrounding villages.

It can be said therefore that tourism has become a key factor in the preservation of national parks for posterity. It helps to ease the burden cast on governments to provide subsidies for their upkeep, a situation that was a disincentive to park administrators to dedicate themselves to their task. It makes it easier to convince politicians that in certain instances the declaration of a protected area should be given priority over clearing for development that may yield dubious results.

The impact of tourist development on the villages in the vicinity of the park can cause socio-economic problems. The villagers resent the double blow that has been dealt. On the one hand, they feel that they have been dispossessed of vast areas of their country and, on the other, that the state is using it for what they perceive as the benefit of tourists instead of their own upliftment. This is manifested in the form of organized poaching, illicit clearing and agitation for parcels of land from the park for village expansion, which immediately brings the management into conflict with the politicians, who espouse the cause of the people.

The need, therefore, for the development of a strategy based on scientific study, experience and common sense should be addressed in formulating a management plan for each park, for there has to be a balance between this and development necessary for visitors.

Making national parks pay

There are four principal channels through which tourist currency can be made to flow into the coffers of both the park administration and the tourism department. These are:

1. Fees levied to enter the park and to hire vehicles and guides.

2. Rentals for tourist lodges, tents and restaurants.

3. Fees from observation towers, special 'game' walks, and the use of movie and video cameras (where applicable).

4. The sale of books, pamphlets and suitable souvenirs.

Apart from the hard currency earned directly, there are the intangibles: employment opportunities in the park and supporting services, profits from catering to tourists requirements, production of saleable goods, accommodation outside the park and so on. Properly channelled, these can make a significant contribution to the economy.

The lure of faraway places

What attracts people to these far-away places? True, the media, especially documentary films on such catchphrases as 'environmental pollution', 'the green house effect' or 'acid rain' arouse interest globally, but there is no doubt that those on animal life are the most appealing. People from urbanized societies that willingly or unwillingly live in 'concrete' jungles are those most appreciative of the natural jungles and crave for even a brief experience within them. Small wonder then that tourists flock to national parks and sanctuaries to see a herd of elephants drinking at a jungle pool or a magnificent tiger lying in dappled sunlight on the forest floor, or listen to a morning chorus of shamas, thrushes and minivets.

East Africa became the Mecca of wildlife tourists and very soon exotic names like Tsavo, Kilimanjaro, Serengeti, the Ngorongoro crater and Murchison Falls rolled off their tongues as though they were new names for the Tower of London, matadors, Venetian gondolas or the Eiffel Tower. Not only did tourists go on safari, paying thousands of dollars for them, but they also began crusading for the conservation of rapidly dwindling numbers of rhinos, elephants, gorillas and chimpanzees. Enormous sums of money were channelled into research projects to find ways and means of saving both animal and habitat, to fight poaching and stop the illegal trade in ivory.

National parks in Asia

During this time the Asian scene hadn't yet unfolded. Now at last the emphasis is shifting to countries such as India, Sri Lanka, Malaysia and Thailand. To the adventurous western tourist, the thinly distributed animals in mostly inaccessible jungles in Asia paled into insignificance beside the millions of antelope, zebra and wildebeeste parading the vast open plains of the Ngorongoro and the Serengeti. But suddenly everybody wants to go to Nepal's Chitwan National Park to 'rub shoulders' with the great one-horned rhino, to Kanha in India to 'stalk', with their cameras, the majestic Royal Bengal tiger straight out of Kipling's *Jungle Book*, or to Sri Lanka's Yala National Park to pull up alongside a family group of the most handsome representatives of the Asian elephant.

The elephant has become a flagship species of wildlife conservation in all 13 countries of Asia in which it still occurs. Forged in prehistoric times and surviving mass destruction during waves of European occupation, the unique bond between man and elephant remains indestructible in Asia, and augurs well for the future of this truly magnificent animal in the wild. (See pages 98-101 for its status.)

It is not merely a bond of sentiment or awe, but one of mutual respect for and trust in each other. One has only to see how proudly a huge tusker, superbly attired for the occasion, carries a shining casket containing sacred relics of the Lord Buddha on its back, or kneels low enough to allow a bridal couple to step into the decorated platform it is carrying, to understand that here is an animal created for a long partnership with man, and a partnership that must be preserved for the benefit of generations yet to be born.

An ever increasing number of westerners are going in search of these incredible encounters. Tourists flock to temple festivals to see elephants in their regalia, to remote villages where some social ritual is in progress or to a forest where they perform the more serious task of hauling timber. And many Asian countries are developing their national parks to make observing elephants simpler. Wild herds can be seen in Khao Yai National Park in Thailand, in India's Kaziranga or Bandipur, but nowhere do they seem to be closer to a tourist than in Sri Lanka's Yala National Park.

Elephant-spotting in Yala National Park

There, in one of the park's six 'blocks', some 60 elephants mill around in 135km^2(52 miles^2) of high forest, rockscapes and low scrub. Criss-crossed with seasonal streams and interspersed with

Below: Family groups of Asian elephants take to the water in Yala National Park in Sri Lanka. In this superb open setting in the southeastern corner of the island tourists can watch and photograph groups of elephants, as well as other wild animals, fulfil their relatively undisturbed lives.

lakes, the scrub frequently parts to give stunning vistas of the blue Indian Ocean. This multiplicity of ecological niches gives rise to prime elephant habitat and its open scenery makes elephant watching from a safe distance the easiest thing in the world.

In a two-hour 'game-run' from 6am to 8am several thrills may be experienced – a lone bull will amble along the main track with no intention of even looking behind him until he finds his own entrance into the scrub, a small family group will be defying orders to grab that last bunch of leaves before going home, or trumpeting mothers will be warning their offspring to stay close to each other. The evening run from 4pm to 6pm is even more rewarding. Herds will converge on the grassy plains or at large watering places and this is when tourists will get their fill of elephant family life. Endearing scenes of young cousins at play, an austere matriarch seemingly interested only in scraping grass off the plain, but actually watching every move of her wards (as well as the tourists) and the hilarious spectacle of adult elephants rolling in the water, often submerged with only the tip of the trunk showing like a periscope, will live long in the memory of the viewer and urge him to return.

If there are scores to be settled by competing bulls, this is the time it is done. The she-elephant in question feeds nonchalantly as the two suitors approach and begin their sparring. The contest is monitored by the leader who, in her wisdom, decides which is the better and cold shoulders the other.

Tourists have only to move around the park slowly and in silence, and the guide, reading the sign language of colleagues in passing vehicles, will take them to other animals that are out that evening – leopard, sloth bear, wild boar and deer. Such scenes in·a national park help replace an inborn fear of animals with an understanding and respect for them.

The way forward

The development of national parks as sources of revenue from tourists is spreading throughout Asia. Besides Chitwan, Kanha and Yala already mentioned, Malaysia's Taman Negara, Thailand's Khao Yai, Indonesia's Ujong Kulaong and China's Xishuangbanna in the salubrious south are parks that are rapidly preparing for tourism's swift march eastwards.

The Khao Yai National Park in Thailand merits special mention here for it provides a model for politicians beleaguered by their constituents opposing the wresting of land from them. Through cooperation between park management and villagers, the latter have formed a conservation society whose members are trained to act as guides within the park.

The Asian Elephant Specialist Group

On paper, the Asian elephant still has a wide distribution, occurring in 13 countries: India, Sri Lanka, Bangladesh, Nepal, Bhutan, Peninsular Malaysia, Indonesia (Sumatra), Sabah, Thailand, Cambodia, Laos, Vietnam and China. However, this impressive range is misleading, for nowhere are they plentiful, nor is their future assured, as they are driven from their home ranges into ever-diminishing pockets of jungle. Indeed, the total estimated population in its entire range is between 35,000 and 55,000 in 500,000km^2(193,000 miles^2) of discontinuous plantation forest and jungle. (See also pages 98-101.)

These countries have not only the elephant in common but also the will to protect them for the benefit of future generations. With the help of the Species Survival Commission (SSC) of the International Union for Conservation of Nature and Natural Resources (IUCN) and the World Wide Fund for Nature (WWF), conservationists in these countries have banded together to form an Asian Elephant Specialist Group (AESG). This group has many objectives but the principal ones consist of compiling scientific information on the threats leading to the decline of the elephant, which will help convince governments on necessary conservation actions, the sharing of knowledge and expertise between countries to help solve problems arising from man/elephant conflict and persuading the people of each country to participate in programmes aimed at protecting elephants and their habitats.

In its 12 years of existence, the AESG has made significant progress. Members feel free to discuss problems and arrive at solutions at the regular meetings and workshops organized in different countries and through the publication of a newsletter. Since 1989, the AESG has maintained an Asian Elephant Conservation Centre in Bangalore, India, which is capable of coordinating all group activities and ministering to the needs of member countries that seek advice in elephant conservation.

To underscore the importance of concerted action, IUCN has recently published an action plan for Asian elephant conservation and is in the process of implementing it. By these timely actions we wish to ensure that the habitat of the Asian elephant will not be further reduced or completely destroyed, as has happened in western Asia, Afghanistan and Java during the last two thousand years.

Despite the thinning out of elephant populations in the countries of its present range, the reverence for these noble animals and the desire to protect them as national treasures have in no way diminished. Backed by international concern and support, the Asian elephant still has a fighting chance to survive the havoc caused by exploding populations' demand for more land for agriculture and economic development. There is fresh hope for them as more nations accept the World Conservation Strategy and prepare their own national strategy based on IUCN's formula that economic development is not feasible without conservation. If we do not work with all our strength and all our determination towards protecting it during our lifetime, we shall be denying posterity the companionship, enjoyment and usefulness of a truly remarkable animal.

The fees charged for this service go to the villagers themselves. Villagers also run cooperative shops close to the park, which are stocked with items required by or of interest to tourists. Furthermore, villagers are permitted to continue collecting the forest products upon which they traditionally depended for their livelihood. A spin-off from this situation is a feeling that the park 'belongs' to the villages and that they stand to benefit from tourism.

Such far-sighted and radical thinking also exists in a few other countries where a symbiotic relationship exists between park managers and villagers. Applying this formula to all protected areas is the best insurance against a demand for settlement within them, and will also enable countries to increase the number of protected areas for wildlife without meeting the hostility and suspicion that hitherto were the biggest obstacles to taking such a step. And these new areas can be selected for species diversity, climatic variability and watershed and catchment protection.

Through the significant contribution tourism can make towards economic development it can also be recognized as a key factor in the preservation of national parks for posterity. Tourism also paves the way for the local inhabitants on the periphery of national parks and reserves to become partners in conservation. The earlier concept of a national park as a 'Garden of Eden' for the privileged has been replaced by a more realistic perception that 'conservation is the human use of natural resources'.

HOW TO PHOTOGRAPH WILD ELEPHANTS

It may seem fairly easy to photograph a big beast such as the elephant. If you aim your camera at an elephant you obviously cannot miss getting it somewhere in the frame! To get a *good* picture of elephants, however, is not that easy. As with all other wild creatures, successful photography requires a great deal of knowledge of the animal, proper planning, the right equipment, patience, courage, a good eye for a picture and a bit of luck. If you are very successful, you might even be able to get some of your 'elephants' published!

Where to find elephants

First of all you have to go to the right places to photograph elephants. Elephants are found in 13 Asian and 33 African countries, but not all of these are ideal places for photographing them. The Asian elephant is mainly an animal of dense rain forest, often in rugged mountainous terrain. In most Asian countries you can spend days wandering through the elephant's habitat without getting even a glimpse of these creatures. Your only way of seeing them may be to wait at a natural salt lick and hope that some of them will visit it. Two exceptions to this are India and Sri Lanka. Here they can be easily seen and photographed in certain wildlife parks.

In India the best places to see elephants are Nagarhole National Park, Bandipur National Park, Mudumalai Sanctuary and Periyar Tiger Reserve in the south, Corbett National Park in the north and Kaziranga National Park in the north east. In some of these, such as Corbett and Kaziranga, the viewing of elephants is seasonal, usually during the dry months between January and April. In all these parks, except Periyar, you can go on elephant-back to see and photograph wild elephants. In Periyar you do it in a different way: you go by boat around a reservoir and see them grazing on the meadows along the shore or even swimming across the lake. One outstanding place in Sri Lanka for seeing elephants is the Yala National Park in the south west.

In Africa there is a much wider choice of places for viewing the savanna elephant than the forest elephant. Amboseli and Tsavo in Kenya, Lake Manyara, Selous and Ruaha in Tanzania, Hwange (formerly Wankie) in Zimbabwe, Luangwa Valley in Zambia and Kruger in South Africa are some of the best places to see the savanna elephant. Zaire, Gabon and Congo are strongholds of the forest elephant, but this is much more difficult to observe.

Above: Tourists watch and photograph elephants from the verandah of their lodge in Aberdares National Park, Kenya.

Choosing the best location

When you visit a park with the specific intention of photographing elephants, the best locations are of course waterholes. Not only during the dry season, but even during the rainy months, elephants come to drink and bathe at a pond or a river. Many parks have watchtowers from which you can safely watch and photograph elephants. Elephants generally begin to come to water after 11am. In the tropics, photography is possible until 5 or 6pm.; after that the light is too poor for good pictures.

A waterhole is a good place to photograph elephants not only drinking, bathing and wallowing, but also in a variety of other situations. A bull may court and mate with a cow elephant, two bulls may have a sparring match, elephants in a family interact socially in many ways, or a sick or old elephant may even come to die at a waterhole. After a bath they may dust themselves and begin feeding on plants in the vicinity. Your goal must be not only to take portraits of bulls or herds, but also to capture some of the interesting and diverse behaviours they indulge in – a calf putting its trunk into the mouth of its mother to sample a titbit, a youngster clambering playfully on another's back, bulls clashing their tusks together or, if you have the nerves, a matriarch staging an impressive mock charge ending in a cloud of dust a few paces away from you. You are fairly safe in a vehicle, but make sure that the ignition responds immediately . . . just in case! Elephants can be very dangerous.

What sort of camera to use?

The camera you use is really your personal choice. A 35mm single-lens reflex is most convenient when travelling. A motor-driven camera is very useful for action pictures of a charging elephant. I have found that the most convenient lens to use when photographing elephants is a 70-210mm or 80-200mm focal length zoom in the medium telephoto range. Most often I end up using the lens at its longest focal length, but many times I have photographed herds or even a single elephant with the lens set at 70mm when I have got very close to them. I also use a 200mm fixed focal length telephoto for the superior picture quality it gives compared to a zoom lens. A 2x converter or a lens of 300mm or 400mm focal length is useful at waterholes, when a herd or a lone bull may be more than 100m(110yd) away. In such cases a monopod or a tripod is necessary to get shake-free pictures.

Unless it is very bright I use a lens at its widest aperture – f4 or 5.6 – in order to go for the highest possible shutter speed to prevent camera shake. A useful rule of thumb is to use a shutter speed that is at least as fast as the focal length of the lens. For instance, with a 200mm lens this should be 1/250 of a second shutter speed.

Above: This one-tusked bull Asian elephant was photographed at close quarters with a standard focal length lens. It can be extremely dangerous to approach elephants this close.

Below: When photographing elephants at a distance across a swamp or grassland, a lens with a focal length of 300mm or 400mm can produce dramatic pictures in safety.

If you have a steady hand you may be able to go down to 1/125 shutter speed. With some support for the camera this can even be as low as 1/60 of a second.

Films and film speed

When you are photographing elephants in the open your best choice of colour transparency film would be one with a speed of 64 ISO, but this is of limited use inside a forest, especially on cloudy days. A film speed of 100 ISO is a good choice for use both in the open and under the forest canopy. You can still manage a 1/125 shutter speed in a forest environment with this film. I do not like the colour balance in transparency film with 400 ISO rating and so rarely use them. Transparency film with a speed rating of 200 ISO is an excellent compromise, which has sufficiently fine grain and good colours. The problem with prepaid films is that you may not be able to get it processed in the country in which you photograph elephants; be sure you have a supply of prepaid mailers for getting your rolls promptly processed. I also keep a camera body loaded with 400 ISO black-and-white film for use in poor light. The art of black-and-white photography is unfortunately dying out; this is regrettable, because elephants are especially good subjects for this medium.

Composing your photographs

It is important to pay attention to the angle of light when photographing elephants. If you plan to wait at a waterhole for a few days, be sure to take note of the elephants' path to the water and the sun's track during the hours you are going to be present. If elephants are going to be lit from the back when they come for water in the afternoon you may want to shift your position to get more frontal lighting on them. You may wish to take some dramatic silhouettes of elephants during sunset or when they are dusting themselves with red soil. In any case, midday is not a good time to photograph them if the sun is shining brightly. The harsh shadows on the lower half of the elephant do not make an aesthetic picture. You may wait for a passing cloud before clicking in order to reduce the contrast. If you have no other choice, make sure that you expose for the shadows; you may have to overexpose by one stop as compared with what your light meter prescribes. If your camera has matrix metering this may be automatically taken care of. When you photograph elephants in or near water a great deal of light is reflected from the water's surface that fools your light meter into underexposure; open up your aperture by half or one stop to expose correctly for the elephants. In many instances you simply have to be satisfied with whatever you get.

When composing elephants in your viewfinder, pay attention to their habitat. You may wish to take full-frame shots of a lone bull or a family of elephants. All your pictures should not be composed this way. If you have a zoom lens, set it to a shorter focal length if necessary, place the elephants in the foreground and show that forest, lake or mountain in the background. Frame an entire acacia tree along with that elephant standing beneath it. Get a low angle shot if you can, to make the elephants appear even more formidable. But in whatever manner you photograph elephants, do not take foolish chances with them. Both in Africa and in Asia photographers have been killed by their subjects. Take care, have fun and return from your safari intact with pictures to show your friends.

SELECTED BIBLIOGRAPHY

ORIGINS & EVOLUTION/ANATOMY & PHYSIOLOGY
Pages 12-47
By Dr. Jeheskel Shoshani

Benedict, F.G. (1936) *The physiology of the elephant*. Carnegie Institution of Washington (Publication No. 474), Washington, D.C., 302pp.

Carrington, R. (1958). *Elephants: a short account of their natural history, evolution and influence on mankind*. Chatto and Windus, London, 285pp.

Coppens, Y., Maglio, V.J., Madden, C.T., Beden, M. (1978). Proboscidea. Pp. 336-367, in *Evolution of African mammals* (Maglio, V.J. and Cooke, H.B.S., eds.). Harvard Univ. Press, Cambridge, Massachusetts, 641pp.

Deraniyagala, P.E.P. (1955). *Some extinct elephants, their relatives and the two living species*. Ceylon Nat. Mus., Colombo, 161pp.

Eltringham, S.K. (1982). *Elephants*. Blandford Press, Poole (Dorset, England), 262pp.

Hanks, J. (1979). *A Struggle for Survival: The Elephant Problem*. Country Life Books (Hamlyn Publishing Group), Middlesex and Mayflower Books, New York, 176pp.

Laursen, L., and Bekoff, M. (1978). *Loxodonta africana*. *Mammalian Species* **92**, 1-8.

Laws, R.M. (1966). Age criteria for the African elephant (*Loxodonta a. africana*). *East African Wildlife Journal* **4**, 1-37.

Maglio, V.J. (1973). Origin and evolution of the Elephantidae. *Trans. Amer. Phil. Soc.*, **63(3)**, 1-49.

Mariappa, D. (1986). *Anatomy and histology of the Indian elephant*. Indira Publishing House, Oak Park (Michigan), 209pp.

Osborn, H.F. (1936). *Proboscidea*. The American Museum of Natural History, New York, Volume 1:xl + 1-802pp. (page 802 includes *Errata*).

Osborn, H.F. (1942). *Proboscidea*. The American Museum of Natural History, New York, Vol. II:xxvii + 805-1675 (plus one *errata* page).

Poole, J.H., and Moss, C.J. (1981). Musth in the African elephant, *Loxodonta africana*. *Nature* **292(5826)**, 830-831.

Roth, V.L., and Shoshani, J. (1988). Dental identification and age determination in *Elephas maximus*. *Journal of Zoology (London)*, **214**, 567-588.

Savage, R.J.G., Long, M.R. (1986). *Mammal evolution: an illustrated guide*. British Museum (Natural History), London, 259pp.

Shoshani, J., Eisenberg, J.F. (1982). *Elephas maximus*. *Mammalian Species* **182**, 1-8.

Shoshani. J., *et al* (75 co-authors) (1982). On the dissection of a female Asian elephant (*Elephas maximus maximus* Linnaeus, 1758) and data from other elephants. *Elephant* **2(1)**, 3-93.

Sikes, S.K. (1971). *The natural history of the African elephant*. Weidenfeld and Nicholson, London, 397pp.

Silverberg, R. (1970). *Mammoth, Mastodon and Man*. McGraw-Hill Book Co., New York, 223pp.

Tassy, P., Shoshani, J. (1988). The Tethytheria: elephants and their relatives, pp 283-315. In Benton, M.J.(Ed). The phylogeny and classification of the tetrapods. Volume 2: *Mammals*. The Systematic Association, the Linnean Society and the Palaeontological Association of London, 329pp.

SOCIAL LIFE Pages 48-63
By Dr. P.C. Lee

Douglas-Hamilton, I. (1972) *On the Ecology and Behaviour of the African Elephant*. D.Phil. Thesis, University of Oxford.

Eisenberg, J.F. and Lockhart, M. (1972) An ecological reconnaissance of Wilpattu National Park, Ceylon. *Smithsonian Contributions to Zoology* **101**, 1-118.

Gadgil, M. and Nair, P.V. (1984) Observations on the social behaviour of free ranging groups of tame Asiatic elephant (*Elephas maximus* Linn). *Proceedings of the Indian Academy of Science* **93**, 225-233.

Hanks, J. (1979) *A Struggle for Survival: The Elephant Problem* Country Life Books (Hamlyn Publishing Group), Middlesex and Mayflower Books, New York.

Laws, R.M., Parker, I. and Johnstone, R.C.B. (1975) *Elephants and their Habitats*, Clarendon Press, Oxford.

Lee, P.C. (1986) Early social development among African elephant calves. *National Geographic Research* **2**, 388-401.

Lee, P.C. (1987) Allomothering among African elephants. *Animal Behaviour* **35**, 278-291.

Leuthold, W. (1977) Spatial organization and habitat utilization of elephants in Tsavo National Park, Kenya. *Zeitschrift fur Saugetierkunde* **42**, 358-379.

McKay, G.M. (1973) Behaviour and ecology of the Asiatic elephant in southeastern Ceylon. *Smithsonian Contributions to Zoology* **125**, 1-113.

Moss, C.J. (1988) *Elephant Memories*. Morrow, New York.

Moss, C.J. and Poole, J.H. (1983) Relationships and social structure of African elephants. In *Primate Social Relationships: An Integrated Approach* (edited by R.A. Hinde) pp315-325 Cambridge University Press, Cambridge.

Poole, J.H., Payne, K., Langbauer, W.R. and Moss, C.J. (1988) The social context of some very low frequency calls of African elephants. *Behavioural Ecology and Sociobiology* **22**, 385-392.

Rapaport, L. and Haight, J. (1988) Some observations regarding allomaternal caretaking among captive Asian elephants (*Elephas maximus*). *Journal of Mammalology*.

Sukumar, R. (1989) *The Asian Elephant: Ecology and Management*. Cambridge University Press, Cambridge.

REPRODUCTION Pages 64-77
By Dr. P.C. Lee

Eisenberg, J.F., McKay, G.M. and Jainudeen, M.R. (1971) Reproductive behaviour of the Asiatic elephant (*Elephas maximus maximus* L). *Behaviour* **38**, 191-225.

Hall-Martin, A.J. (1987) The role of musth in the reproductive strategy of the African elephant. *South African Journal of Science* **83**, 616-620.

Hanks, J. (1979) *A Struggle for Survival: The Elephant Problem.* Country Life Books (Hamlyn Publishing Group), Middlesex and Mayflower Books, New York.

Hess, D.L., Schmidt, A.M. and Schmidt, M.J. (1983) Reproductive cycle of the Asian elephant (*Elephas maximus*) in captivity. *Biology of Reproduction* **29**, 767-773.

Jainudeen, M.R., McKay, G.M. and Eisenberg, J.F. (1972) Observations on musth in the domesticated Asiatic elephant. *Mammalia* **36**, 247-261.

Laws, R.M. (1969) Aspects of reproduction in the African elephant, *Loxodonta africana. Journal of Reproduction and Fertility* **6**, 193-217.

Laws, R.M., Parker, I. and Johnstone, R.C.B. (1975) *Elephants and their Habitats* Clarendon Press, Oxford.

Lee, P.C. and Moss, C.J. (1986) Early maternal investment in male and female African elephant calves. *Behavioural Ecology and Sociobiology* **18**, 352-361.

Moss, C.J. (1983) Oestrous behaviour and female choice in the African elephant. *Behaviour* **86**, 167-196.

Moss, C.J. (1988) *Elephant Memories* Morrow, New York.

Niemuller, C.A. (1989) *Hormonal and Biochemical Changes Associated with Musth in the Captive Male Asian Elephant (Elephas maximus).* MSc. Thesis, University of Guelph, Ontario.

Poole, J.H. (1987) Rutting behaviour in African elephants. *Behaviour* **102**, 283-316.

Poole, J.H. (1989) Mate guarding, reproductive success and female choice in African elephants. *Animal Behaviour* **37**, 842-849.

Poole, J.H., Kasman, L.H., Ramsay, E.C. and Lasley, B.L. (1984) Musth and urinary testosterone concentration in the African elephant (*Loxodonta africana*). *Journal of Reproduction and Fertility* **70**, 225-260.

Rasmussen, L.E.L., Hess, D.L., and Haight, J.D. (1990) Chemical analysis of temporal gland secretions collected from an Asian bull elephant during a four month musth episode. *Journal of Chemical Ecology* **16**, 2167-2181.

Sukumar, R. (1989) *The Asian Elephant: Ecology and Management*, Cambridge University Press, Cambridge.

DISEASE & MORTALITY Pages 102-115
By James Barnett

Caple, I.W., Jainudeen, M.R., Buich, T.D. and Song, C.Y. (1978). Some clinico-pathologic findings in elephants (*Elephas maximus*) infected with *Fasciola jacksoni. J. Wildl. Dis.* **14**, 110-115.

Clark, H.W., Loughlin, D.C., Baily, J.S., Brown, T.McP. (1980) Mycoplasma species and arthritis in captive elephants. *J. Zoo An. Med.* **11(1)**, 3-15.

Condy, J.B. (1974). Observations on internal parasites in Rhodesian elephant, *Loxodonta africana.* Blumenbach 1797. *Proc. Trans. Rhod. Sci. Assoc.* **55**, 67-99.

Corfield, T.F. (1973). Elephant mortality in Tsavo National Park, Kenya. *East Afr. Wild. J.* **11**, 339-368.

Dillman, J.S. and Carr, W.R. (1970). Observations on arteriosclerosis, serum cholesterol and serum electrolytes in the wild African elephant (*Loxodonta africana*). *J. Comp. Path.* **80**, 81-87.

Douglas-Hamilton, I. and Douglas-Hamilton, O. (1975). *Among the elephants.* Collins and Harvill Press, London.

Eltringham, S.K. (1982). *Elephants.* Blandford Press, Poole, Dorset.

Evans, G.H. (1910). *Elephants and their diseases.* Government Printing, Rangoon, Burma.

Gopal, T. and Rao, B.U. (1984). Rabies in an Indian Wild Elephant Calf. *Indian Vet. J.* **61**, 82-83.

Graf, von. Z., Meszaros, J., Boros, G. (1980). Diseases of elephants. *Erkrankungen der Zootiere*, Arnhem, 241-245.

Hanks, J. (1979). *A Struggle for Survival; The Elephant Problem.* Country Life Books (Hamlyn Publishing Group). Middlesex and Mayflower Books, New York.

Jackson, P. (1990). *Elephants.* Endangered Species Series. Apple Press Ltd., London.

Jansenn, D.L., Karesh, W.B., Cosgrove, G.E. and Oosterhuis, J.E. (1984). Salmonellosis in a herd of captive elephants. *Javma* **185 (11)**, 1450-1451.

Karesh, W.B., and Robinson, P.T. (1985). Ivermectin treatment of lice infestations in two elephant species. *Javma* **187 (11)**, 1235-1236.

Kretzschman, C.K. and Kuther, H. (1972). Course and aetiology of elephant pox in the zoological garden of Magdeburg. *Erkrankungen der Zootiere*, Wroclaw, 97-210.

Kuntzo, Von A. (1979). Clinical aspects of colic in elephants. (*Elephas maximus*). *Erkrankungen der Zootiere*, Mulkouse, 197-210.

Laws, R.M. (1966). Age criteria for the African elephant (*Loxodonta africana*). *E. Afr. Wildl. J.* **4**, 1-37.

Laws, R.M. and Parker, I.S.C. (1968). Recent studies on elephant populations in East Africa. *Symp. Zool. Soc. Lond.* **21**, 319-359.

Lee, P. (1990). *Growth and reproduction in African elephants.* Lecture presented to British Ecological Society – Tropical Ecology Group at a Symposium on elephants, Wolfson College, Cambridge.

Long, E.M. (1980). Observations on growth and molar change in the African elephant. *Afr. J. Ecol.* **18**, 217-234.

McGavin, M.D., Walker, R.D., Schroeder, E.C., Patton, C.S., McCracken, M.D., (1983). Death of an African elephant from probable toxaemia attributed to chronic pulpitis. *Javma.* **183 (11)**, 1269-1273.

Moss, C. (1988). *Elephant Memories.* Elm Tree Books.

Mustafa, A.H.M. (1984). Isolation of anthrax bacillus from an elephant in Bangladesh. *Vet. Rec. (1984).* **114**, 591.

Osman, W.C., Barker, W., Stockley, C.H., Pitman, C.R.S., Offerman, P.B., Rushby, G.G. (1953). *The Elephant in East Central Africa.* A Monograph. Rowland Ward Ltd.

Pilaski, Von. J., Schaller, K., Matern, B., Kloppel, G., Mayer, H. (1982). Outbreaks of Pox among Elephants and Rhinoceroses. *Erkrankungen der Zootiere*, Veszprem, 257-265.

Pilaski, Von. J., Magunna, E., Hagenbeck, C. (1985). Pox of Asian Elephants (*Elephas maximus*) in Carl Hagenbeck Zoo Park, Hamburg. *Erkrankungen der Zootiere*, St. Vincent/Torino, 437-447.

Saunders, G. (1983). Pulmonary *Mycobacterium tuberculosis* infection in a circus elephant. *Javma* **183 (11)**, 1311-1312.

Schmidt, M. (1986). *Proboscidea (Elephants), in Zoo and Wild Animal Medicine.* Fowler, M.E. (Ed.) 2nd Edition. W.B. Saunders Company, Philadelphia and London.

Sikes, S.K. (1969). Habitat and cardiovascular disease: observations made on elephants (*Loxodonta africana*) and other free-living animals in East Africa. *Trans. Zool. Soc. Lond.* **32**, 1-104.

Sikes, S.K. (1971) *The World Naturalist. The Natural History of the African Elephant.* Weidenfield and Nicolson, London.

Skinner, J. (1990). *Elephant Management in Southern Africa – an historical perspective.* Lecture presented to British Ecological Society – Tropical Ecology Group at a Symposium on Elephants, Wolfson College, Cambridge.

Westhuysen, O.P. Von der (1938). A monograph of the Helminth Parasites of the Elephant. *Onderstepoort Journal of Veterinary Science and Animal Industry.* **10**, 49-190.

INDIAN MYTHS AND HISTORY Pages 130-147
By Dhriti K. Lahiri-Choudhury

The references to elephants in Vedic literature have been supplied by Professor Samiran Chakrabarty, Director of The School of Vedic Studies, Rabindra Bharati University, Calcutta. The Vedic references to elephants have been gleaned mostly from A.A. Macdonell and A.B. Keith, *Vedic Index of Names and Subjects*, 2 Vols, 1912; repr. Delhi: Motilal Banarasidass, 1982.

The chronology of Vedic literature featured in the chapter is as follows:

I. Rigveda Samhita I-IX (II-IX are the earliest) 1500-1200-1000 BC.

II. Rigveda Samhita X, Atharvaveda Samhita

III. Maitrayani Samhita – Krishna (Black) Yajurveda about 800 BC.
　　Mantra parts of Taittiriya Samhita – Krishna (Black) Yajurveda
　　Vajasaneyi Samhita – Madhyandina and Kanva recensions of White Yajurveda

IV. Aitareya Brahmana I-V – Rigvedic 650/600 BC.
　　Brahmana parts of Taittiriya Samhita
　　Panchavimsha Brahmana – Samavedic

V. Satapatha Brahmana – White Yajurvedic

VI. Jaiminiya Upanishad Brahmana – Samavedic

VII. Brihadaranyaka Upanishad – White Yajurvedic
　　Chandogya Upanishad – Samavedic

VIII. Nirukta
　　Adbhuta Brahmana
　　(Klaus Mylius. *Geschichte der Literatur im alten Indien.* Leipzig, 1983).

Other source material for the chapter is as follows:

Abu'l-Fazl Allamai. *A'in-i Akbari.* Tr. H. Blockmann. Calcutta:Asiatic Society of Bengal, Series Bibliotheca Indica, 1873. 2nd ed. revised by D.C.Phillott. Calcutta:Royal Asiatic Society of Bengal, Bibliotheca Indica, work no. 61, vol. I, issue no. 1492, New Series, 1939.

Cowell, E.B. Ed. *The Jataka or Stories of Buddha's Former Births.* 7 Vols., Cambridge University Press, 1895-1913.

Keith, A.B. tr. *The Veda of the Black Yajus School entitled Taittiriya Samhita*, Harvard Oriental Series, Vol. XVIII, 1914; repr. Delhi: Motilal Banarasidass, 1967.

Keith, A.B. tr. *Rigveda Brahmanas*, Harvard Oriental Series, Vol. XXI, London, 1920; repr. Delhi: Motilal Banarasidass, 1981.

Price, David. Tr. *Autobiographical Memoirs of the Emperor Jahangueir.* 1829; repr. Calcutta:Editions Indian, 1972.

Sarkar, J.N. *Military History of India*, Calcutta:Orient Longmans, 1960; 2nd impression, 1960.

Shamasastry, R. tr. *Kautilya's Arthashastra*, Mysore, 1956.

Wilson, H.H. tr. *The Rig-Veda Samhita* 1850; repr. New Delhi: Cosmo Publications, 1977.

THE IVORY TRADE Pages 148-157
By Richard Luxmoore

Barbier, E.B., Burgess, J.C., Swanson, T.M., Pearce, D.W. (1990). *Elephants, economics and the ivory trade.* Earthscan, London, 154pp.

Caughley, G., Dublin, H. and Parker, I. (1990) Projected decline of the African elephant. *Biological Conservation* **54**, 157-164.

Ivory Trade Review Group (1989). *The ivory trade and the future of the African elephant.* Report prepared by the 7th Conference of the Parties to CITES.

Milner-Gulland, E.J., and Mace, R. (1991). The impact of the ivory trade on the African elephant *Loxodonta africana* as assessed by data from the trade. *Biological Conservation* **55**, 215-229.

Parker, I.S.C. (1979). *The Ivory Trade.* Consultancy report on behalf of the US Fish and Wildlife Service and IUCN. 4 vols.

Pilgram, T. and Western, D. (1986). Inferring the sex and age of African elephants from tusk measurements. *Biological Conservation* **36**, 39-52.

KEEPING WILD ELEPHANTS AT BAY Pages 166-169
(Part of CONSERVATION)
By Dhriti K. Lahiri-Choudhury

Anderson, David and Grove, Richard (Eds) (1987) *Conservation in Africa: People, Policies and Practice.* Cambridge University Press.

Bell, R.H.V. and McShane-Caluzi, E. (Eds) (1986) *Conservation and Wildlife Management in Africa.* Peacecorps, Washington.

Blair, J.A.S., Boon, G.G. and Noor, N.M. (1979) Conservation or Cultivation: the confrontation between Asian Elephant and land development in Peninsular Malaysia. *Land Development Digest* **2**, 27-59.

Blair, J.A.S., and Noor, N.M. (1979) Incompatible Neighbours. *Proceedings of the Elephant Damage Workshop held at the FELDA Institute of Land Development, Trolak, Perak.*

Jackson, P. (1990) *Elephants.* Endangered Species Series. Apple Press Ltd., London.

Lahiri-Choudhury, D.K. (1975) A report on Elephant Depredation in Jalpaiguri Forest Division and part of Madarihat Range of Cooch Behar Forest Division in North Bengal. *Calcutta: Report submitted to West Bengal Forest Department.* (pp 60; maps 10).

Lahiri-Choudhury, D.K. and Bardhan Roy, B.K.(1982). Chase without Capture: an Exercise in Anti-elephant Depredation Measures in Kurseong Forest Division of Northern Bengal. Paper presented at the *International Workshop on Management of Elephants in the Wild and in Captivity* held at Jaldapara, West Bengal in 1982.

Proceedings of the International Workshop on the Management of Elephants in the Wild and in Captivity. (1982). Calcutta: Northeast India Task force of Asian Elephant Specialist Group of IUCN/SSC.

Sale, J.B., and Berkmuller, K. (1988). Manual of Wildlife Techniques for India. *Field Document No. 11 (FO:IND/82/003 July 1988).* Dehra Dun: Wildlife Institute of India and FAO.

Seidensticker, John (1984) *Managing Elephant Depredation in Agriculture and Forestry Projects.* Washington D.C.: World Bank.

Sukumar, R. (1989) *The Asian Elephant: Ecology and Management,* Cambridge University Press, Cambridge.

Sukumar, R. (1991) The management of large mammals in relation to male strategies and conflict with people. *Biological Conservation* **55**, 93-102.

Western, David and Pearl, Mary (1989) *Conservation for the Twenty-first Century.* Oxford University Press, Oxford and New York.

TOURISM AND NATIONAL PARKS Pages 174-177
(Part of CONSERVATION) By Lyn de Alwis

Abrahams, E. Anthony. Tourism Promotion: A shared place in the Sun. *PARKS (An international journal for managers of national parks and other protected areas)* Volume 7, No. 4 (Jan-March 1983).

Sankhala, K.S. *National Parks.* Published by the Wildlife Preservation Society of India. Dehra Dun, India.

Manning, Robert. Strategies for Managing Recreational Uses of National Parks. *PARKS,* Volume 4, No. 1.

AUTHORS' ACKNOWLEDGEMENTS
Dr. J. Shoshani would like to acknowledge the help of the following people: Gary H. Marchant for advice on the illustrations of extinct and living proboscideans, as well for providing the original drawings for the internal organs of an elephant and the cross section of the trunk. Sandra Lee Shoshani and Jules L. Pierce for proofreading. The Library of the Elephant Interest Group for invaluable reference material during the writing process.

PUBLISHER'S ACKNOWLEDGEMENTS
The publishers would like to acknowledge the reference sources for the following illustrations featured in this book. These acknowledgments are based on the most complete information available at the time of compilation.

Page 15: Data supplied by J. Shoshani. Page 16-17: Overall configuration provided by J. Shoshani. Individual portraits are reductions of those used on succeeding pages (see below). Page 19: Side view of *Palaeomastodon* jaw based on an illustration in *Proboscidea* by Henry Fairfield Osborn, Volume 1 (1936), published by. The American Museum of Natural History, New York. (Volume 2 was published in 1942 and details of it are listed in the selected bibliography under 'Evolution'). Top views of teeth based on material from Maglio, V.J. (1973). Origin and evolution of the Elephantidae. *Trans. Amer. Phil. Soc.,* **63(3)**, 1-49. Page 20: Based on skull illustrations by Osborn and material in *Mammal Evolution – an illustrated guide* by R.J.G. Savage and M.R. Long, British Museum, (Natural History), 1986. Page 21: After Osborn. Page 22: After Osborn. Page 23: After Osborn. Page 24: After Osborn. Page 25: After Osborn (1942) and R.J.G. Savage and M.R. Long (1986). Page 26: After Osborn (1942). Page 27: After Maglio (1973). Page 28: After Osborn. Page 35: Based on an original illustration by Gary H. Marchant, research by J. Shoshani. Page 36: Based on an illustration in *Elephants* by Dr. S.K. Eltringham (1982), Blandford Press. Page 39: Based on an original illustration by Gary H. Marchant, research by J. Shoshani. Page 40: Skull based on an illustration in *The Vertebrate Skeleton* by S.H. Reynolds, 2nd edition (1913), Cambridge University Press. Teeth based on an illustration by John E. Dallman. Page 41: Based on a number of reference sources – the teeth are after Laws (1966); Sikes (1971); Roth and Shoshani (1988). Page 45: Based on an original drawing by Gary H. Marchant. Page 49 Data supplied by Dr. P.C. Lee. Page 50: Data supplied by Dr. P.C. Lee. Page 52: Based on material in Poole, J.H., Payne K., Langbauer, W.R. and Moss, C.J. (1988) The social context of some very low frequency calls of African elephants. *Behavioural Ecology and Sociobiology* **22**, 385-392. Page 54-55: Based on material in *Elephant Memories* by Moss, C.J. (1988), Morrow, New York, and on Moss & Poole (1983). Pages 56 and 57: Data supplied by Dr. P.C. Lee. Page 58: Data from W.K. Lindsay and P.C. Lee. Page 69: Based on an illustration (after Short, 1972) in *A Struggle for Survival: The Elephant Problem* by J. Hanks (1979) Country Life Books/Hamlyn Publishing Group, Middlesex and Mayflower Books, New York. Page 71: Data supplied by Dr. P.C. Lee. Page 72: After J. Hanks (1979). Page 73: Data supplied by Dr. P.C. Lee. Page 75: Based on figure 13 in Rutting behaviour in African elephants, Poole, J.H. (1987). *Behaviour* **102**, 283-316. Page 97: Map based on Iain Douglas-Hamilton (1979) *African Elephant Management Plan,* IUCN/WWF/NYZS, Elephant Survey and Conservation Programme. Page 98-9: Map compiled from information in *The Asian Elephant: Ecology and Management* by R. Sukumar (1989), Cambridge University Press. Page 105: After J. Hanks (1979). Page 110: Based on Observations on arteriosclerosis, serum cholesterol and serum electrolytes in the wild African elephant (*Loxodonta africana*) by J.S. Dillman and W.R. Carr, *J. Comp. Path.* 80, 81-87. Page 149: Calculated from the tusk weight-age relationship of savanna elephants derived from Pilgram and Western (1986). Page 152-3: Compiled from data collected by I.S.C. Parker (Parker, 1979) and the Ivory Trade Review Group (1989). Page 154: Compiled by Richard Luxmoore from overseas trade statistics of Hong Kong and Japan. Page 159: Map based on maps in *Conservation Biology,* 1, No. 3, October 1987 and in *The Asian Elephant: Ecology and Management* by R. Sukumar (1989), Cambridge University Press. Page 168-9: After Blair, J.A.S. and Noor, N.M. (1979); Sale, J.B. and Berkmuller, K. (1988) and from sketches provided by D.K. Lahiri-Choudhury.

INDEX

Page numbers in **bold** indicate major references, including accompanying photographs and illustrations. Page numbers in *italics* indicate captions to other photographs and illustrations. Less important text entries are shown in normal type.

PICTURE CREDITS

Artists
Copyright of the artwork illustrations on the pages following the artists' names is the property of Salamander Books Ltd., except where indicated. The artwork illustrations have been credited by page number.

Bob Bampton (Bernard Thornton Artists, London): 17(*Platybelodon*), 25
Andrew Beckett (Garden Studio): 54-55
Rod Ferring: 16-17(base artwork), 35, 39, 41(base artwork), 45, 49, 50, 52(graph), 56, 57, 58, 69, 71, 72, 73, 75, 97, 98-99, 110, 149, 152-153, 154, 159, 168-169
Matthew Hillier: 32-33
Maggie Raynor: 40, 105, 107
Eric Rowe(Linden Artists): 52(portraits)
John Sibbick © John Sibbick: 16(*Moeritherium*), 20
Glenn Smith: 15, 16-17(line work), 19, 20-28(comparative size symbols), 36, 41(line work)
Todd G. Telander © Todd G. Telander: 16-17(all except *Moeritherium* and *Platybelodon*), 21, 22, 23, 24, 26, 27, 28

Photographers
The publishers wish to thank the following photographers and agencies who have supplied photographs for this book. The photographs have been credited by page number and position on the page: (B) Bottom, (T) Top, (C) Centre, (BL) Bottom Left, etc.

Lyn de Alwis: 128, 129

Ardea London Ltd: 43(P. Morris), 126(BL), 160-1(B, Joanna van Gruisen), 170(Francois Gohier), 174(Chuck McDougal)

Biophoto Associates: 42(T)

Bridgeman Art Library, London: 141(Christie's, London), 151(B, British Library/London)

Dhriti K. Lahiri-Choudhury: 130, 131(B), 132, 133, 134, 135, 136, 138, 139, 140, 143, 144, 145, 166, 167, 169(C)

Bruce Coleman Ltd: 13(Jeff Foott), 79(B, Dieter and Mary Plage), 87(T, Alain Compost), 104(Dieter and Mary Plage), 118(Dieter and Mary Plage), 119(Dieter and Mary Plage), 125(T, M. Freeman), 125(B, Dieter and Mary Plage), 176(Dieter and Mary Plage)

C.M. Dixon: 131(C), 137

Mary Evans Picture Library: 150

Images of Africa Photo Bank: Endpapers(Carla Signorini Jones), 27(David Keith Jones), 34(David Keith Jones) 38(T, Carla Signorini Jones), 38(B, David Keith Jones), 40(David Keith Jones), 41(David Keith Jones) 44(David Keith Jones), 45(BL, David Keith Jones), 46(Carla Signorini Jones), 48(David Keith Jones), 50(David Keith Jones), 51(B, David Keith Jones), 53(T, David Keith Jones), 58(T, David Keith Jones), 59(David Keith Jones), 65(David Keith Jones), 70(B, David Keith Jones), 72(David Keith Jones), 74(B, David Keith Jones), 75(Carla Signorini Jones), 78(David Keith Jones), 80(David Keith Jones), 81(David Keith Jones), 83(BR, David Keith Jones), 89(BR, David Keith Jones), 90-1(David Keith Jones), 92(Willi Rader), 94-5(David Keith Jones), 102(David Keith Jones), 103(T, David Keith Jones), 106(T, David Keith Jones), 108(David Keith Jones), 109(T, Brian Shorter), 109(B, David Keith Jones), 111(David Keith Jones), 113(T, David Keith Jones), 114(David Keith Jones), 115(David Keith Jones), 148(David Keith Jones), 152(Daphne Sheldrick), 158(David Keith Jones), 168(David Keith Jones), 172-3(Peter Tilbury), 175(David Keith Jones), 178(David Keith Jones), 179(B, David Keith Jones)

Frank Lane Picture Agency Ltd: Title-page(Konrad Wothe), 10(Silvestris), 30(Terry Whittaker), 37(BR, Tony Wharton), 37(BL Terry Whittaker), 42(B, Fritz Polking), 45(BR, Silvestris), 47(Frants Hartmann), 62-3(Philip Perry), 67(B, Mandal Ranjit), 68(B, Frants Hartmann), 70(T, Silvestris), 82(Silvestris), 84(Frants Hartmann), 88-9(Eric Hosking), 105(Terry Whittaker), 116(Leonard Lee Rue III)

Dr. Phyllis C. Lee: 53(B), 58(B), 64, 68(T), 71, 74(T), 76-7

Richard A. Luxmoore: 155(B)

The Mansell Collection: 146

Natural Science Photos: 8(A. Watts), 12(C. & T. Stuart), 17(T, P.H. & S.L. Ward), 31(B,C. Jones), 36(C. & T. Stuart), 39(K. Jayaram), 51(T, Mark R. Stanley Price), 56(Mark R. Stanley Price), 57(C. & T. Stuart), 60(C. & T. Stuart), 61(C. Jones), 66-7(T, C. & T. Stuart), 83(CL, P.H. & S.L. Ward), 93(Martin Harvey), 96(C. & T. Stuart), 106(B, C & T Stuart), 107(Lex Hes), 110(P.H. & S.L. Ward), 112-3(B, Mark R. Stanley Price), 117, 121(P.H. & S.L. Ward), 122-3(K. Jayaram), 124(P.H. & S.L. Ward), 126-7, 147, 151(T, K. Jayaram), 155(T, Stephen M. Davis), 156-7(J.C. Pasieka), 162, 163(Stephen M. Davis), 164-5(Mark R. Stanley Price), 171(P.H. & S.L. Ward)

Oxford Scientific Films: 19(Charles Palek)

Photo Researchers Inc.: 37(T, Okapia)

Jeheskel Shoshani: 14, 25, 28(Marion Barnhart), 29(T)

R. Sukumar: 31(T), 49, 54, 69, 74(C), 79(C), 85, 86-7, 100-1, 101, 103(B), 120, 159, 161(T), 169(T), 179(T)

Tass News Agency: 29(B)

Werner Forman Archive: 149

Zefa Picture Library (UK) Ltd.: 5(Superstock)